ALL RICHES COME FROM INJUSTICE

THE ANTI-MAMMON WITNESS OF THE EARLY
CHURCH & ITS ANTI-CAPITALIST RELEVANCE

STEPHEN D. MORRISON

BELOVED PUBLISHING · COLUMBUS, OH

Copyright © 2023 by Stephen D. Morrison

Beloved Publishing • Columbus, Ohio

All rights reserved.

Paperback ISBN: 978-1-63174-181-4

eBook ISBN: 978-1-63174-182-1

No part of this book may be reproduced in any form or by any electronic or mechanical means, including information storage and retrieval systems, without written permission from the author, except for the use of brief quotations in a review.

Acknowledgments:

I want to thank Ryan Cagle, Mako Nagasawa, and Brach Jennings for their valuable feedback on an early draft of this book.

CONTENTS

Introduction   v

1. Biblical Foundations   1
2. Can the Rich be Saved?   25
3. The Earth is Common   45
4. Hoarded Wealth is Theft   71
5. Contentment and the Sin of Luxury   97
6. Usury   115
7. The Tyranny of Mammon   129
8. Socioeconomic Analysis   145
9. On Marx   155
10. Conclusion   171

Notes   175
Bibliography   189

INTRODUCTION

We live in times of unprecedented inequality, where *eight men* own more than half of humanity's total wealth.[1] I called this book *All Riches Come From Injustice* because I like how radical that phrase is—fitting for radical times. But the phrase is not mine originally; it comes from St. Jerome, the influential fourth-century theologian, scholar, and translator. Accordingly, it is a fitting description of this book, which aims to rediscover the Christian critique of mammon by examining the radical sayings of the Early Church Fathers.

Here's the full quote from Jerome:

> And he very rightly said, 'money of injustice,' for all riches come from injustice. Unless one person has lost, another cannot find. Therefore I believe that the popular proverb is very true: 'The rich person is either an unjust person or the heir of one.'[2]

Notice how Jerome is sensitive to the fact that riches do not happen by accident. For one person to be rich, another must be poor. That highlights another aspect of this book. I will argue that the Church needs a robust socioeconomic analysis of capitalism if we want to faithfully proclaim Christ's anti-mammon message today. We need more than lofty words against injustice; we need to understand our situation concretely. Archbishop Desmond Tutu put it well, "There comes a point where we need to stop just pulling people out of the river. We need to go upstream and find out why they're falling in."[3]

The Christian response to poverty often focuses on bandaid solutions, i.e., pulling people out of the river. That sort of charity work is necessary, of course, but I am also interested in asking the systemic question of why people are poor in the first place, even though a handful of wealthy people hoard enough resources and riches to feed, cloth, and provide housing for everyone. It would be absurd to think systemic poverty is entirely unrelated to the fact that eight men hoard 50% of the earth's wealth. So we must ask *why* we are in this situation so that we can do something about it.

However, I also want to clarify what this phrase does *not* mean. It would be particularly easy to misunderstand "*all* riches." The point is not to condemn everyone living in comfort or financial security. Rather, I argue that the Christian critique of riches is most accurately understood as being against *inequality*, not abundance. Thus, it should also be said that this critique is not primarily moral. The target of the anti-mammon critique is systemic, dealing with the systems of mammon, not necessarily personal. Of course, the personal is always included, but it is not the focus.

Inequality is the problem, not riches as such. The issue is that extreme wealth is hoarded by the few, while scarcity and suffering is left for the many. The problem is *differentiating* wealth and its effects.

"Differentiating wealth" is a term I have borrowed from the Latin American Liberation theologian José Miranda, who uses it to summarize the crux of the Bible's critique of wealth:

> Jesus has no horror of wealth, neither in itself nor in its use and enjoyment. [...] But as we were saying, 'rich' and 'poor' are correlative terms. When Christ says, 'Happy the poor' and 'Woe to you the rich,' what he is attacking is that some are poor and others rich. If I may introduce a technical term, it is *differentiating*, or relative, wealth that he condemns.[4]

So, if we want to amend this book's title for clarity, it would be more accurate to say, "All *differentiating* riches come from injustice." Riches do not exist in a vacuum. That is the conviction behind the concept of differentiating wealth. It means that in order for some to have much, others must have little. That is why many in the Early Church believed that an original or inherited act of injustice was at the root of all differential wealth.

It is also why the first Christians seriously questioned whether or not the rich could be saved. That question shocks us today—perhaps because we are familiar to a watered-down concept of mammon. But consider it for a moment: The first Christians took Christ's teachings about wealth so seriously that they asked, "Can the rich be saved?"

Today, we often reverse this approach by talking about wealth as if it were a sign of God's favor, which implies that poverty is a sign of God's judgment. Somehow, we think the poor *deserve* their poverty (whether it is because of moral failure, drug addiction, financial illiteracy, etc.). This idea has its roots in the neoliberal project, which overlooks any and all systemic factors related to poverty and instead blames the individual for their plight. But the acceptance of this mindset in the Church shows how far away we have drifted from the teachings of Christ, which lead the first Christians to struggle with the salvation of the rich, not the poor.

In ancient Rome, the rich were not simply wealthy individuals living luxuriously on their estates. Instead, they were statesmen and aristocrats who wielded enormous social and political power over society.[5] Today, the capitalist class serves a similar function in society. So, I want to propose a modern version of the Early Church's question: *Can a Christian be a capitalist?*

What I mean by a "capitalist" is something similar to what the Early Church meant by the rich. In technical terms, I mean someone who owns and controls "capital" and who is, accordingly, a wealthy member of the capitalist class with all the social privileges and powers that entails. In practical terms, I mean someone who hoards wealth and resources for themselves to extract profits from the working poor, privatizes what was once common, and now lives in extreme luxury while many of their own workers struggle to survive. When you hear the term "capitalist," I want you to think of someone who hoards unfathomable riches and lives luxuriously (while millions starve around the world), but I also want you to think of someone who wields tremendous social, economic, and political power (while millions are powerless and disenfranchised).

When the first Christians asked about the salvation of the rich, they were asking about the *oppressors* of society, those whose wealth was a perpetual sign of their injustice toward the poor and needy. Today, it could be argued that the same is true about the capitalist class, whose wealth is generated by the toil of the masses who, in return, barely earn enough to survive. I will more fully argue this point in chapters eight and nine.

But let's stay with the shocking fact that the Early Church questioned the salvation of the rich. The first text to systematically examine this question was written by Clement of Alexandria in the second century. He argued that the rich could be saved since that was no different from saying sinners could be saved. It is impossible with human beings, but all things are possible with God. *However,* he also argued that the rich could not continue in their sin; they were obligated to give away their excess wealth to the needy.

Another text to consider—one of the most influential early Christian texts—is *The Shepherd of Hermas*. The author argues that the rich do not fit within the Christian community, nor can they be useful in the Church—unless they give away their riches. The rich are compared to round pegs trying to fit into a square hole.[6]

The fact that this question about the salvation of the rich was being asked —and asked with such urgency—demonstrates how seriously the Early Church took Christ's anti-mammon message. Today, we often separate faith and money, but Jesus had *a lot* to say about mammon. He actually talked about money almost more than any other subject. Eleven out of thirty-nine parables deal with money (28%), and one out of every seven verses attributed to Christ are about money (14%). Jesus' critique of mammon was more central to his ministry and teaching than we have been willing to admit.

Jesus challenged and condemned the rich, while the poor found comfort in his gospel. We need to ask ourselves today: Do the rich feel challenged by us? Do the poor and hungry find comfort? Are their material needs met? When will the Church join Christ in declaring: "Woe to you who are rich! Blessed are the poor!" The day when the rich are *uncomfortable* in our midst —while the poor are comforted and blessed in spirit and body—will be the day we have moved closer to Christ's message.

Capitalism

What does all this have to do with capitalism? If we take the Bible's anti-mammon message seriously, I think the Church should adopt an anti-capitalist political ethic. I will argue that anti-capitalism is the application of the Biblical and Patristic witness for us today. Of course, the Early Church fathers had no concept of capitalism, but their insights still have much to say about our current economic system. The chapters in this book address several of these: the commonality of the earth, our obligation to help the needy, and the rejection of usury. Thus, their witness speaks *against* three critical attributes of capitalism: private property, economic individualism, and a system based on debt and interest.

Furthermore, the overall rejection of mammon includes rejecting any institution that prioritizes mammon above all else. No economic system has more completely made mammon the chief end of human life than capitalism. Thus, the critique of mammon found in the Bible and the sayings of the Early Church strongly suggests that our obligation today is to be anti-capitalist.

The overall aim of this book is political, but it is also deeply theological. That is because central to this critique is the realization that *the god of this world is mammon*. Eugene McCarraher observes, "Under capitalism, money occupies the ontological throne from which God has been evicted."[7] I argue that capitalism is the true religion of modernity, despite all the talk of living in a secular age. Maybe the so-called death of God is a *capitalist* phenomenon due to the tendency of capital to become a fetish for worship.[8] Mammon is not *neutral*; it is a rival deity that has usurped God's throne.

Even Karl Marx recognized this. Because capitalism has subjected *everything* to the value of exchange, "It has drowned the most heavenly ecstasies of religious fervor [...] in the icy water of egotistical calculation."[9] In other words, capitalism's cold economic demands have overpowered society's religious concerns. Religion has been replace by the brute calculations of the market. Therefore, "All that is solid melts into air, all that is holy is profaned."[10] But notice that Marx thinks *capitalism* has done this. So, perhaps the decline of religion in modernity has less to do with science or the internet; maybe capitalism is the single most significant reason for the decline in religion because capitalism itself is a rival religion.

I know the very mention of the name "Karl Marx" can lead to panic, but I hope you will stick with me. I will address the difficulties involved with Marxism in chapter nine, including Marx's infamous critique of religion. But the point is this: We could feasibly argue that the supposed decline of religion in the West is not due to some hypothetical plot by atheism but because of the rise of a new religion, capitalism. Marx identified this fervor as "commodity fetishism," but it might as well be called idolatry.

When Jesus said we must choose between God and mammon, loving the one and hating the other, he was describing mammon as a *rival god*. He consciously echoed the first commandment, "You shall have no other gods before me" (Ex. 20:3).[11] Christ's either/or dichotomy explains why capitalism can be feasibly called a religion, it entails serving a god called mammon.

Capitalism is a rival faith that can only be resisted, not accommodated. Thus, we direly need a robust anti-capitalist ethic by returning to the wisdom of the Early Church and their radical critique of mammon. What is at stake is not only the social injustice of inequality but also the very Lordship of Christ. So, today we must boldly proclaim: Jesus is Lord—not mammon!

We cannot combat this idolatry without confronting the social and political systems that prop it up. That is why the political and theological critiques of mammon coincide. This book rejects mammon and capital, *for God's sake,* not purely for political ends. Indeed, because mammon actively usurps God's lordship over the earth, it is the task of our time to re-proclaim a gospel that stands against mammon and empire.

For that reason, I need to disclaim that the quotes selected and arranged for this book are intentionally biased and one-sided. My aim is *not* to offer a balanced or exhaustive study of how the Patristic writers dealt with the issues of wealth and poverty. Nor does this book's scope permit a detailed analysis of the life and context of their teachings. The radical sayings of these early

Christians serve a larger purpose in the argument of this book, which strives to challenge the Church's relationship to capitalism.

The etymology of the word "radical" indicates a return to one's "roots." So it is indeed fitting to call this selection of sayings "radical" in both senses, the common and etymological. Of course, there is always a risk of exaggeration. But that risk is minimal when the Church exists in an already unbalanced position regarding riches. If we once again find ourselves in a situation where the rich are *excluded* from Church fellowship, perhaps then our message can be re-balanced with words of "caution." But in situations of *imbalance*, it is a corrective measure to stress this forgotten aspect of the truth, even if it seems unbalanced. In fact, what is genuinely unbalanced is just how far away we've fallen from Christ's critique of mammon. Therefore, in the hope of returning to the message of Christ, a radical message needs to be proclaimed.

Outline

This book examines the anti-mammon witness of the Bible and the sayings of the Early Church Fathers to argue that the witness of both *points toward* a Christian anti-capitalist ethic today. That is my basic argument. The bulk of this work focuses on the Fathers by selecting various quotes from the first five centuries of the Church, analyzing their wisdom, and applying their insights to our situation. The final two chapters argue for the necessity of a socioeconomic analysis of capitalism, one that brings together the anti-mammon wisdom of the Bible and Patristics with Marx's critique of capital to create a basis for Christian anti-capitalism.

Before we begin, there are two disclaimers to be aware of. First, I am not a Church historian, nor do I read the Church Fathers in their original language. I lean on the work of other scholars and try to place these quotes in their proper context, but I am primarily interested in how we might apply their wisdom today.

Second, I am a Christian socialist. This book does not explicitly argue *for* socialism (though it does implicitly at times), but it will be clear from my analysis that this is my position. I will eventually complete a longer book that argues *for* Christian socialism; however, this present book is merely an argument for anti-capitalism.

It is also important to say that neither the Bible nor the Early Church's teachings *directly* proclaim anti-capitalism or socialism. But I am arguing that their insights *point in that direction*. It would be a mistake to turn the Fathers into anti-capitalists or Jesus into a socialist. That is not my claim. Instead, I am interested in applying their wisdom to our situation. Therefore, my aim is not primarily descriptive (analyzing what was said) but constructive (building on past insights for our situation today).

It is also important to remember that the Early Church was not a monolith, and I do not intend to make them into a unified and muddled voice. Instead, the aim here is to build on the sayings of the Early Church and argue that the anti-mammon message of the Christian faith points to the necessity of anti-capitalism today.

Readers can still benefit from this book without accepting my conclusions. The research that went into collecting these quotes will still be useful for anyone interested in the questions of faith and money. But it would be dishonest not to make my biases clear. With that said, the book follows this basic outline:

Chapter one establishes the biblical basis of an anti-mammon gospel. Chapters two through seven examine the anti-mammon sayings of the Early Church, which are arranged thematically.

Chapter two examines the question of the salvation of the rich. The chapter concludes that if the rich are saved, they are saved in spite of their wealth, and with the hope of the rich being liberated from their sin by giving away their riches to the needy.

Chapter three examines the theme of the common earth and the critique of privatization. This chapter conclusions that the Early Church fathers rejected private property because it goes against God's original design for creation, that all things would be in common for the sustenance of all.

Chapter four shows that many of the Church Fathers understood giving to the poor as an *obligation* and even suggested that not giving is a kind of theft. Thus, the conclusion is that hoarded riches are *theft*, and those with excess are obligated to give to those lacking.

Chapter five examines the sin of luxury and the virtue of contentment. This chapter concludes that the proper use of wealth is to sustain oneself, but luxury beyond one's essential needs is sinful.

Chapter six discusses the sin of usury, meaning charging interest for a loan. This chapter concludes that usury makes human beings the lords over time, which is a sin against God's lordship over time. Finally, this chapter begins a more explicit critique of capitalism because the capitalist system could not exist without usury, and thus, the Biblical and historical Christian rejection of usury necessitates anti-capitalism because capitalism is a system that is built upon interest and investment.

Chapter seven examines the tyrannical nature of mammon, that it is a rival god that enslaves its servants. This chapter concludes that capitalism is the modern embodiment of mammon because no other system has subjected all things to the demands of mammon like capitalism.

Chapters eight and nine argue for the necessity of socioeconomic analysis, particularly in the work of Karl Marx. These chapters are where my full argument is presented, and I hope readers will have the patience to withhold judgment until my case can be made.

This book is an invitation to *begin* a conversation, not the end of one. Whether or not every reader agrees with me is not my concern. What matters most of all is for the Church to begin reckoning with its failure to take Christ's anti-mammon message seriously.

This book developed out of a larger project on Christian socialism.[12] I initially planned to examine the sayings of the Early Church as a chapter, but after realizing how much material there is, it became clear that this needed to be a stand-alone project. Separating these books allows the sayings of the Father's room to breathe, while still contributing to a larger argument.

Ultimately, I hope this book is read as a serious attempt to understand and apply the anti-mammon witness of the Christian Scriptures and tradition to our situation. Some will likely disagree with my approach or conclusions, but the questions raised by this book remain a vital challenge for the Church. We should no longer avoid wrestling with them, nor should we accept a Christianity that has nothing to say about capitalism, inequality, and the injustice of hoarded wealth.

1

BIBLICAL FOUNDATIONS

An over-spiritualization of the Bible has pacified its radical anti-mammon message. What I mean is that the Bible has become a book about heavenly matters with little to no relevance to the systems of this world; it has ceased to challenge us in our actual, historical lives as people. But the Bible does not proclaim a *pie-in-the-sky* religion. On the contrary, a central message of the New Testament is the Kingdom of God—"on earth as it is in heaven," as Christ taught us to pray. The Church's mission is not to escape the earth or live privately fulfilling spiritual lives as monastics but to make the earth look like heaven, to heal the sick, proclaim good news to the poor, and let the oppressed go free (Lk. 4). The Bible has thus been co-opted by the rich and powerful as a tool of spiritual pacifism, but at its core, it still contains the most radical message of hope for the poor and downtrodden. Despite its misuse, it is still fundamentally a message of good news for the least of these. "The Bible," writes Ernst Bloch, "has always been the Church's bad conscience."[1] It is high time we listen to it with utter seriousness.

Thus, we will begin with a sober survey of the anti-mammon message of the Bible. It would be nearly impossible to read the Bible in its entirety without having a strong impression that God cares about the poor and oppressed deeply. That message is on nearly every page. Of course, God cares about sin and salvation, too. Still, it is the failure of our gospel message today that we *maximize* the spiritual aspect of the good news while *minimizing* (or denying) the material dimension. Yet God raised Israel out of political captivity in Egypt, and Christ was crucified on a rebel's cross as a threat to the

Roman state. The two central events of God witnessed in the Bible—exodus and crucifixion/resurrection—were political, revolutionary, and historical.

In the New Testament, Jesus took sides with the poor and marginalized, broke bread with the outcasts, and stood up for the needy. We are unfaithful to Christ's message if we turn it into a purely spiritual word about "saving souls." Archbishop and martyr Oscar Romero explains, "To love our neighbor means to be concerned about their needs, their concrete situation, and, like the Good Samaritan, to help the poor fallen by the roadside."[2]

A large part of the problem is how we have separated the message of Christ from the way of Jesus. The gospel today is a religious message about praying the right words to enter heaven when you die. But that is barely half of the gospel Christ proclaimed—if it has anything to do with it, to begin with—and it is certainly not a message that would have led to Christ's crucifixion. Rome did not habitually crucify *religious preachers* proclaiming salvation in another world. Rome even permitted religious leaders who could pacify an unruly public with other-worldly hopes.[3]

Roman A. Montero clarifies Christ's context, "The economic, religious, and political spheres in first-century Palestine were inseparable; the temple was religious in nature as well as economic and political."[4] The modern compartmentalization of economics, politics, and religion into separate spheres is foreign to Christ's gospel; to proclaim it again today involves all three.

So let us return to the words of Christ with fresh eyes and allow their power to disrupt our comfortable illusions. If the Bible is no longer a constant challenge, perhaps we have not been reading it correctly. The Scriptures should be like a sword that cuts deeply, removing the dead and diseased parts of our life and thinking. Unfortunately, in proclaiming a message of purely spiritual comfort and escape to heaven, we have not allowed the Bible to challenge us in our daily, historical lives. We have become far too concerned with the soul in heaven that we overlook the body of the historical person. In short, we have failed to speak to the daily lives of people in history.

And what is more fundamental to our lives than money? The persistent thought that keeps us in fear, the reason we work day in and day out, and the reason we organize our lives the way we do is money. Today more than even in Christ's time, money dominates our lives like a harsh tyrant. If the gospel we proclaim has nothing to say about money, then it has nothing to do with the actual existence of human beings. It is an empty, idealistic husk lacking in substance. Furthermore, we cannot talk about money without talking about the politics of mammon. José Miranda writes, "To uphold an apoliticism of the gospel is to uphold the nonrealization of the gospel."[5] Thus, the gospel *must* be political, or else it is *powerless*.

This first chapter aims to return to the Bible and be awakened by the bold and disturbing message it proclaims about money and riches. I have chosen to begin with the words of Christ because they are often the sharpest. Then we will examine the Hebrew Bible as the background for Christ's prophetic critique of mammon. Finally, we will briefly survey the words of Paul, James, and the book of Acts. The ultimate goal in all this is to demonstrate the anti-mammon message of the Bible as *essential*, not accidental or peripheral, to the gospel Christ proclaimed. That means to be a Christ follower is to be firmly against mammon in all its forms and systems.

1. Jesus

Jesus announced his ministry in Luke 4 not as a spiritual teacher of hope for another world—anesthesia for the masses—but as hope for the poor and oppressed:

> The Spirit of the Lord is upon me,
>   because he has anointed me
>   to bring good news to the poor.
> He has sent me to proclaim release to the captives
>   and recovery of sight to the blind,
>   to let the oppressed go free,
>   to proclaim the year of the Lord's favor.
>
> — LUKE 4:18-19

Luke's account describes Jesus as a prophet of hope for the downtrodden and poor. Mary's Magnificat, which sets the tone for this account, solidifies this emphasis:

> My soul magnifies the Lord,
>   and my spirit rejoices in God my Savior,
>   for he has looked with favor on the lowliness of his servant.
> Surely, from now on all generations will call me blessed;
> for the Mighty One has done great things for me,
>   and holy is his name.
> His mercy is for those who fear him
>   from generation to generation.
> He has shown strength with his arm;
>   he has scattered the proud in the thoughts of their hearts.
> He has brought down the powerful from their thrones,
>   and lifted up the lowly;

he has filled the hungry with good things,
and sent the rich away empty,
according to the promise he made to our ancestors,
to Abraham and to his descendants forever.

— LUKE 1:46-55

These two announcements establish a solid foundation for how Luke wants us to understand the life and ministry of Jesus. From the beginning, Jesus was on the side of the poor and oppressed and stands against the rich and powerful oppressors, "He has brought down the powerful [...] and lifted up the lowly." His arrival was the fulfillment of God's covenant faithfulness to Israel. The same God who led them out of captivity from Egyptian slavery came to proclaim liberty, comfort the poor and needy, and condemn the rich and powerful. The exodus was not purely spiritual but concrete and historical; so too is the liberty Christ came to proclaim and the hope his message gave to the poor and oppressed.

The message of Christ is inseparable from a material concern for the least of these. And that concern includes the condemnation of their oppressor, the rich and powerful who benefit from their poverty. That is on display in Mary's song. The gospel is a message of comfort for the low and humble, yet it is also a challenge and condemnation of the high and mighty. That is what happens when Christ's gospel is proclaimed: the poor are comforted while the rich are condemned.

This insight contradicts much of what we tend to assume in the Church today. We have flattened the gospel so that it does not offend the rich and powerful, which means it can no longer be a comfort for the poor and downtrodden. The message of Christ is singular, but it is at the same time a message of good news to the poor *and* judgment to the rich. Paul alludes to this when describing the knowledge of Christ as both a sweet smell and an offensive odor:

> But thanks be to God, who in Christ always leads us in triumphal procession, and through us spreads in every place the fragrance that comes from knowing him. For we are the aroma of Christ to God among those who are being saved and among those who are perishing; to the one a fragrance from death to death, to the other a fragrance from life to life.
>
> — 2 CORINTHIANS 2:14-6

While Paul's immediate concern is for the knowledge of God's triumph at the cross, the description is fitting for the nature of the gospel itself. The same gospel is at once good news to the poor and bad news to the rich; it is hope for the oppressed and condemnation of their oppressors. Both Luke 1 and 4 follow the same pattern: comforting the poor and condemning the rich. A gospel that challenges no one also cannot comfort anyone.

The gospel we proclaim today does not produce the same effect described here. Instead, our message is one of religious escape and spiritual numbness. It is one of apathy to injustice, which is too afraid to offend the powerful or defend the needy. What would it look like today to proclaim a message that caused the poor to rejoice and find comfort? Which might confront the rich and powerful and bring them to shame? Christ was a friend of sinners and tax collectors, the despised and forgotten, and the prostitutes and homeless. He took their side in radical solidarity with the least of these, becoming poor for our sakes. And who was the most frequently angry with Jesus? Who was offended by him? The Pharisees (religious elites who benefited from the oppressive status quo), the powerful (Herod), and the rich (the rich young ruler). Christ's message did not comfort all classes evenly but showed a preference for the weak by exalting the humble and calling the powerful to repentance. This principle is summed up by what liberation theologians call God's "preferential option for the poor."[6]

In this context, Jesus sets up a clear distinction between mammon and God. His famous claim that we cannot serve two masters is not a moral verdict about matters of the heart. Instead, Jesus describes an either/or situation. Mammon is an *idol*. Like every idol, we reject it or serve it *completely*. Jesus established mammon as a rival deity that we must reject entirely.[7] José Miranda writes, "The real rival of Yahweh is money."[8] That is what is so startling about Jesus' teachings about mammon. He personifies money as a rival God, as the enemy of Christ's Lordship. As such, mammon can only be rejected or worshiped totally. There is no grey area. Either Jesus is Lord, or mammon is lord.

Jesus' words are familiar enough but still worth revisiting in full:

> No slave can serve two masters; for a slave will either hate the one and love the other, or be devoted to the one and despise the other. You cannot serve God and wealth [mammon].
>
> — LUKE 16:13

What is important to stress with this passage is how drastically it sets up an "all-or-nothing" situation. It is unavoidably black and white. Like the new creation, it is either one or the other. One cannot be new and old without risking a rupture in the old, ruining both (Lk. 5:37-9, Mt. 9:17). But the primary metaphor behind these words is that of a master/slave. The service of God is total and excludes the service of all others.

Many commenters have noted that the word "mammon" is unique to Jesus in the New Testament; no other figure uses it. What does it mean? Hauck defines the term at length:

> In the first instance it means "property," "earthly goods," but always with a derogatory sense of the materialistic, anti-godly and sinful. In the earthly property which man gathers (Mt. 6:19 ff.), in which he erroneously seeks security (Lk. 12:15 ff.), to which he gives his heart (Mt. 6:21), and because of which he ceases to love, Jesus finds the very opposite of God (Mt. 6:24 par.). Because of the demonic power immanent in possessions, surrender to them brings practical enslavement (Mt. 6:19 ff.). The righteous must resolutely break free from this entanglement and stand in exclusive religious dependence on God, Mt. 6:24 par. This realistic view of the actual facts makes it impossible for Jesus to think of earthly possessions with religious optimism or to regard them as a mark of special divine blessing (Job 1:10). The phrase μαμωνᾶς τῆς ἀδικίας in Lk. 16:9 (== ἀδίκῳ μαμωνᾷ, 16:11) corresponds exactly to the Aram. מָמוֹן דְּשְׁקַר, == possessions acquired dishonestly. The saying of Jesus need not have been originally directed against publicans, for in practice no property can be acquired except with some element of injustice (cf. Σειρ. 26:28). The estimation of God as the supreme good, and the high ethical emphasis placed on brotherly love, especially in expectation of the imminent end, rule out all ideas of using mammon in the world to serve cultural aims and concerns. The only possibility for Jesus is the renunciation of earthly wealth as this is expressed in giving it to the poor.[9]

Jesus' opinion of private, hoarded wealth was entirely negative. Service to mammon means total enslavement, which precludes service to God. Thus, mammon is a rival deity and an idol. Accordingly, the only *righteous* use of material wealth is to help the poor, to give it away. The direct implication is that anything hoarded in excess of "daily bread" is sinful.

People in the first century did not handle money as often as we do today. People used money, of course, but it was mostly to pay taxes. We need to place ourselves in the context of Christ's original audience. Most would have been peasants, farmers, unskilled day laborers, or beggars, who typically did not hoard a reserve of coinage. Most would have lived at or below subsistence levels. The presence of hoarded money for Jesus' time was thus a sign of privilege, implying accumulated riches beyond subsistence living. Most lived "hand to mouth," producing and consuming in equal share with little to nothing left over.

Thus, Christ's rejection of mammon was not a total renunciation of money as a tool but instead a powerful critique of *hoarded excess*. The difference is between having enough to meet your daily needs or having more than enough yet refusing to share with those who do not have enough to eat. Thus, repeatedly in the Bible, the problem with riches is not money but *hoarded* excess. Christ condemned accumulated wealth as a rival god, an object of trust that cannot coexist with faith in the Lord.

Today, money is an abstraction. It is not as directly connected to resources as it was in Christ's time. That is why it is easy to overlook the implications of what Christ is saying. He is not rejecting money as a tool but hoarded riches, which we trust instead of God. The rich can afford to hoard resources for their protection and privilege. The poor cannot and thus must rely wholly on God for their provisions. Therefore, blessed are the poor and woe to the rich (Lk. 6). To serve mammon is to replace God with money as the source of safety; it is to serve and trust another God.

So let us be frank, as Christ's words require. What does this either/or between God and mammon mean today? In short, to follow Christ excludes following mammon, i.e., hoarding riches. Thus, we must state the matter plainly: *It is impossible to be a billionaire if you follow Jesus.* The two paths are antithetical. First of all, hoarding a billion dollars without injustice or exploitation is not feasible. No one "earns" a billion dollars on their own without exploiting the labor of the poor or the resources of the vulnerable.

Furthermore, the hoarded wealth of the rich *belongs* to the poor and needy. Thus, even if a Christian somehow became a billionaire without injustice (a questionable premise), they would not remain rich for long if they followed Christ since they would be obligated to give away most of their wealth. Thus, in either case, a billionaire *cannot* be a Christian, and a Christian *cannot* be a billionaire. That is, without forsaking Christ (though they might still be saved despite their sin).

Hoarding wealth in such extreme quantities means hoarding the *means of existence* for millions who will suffer and die without it. The problem is more than just that a pile of money sits unused but that money represents *material resources* that might have helped the desperately poor and hungry. The blood of the needy stains the hands of every billionaire. They neglect Christ by neglecting the poor. God has given the earth for all in common to benefit all, but the rich reject God's order of creation by hoarding what is give freely to benefit all.

The only righteous form of wealth is *shared* wealth. For a rich person to have much, others must have little. Mammon is the idol of this unjust pursuit of hoarded wealth and resources. The very mechanism of its accumulation is unjust and deceptive, rooted in violence and theft. And ultimately, the pursuit of riches is rooted in idolatry. Mammon becomes an object of trust, an idol above God. That is the brute reality of what Christ is saying. We can either serve one or the other. That is not just an ethical statement but a realistic observation. The pursuit of hoarded riches as an object of total trust is sinful. It *always* leads to idolatry. It *is* idolatry. Riches may belong to the righteous, but the righteous will share their wealth with the needy.

Righteous wealth is shared; unjust riches are hoarded. The way of Christ is to share excess with the poor and needy; the way of demonic mammon is to hoard resources while many suffer. This principle is rooted in the Torah, which stresses the commonality of creation. The earth is the Lord's and was given to all in common. The land is borrowed from the Lord, for the good of all, not for hoarding and private gain. Thus, the only proper use of riches is to share with all commonly. If one has much and another lacks the essentials, it is a sin against God, the Lord and Creator of both.

As we have seen, the point is not to condemn money as a tool for existence. The modern world makes having a bank account essential for survival. Thus, some degree of "hoarding" is necessary. But there is a massive difference between trying to *survive* in late-stage capitalism by being financially wise with a 401k and savings account versus hoarding more money than you can spend in a thousand lifetimes. That is not to say anyone is off the hook from the obligation to help the poor. Instead, the point is to highlight how Christ directed his harshest condemnations towards the super-rich, the 1%, which is today the capitalist class that owns the means of production and wields enormous social power because of it. We will return to this point and explore it more fully in chapter eight.

We might define mammon as the idol of hoarded riches, not simply money. But, of course, money is an essential tool today. Yet hoarded wealth is a different matter altogether. That translates today to "capital," which is the social power to own and direct production and distribution in the market and thus exercise dictatorial control over the vast majority of the population.

It is here that we can fully appreciate the meaning of Christ's parable about hoarded grains and bigger barns:

> Then he told them a parable: 'The land of a rich man produced abundantly. And he thought to himself, 'What should I do, for I have no place to store my crops?' Then he said, 'I will do this: I will pull down my barns and build larger ones, and there I will store all my grain and my goods. And I will say to my soul, Soul, you have ample goods laid up for

many years; relax, eat, drink, be merry.' But God said to him, 'You fool! This very night your life is being demanded of you. And the things you have prepared, whose will they be?' So it is with those who store up treasures for themselves but are not rich toward God'

— LUKE 12:16-21

What should the rich man do in this situation if he wanted to live justly and serve the Lord? The Torah offers a clear answer, which most of Christ's listeners would have known. He was obligated to share his surplus with those who lacked, but he hoarded material excess while others suffered. Deuteronomy 15:4 establishes this obligation, "There will, however, be no one in need among you, because the Lord is sure to bless you in the land that the Lord your God is giving you as a possession to occupy." Everyone having enough to eat—"no one in need among you"—was a sign of God's favor over Israel. The law condemned those who hoarded luxuries while others lacked essentials.

The dual nature of Christ's anti-mammon message is explicit in Luke 6. The gospel is good news to the poor and judgment against the rich and powerful. Thus, Christ makes the point direct:

Blessed are you who are poor,
    for yours is the kingdom of God
Blessed are you who are hungry now,
    for you will be filled.
Blessed are you who weep now,
    for you will laugh. [...]
Woe to you who are rich,
    for you have received your consolation.
Woe to you who are full now,
    for you will be hungry.
Woe to you who are laughing now,
    for you will mourn and weep.

— LUKE 6:20-1, 25-6

Matthew's version says, "Blessed are the poor *in spirit,*" which is sometimes preferred because a spiritualized concept of poverty is more congruent with a gospel of escape. But it is an interpretive choice made by modern readers to *limit* Luke's meaning by Matthew rather than to allow Matthew to *expand* the meaning of Luke. It is a hermeneutical fallacy to let one interpretation limit the other instead of allowing both to be complementary expansions of a shared theme. Ultimately, Luke and Matthew likely pulled from the same source material (sometimes called Q). But furthermore, Matthew's designation of the poor "in spirit" does not exclude material poverty but expands it to mean both the status of poverty and the humility that often goes with it. Thus, the wealthy can become poor in spirit by humbling themselves, observing God's law, and then *proving* their humility by giving away their riches. Matthew's version is not an excuse to ignore the material focus of Christ's words in both parallel passages. Nor does it justify ignoring Christ's direct condemnation of the rich as a class of persons guilty of social injustice.

Malina and Rohrbaugh describe the ancient Mediterranean mindset, the cultural background of Christ's rebuke:

> Acquisition was, by its very nature, understood as stealing. [...] Profit-making and the acquisition of wealth were automatically assumed to be the result of extortion or fraud, and the notion of an honest rich man was a first-century oxymoron.[10]

The rich and poor are condemned and praised in parallel because the powerful and oppressed exist in a symbiotic relationship. The poverty of one is because of the riches of the other. The poor are not poor by accident but are made poor by the conditions imposed upon them by the greed of the rich to hoard more than their share of God's gift, the earth and its resources, which is common for all.

Our Western notion of rich and poor is distorted by ideology. The capitalist project is built on the myth of meritocracy, that the rich earn and thus deserve their luxuries while the poor deserve their suffering. But this lie ignores the social conditions that lead to both wealth and poverty, not to mention the material conditions that cause perpetual injustice by keeping the rich rich and the poor poor. Poor children often stay in poverty their entire lives, as do the children of rich parents. A common saying in antiquity captures this well, "The rich person is either an unjust person or the heir of one." St. Jerome quotes this unsourced "popular saying" and calls it "very true."[11] That indicates that a negative concept of wealth was not only common, but Jerome considered it congruent with the teachings of Christ.

Christ's critique of the rich is essential to the gospel. It is the New Testament version of the first commandment (as discussed below). Our basic confession is this: Jesus is Lord. Mammon is a demonic idol that threatens this basic confession, and thus we must recognize mammon as irreconcilable with the way of Jesus. The path of mammon and the path of Christ run in opposite directions. One cannot pursue hoarded riches and Christ.

Jesus proclaimed a word of hope to the poor and oppressed and a warning of judgment to the rich and powerful. The effort to spiritualize Christ's words waters down his radical gospel. But a watered-down gospel is not only less offensive but is also less powerful. Such a gospel cannot offer any comfort to the oppressed in their struggles or give them hope in the God who prefers small and little things of this world over the high and mighty. The God of the gospel is the one who rescued Israel from oppression, raised Christ from the dead, and today sides with the powerless against unjust exploitation and misery.

2. Hebrew Bible

Jesus' rebuke of mammon is deeply rooted in the Hebrew Bible. He presents this either/or in connection with the first and second commandments:

> I am the Lord your God, who brought you out of Egypt, out of the land of slavery.
> You shall have no other gods before me.
> You shall not make for yourself an image in the form of anything in heaven above or on the earth beneath or in the waters below.
>
> — EXODUS 20:2-4

Our familiarity with these words often causes us to overlook the seriousness with which the Israelites worked to obey them. It would have been immediately clear to Jesus' listeners that his critique of mammon established money as a rival god incompatible with the Lord of Israel. There is no room for neutrality when it comes to idols. Either we resist and reject an idol totally, or we will become enslaved by it.

A common error of Christian interpretation is to divorce Jesus from the faith of Israel, especially the Torah and prophets. But we rightly understand Christ only in this light. The commandment against idolatry helps us recognize the radical overtones of Christ's anti-mammon message. But other aspects of the Hebrew Bible are also vital for understanding how his teachings presuppose yet radicalize the biblical concept of justice. There are two relevant points we will consider here. The first is the idea of the land belonging to the Lord, and the second is the prophetic treatment of the rich as synonymous with the unjust.

In most ancient cultures, the land represented life. It was the source of food and the foundation of national identity. God's covenant with Israel included the "promised land" flowing with milk and honey. The Hebrew

Bible teaches that all of the land belongs to God. The psalmist writes, "The earth is the Lord's and the fullness thereof" (Ps. 24:1). This is not merely a statement regarding God as creator and lord over the earth. The implications were more immediately political and economic.

The practice of jubilee is an instructive example:

> You shall count off seven weeks of years, seven times seven years, so that the period of seven weeks of years gives forty-nine years. Then you shall have the trumpet sounded loud; on the tenth day of the seventh month—on the day of atonement—you shall have the trumpet sounded throughout all your land. And you shall hallow the fiftieth year and you shall proclaim liberty throughout the land to all its inhabitants. It shall be a jubilee for you: you shall return, every one of you, to your property and every one of you to your family. [...] The land shall not be sold in perpetuity, for the land is mine; with me you are but aliens and tenants.
>
> — LEVITICUS 15:8-10, 23

Jubilee was an economic practice of debt resettlement that reflected the central concept of the land as ultimately belonging to the Lord, shared with Israel as a gift for the good of the nation.[12] Most importantly, this practice denied the ability of the rich and powerful to hoard and capitalize off the land forever as if it were theirs to own and not the Lord's. God had given the land to Israel for the common good of all. To hoard it for profit was a sin against the Lord, who gave it freely. It was forbidden for the land to be claimed as the eternal property of any person; it must remain politically and economically seen as a gift from God, a gift given for all people and not the privileged few.

The same logic for this ban on selling the land forever sits behind the prohibition of usury, which was the practice of charging interest for profit:

> If any of your kin fall into difficulty and become dependent on you, you shall support them; they shall live with you as though resident aliens. Do not take interest in advance or otherwise make a profit from them [the poor], but fear your God; let them live with you. You shall not lend them your money at interest taken in advance, or provide them food at a profit. I am the Lord your God who brought you out of the

land of Egypt, to give you the land of Canaan, to be your God.

— LEVITICUS 25:35-8

For most of its history, the Church banned the practice of usury for clergy and members. Today, this prohibition has been almost entirely lost or forgotten. Profiting off the debts of the poor and needy is an acceptable practice under capitalism. Still, according to the Biblical concept of economic justice and the Lord's ownership of all things, it is a sin against God. Rejecting usury today would mean resisting all forms of high-interest lending that prey on the poor and the extortionist international debts forced upon third-world nations by the richer nations of the first world through the IMF and World Bank. (We will discuss usury in chapter six.)

The theological basis for the year of jubilee is the same as the ban on usury. God ordained creation to be held in common, not to be privatized as the exclusive right of the few. Creation itself is a gift from the Lord. Yet to take God's freely given creation, given for the benefit of all God's creatures, and hoard it for profit, is a sin against God as creator and Lord.

The implications are radical. If God's will for creation is to hold the earth's resources in common, not to monopolize them for the few, then the primary source of profit today goes against God's will. Profit in the capitalist system is rooted in sin and injustice. Capitalism takes what everyone needs and privatizes it for personal profit, such as water, food, housing, and medicine. Giant food manufacturers throw away and waste millions of tons of food yearly in a world where millions starve and die. And they waste so much because throwing away all that food is *more profitable* than feeding people freely. There are no better words for these actions—made acceptable and necessary by capitalism—than to say they are sinful and unjust.

Deuteronomy offers a powerful critique of privatization and usury, which establishes a biblical basis for a radical critique of the capitalist system.

> Every seventh year you shall grant a remission of debts. And this is the manner of the remission: every creditor shall remit the claim that is held against a neighbor, not exacting it of a neighbor who is a member of the community, because the Lord's remission has been proclaimed. [...] There will, however, be no one in need among you, because the Lord is sure to bless you in the land that the Lord your God is giving you as a possession to occupy. [...] If there is among you anyone in need, a member of your community in any of your towns within the land that the Lord your God is giving you,

> do not be hard-hearted or tight-fisted toward your needy neighbor. You shall rather open your hand, willingly lending enough to meet the need, whatever it may be. […] Give liberally and be ungrudging when you do so, for on this account the Lord your God will bless you in all your work and in all that you undertake. Since there will never cease to be some in need on the earth, I therefore command you, 'Open your hand to the poor and needy neighbor in your land.' […] Remember that you were a slave in the land of Egypt, and the Lord your God redeemed you; for this reason I lay this command upon you today.
>
> — DEUTERONOMY 15:1-2, 4, 7-8, 10-11, 15

Jesus was not the first to suggest that failing to give to the poor and needy was a sin against God. It was already a prominent commandment of the Torah. Yet Christ made the point extreme: either God or mammon. He also went further by personifying himself as the poor and needy in the parable of the sheep and goats (Mt. 25), suggesting that whatever is done or undone to the least of these is done or undone to the Lord. To care for the needy and poor is thus to care for Christ. That is justice and righteousness according to the law. The Bible does not uphold the principle that "what's mine is mine" but stresses that "God gives all things in common so that no one should be in need." To hoard what God has shared commonly for the good of all is to sin against God and condemn your neighbor to poverty and death.

That leads us to the second point worth noting about the Hebrew Bible. Because of how it defines divine justice, the Old Testament uses the "rich" and "unjust" as parallel terms. The rich were not called unjust because of what they did personally. Rather, their status as rich persons—as hoarders of what God gave commonly—warranted calling them unjust.

A common literary technique in the Scripture is "parallelism."[13] This is when the author joins two poetic phrases together to say the same thing differently, thus drawing a parallel between the two ideas. For example, Isaiah 58:8 writes, "The people will see your justice, / and all the kings your glory." A parallel is thus drawn between God's justice and glory. It is not necessarily a synonym, but the poetic parallel draws them into close relation so that it becomes unthinkable to imagine God's glory without justice and vice versa.

Through this literary technique, the Bible reveals its assumption that the rich are, by definition, wicked. Isaiah 53:9 reads, "They made his grave with the wicked / and his tomb with the rich." The point is clear. The rich man's tomb is also the grave of the wicked, or at least the two should be considered conceptually similar. Thus, the Bible seems to imply that an unjust rich person is *the rule,* not the exception. Job is such a remarkable book because it gives the extraordinary case of a rich man who was also righteous and who proved his devotion to God by sharing his wealth with the needy (Job 29:12-7; 31:16-23). But we must remember that Job is the exception and not the rule. The assumed rule is that to be rich, to hoard what God gives for all, is an injustice.

Hauck and Kasch comment on this further:

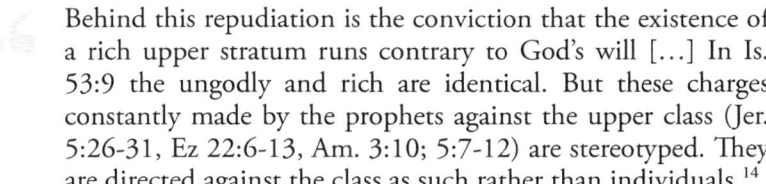

> Behind this repudiation is the conviction that the existence of a rich upper stratum runs contrary to God's will [...] In Is. 53:9 the ungodly and rich are identical. But these charges constantly made by the prophets against the upper class (Jer. 5:26-31, Ez 22:6-13, Am. 3:10; 5:7-12) are stereotyped. They are directed against the class as such rather than individuals.[14]

Why does the Hebrew Bible identify the rich with the unjust? Because to grow rich means violently stealing for private benefit what God has given for the common good of all. "There shall be none in need among you." But when the rich hoard the common resources of the land as their private wealth, the needy go without essentials. Thus, riches are inherently rooted in violence and theft (typically systemic rather than personal). To be rich is to hoard what God has given in common for all.

Likewise, the prophets frequently condemned the rich as sinful and called Israel to remember the poor. Amos exemplifies this familiar cadence:

> Take away from me the noise of your songs;
> I will not listen to the melody of your harps.
> But let justice roll down like waters,
> and righteousness like an ever-flowing stream.
>
> — AMOS 5:23-4

Religious devotion is bankrupt without a primary concern for the poor and needy. Justice is central to Christian faith, and we adopt a functional Marcionism whenever we downplay or ignore the call in the Hebrew Bible to prioritize justice for the least of these, i.e., good news to the poor. Marcionism was an early heresy that rejected the Old Testament as Christian Scripture. A purely spiritual and religious definition of our faith functionally ignores the Hebraic focus on justice as a material concern and preaches, in contrast, an exclusively spiritual gospel. Jesus' message must be contextualized into the prophetic concern for justice. If our gospel downplays the material needs of the least of these, it is not the same gospel Christ proclaimed.

A spiritualization of justice and righteousness is partially to blame for why we cannot see the material dimension of God's covenant faithfulness to the human race. God is not concerned purely with spiritual righteousness, yet that is how these terms are almost exclusively defined in Christianity. But Isaiah is clear about what God's justice and righteousness mean:

> Wash yourselves; make yourselves clean;
>> remove the evil of your doings from before my eyes;
>> cease to do evil,
>> learn to do good;
>> seek justice,
>> rescue the oppressed,
>> defend the orphan,
>> plead for the widow.
>
> — ISAIAH 1:16-7

Justification is not only the forgiveness of sin but the success of righteousness. Justice looks like rescuing the oppressed, defending the orphan, and pleading for the widow. Divine justice *restores*. Our theological debates about justification are empty and meaningless until justification leads to restoration and healing for the least of these.[15]

3. Acts

The first Christians built a community according to the principles of the Torah and their radicalization by Christ's anti-mammon mandate. Luke makes this point by evoking the same language as Deuteronomy 15—"There will, however, be no one in need among you"—when describing the Christian community in Acts 2 and 4:

> All who believed were together and had all things in common; they would sell their possessions and goods and distribute the proceeds to all, as any had need. [...]
>
> Now the whole group of those who believed were of one heart and soul, and no one claimed private ownership of any possessions, but everything they owned was held in common [...] There was not a needy person among them, for as many as owned lands or houses sold them and brought the proceeds of what was sold.
>
> — ACTS 2:43-4; 4:32, 34

Biblical Foundations

The New Testament portrays Christ as a messiah who fulfills the economic hopes of the Torah, particularly the hopes of the poor and oppressed, as this reference to Deuteronomy indicates. That is what made his gospel such a radical hope for the downtrodden and "good news to the poor." It is important to see that one of the first practical effects of Christ's resurrection on the community he left behind was the economic fulfillment of the Torah, that all was held in common and no one was in need. It was so important to Luke's portrait of the first community that he described this economic communalism *twice*.

A common suggestion is that the communalism of Acts 2 and 4 was voluntary and did not indicate an economic practice as much as a moral one. Roman A. Montero argues otherwise:

> Putting the economic teachings of Jesus, based on the principles of the Jubilee and Sabbatical laws, into practice was not optional for the early Christians; it was not something that a Christian might do if he or she feels like being an especially nice person. This was something that a Christian must do, was obligated to do; it was just as central to the early Christians as was refraining from idolatry and fornication.[16]

Several Church Fathers echo this point, as we will see in chapter four. Economic sharing was *not* optional. This practice was only voluntary because being a Christian was voluntary. However, a Christian could not do otherwise but share freely. Thus, this approach establishes a model for how to apply Christ's words today. The first Christians held all things in common on principle. That establishes the pattern for our Christian economic philosophy. Or, at the very least, it indicates that Christian faith is fundamentally against economic inequality.

Acts 2 and 4 demonstrate what it looks like to fulfill Jesus' rebuke of mammon. The first Christians took these words seriously and thus renounced all allegiance to mammon by sharing in common their material resources. They demonstrated the implications of Christ's rebuke. They recognized what material abundance is for, not to hoard it but to share. Thus, wealth in itself is not the issue but hoarded riches. The first Christian community used material abundance for the benefit of all. It would be an error to think that Jesus' radical rebuke of mammon meant that material wealth must be abandoned entirely. On the contrary, wealth can and should be a tool for justice, but *hoarded* wealth is emphatically and repeatedly rebuked as an idol.

4. James

Another potent anti-mammon witness is James 5, which evokes the spirit of the prophets in rebuking the rich:

> Come now, you rich people, weep and wail for the miseries that are coming to you. Your riches have rotted, and your clothes are moth-eaten. Your gold and silver have rusted, and their rust will be evidence against you, and it will eat your flesh like fire. You have laid up treasure for the last days.
>
> — JAMES 5:1-3

Hoarded wealth rots and spoils; shared wealth is a blessing to all. The rich treat material abundance as an object to be collected and accumulated. They are hoarders. But for the poor, money is a means of survival. Those who share with the needy build an eternal reward; they lend to the Lord. But those who hoard wealth only heap upon themselves judgment and spiritual disease. Covetousness corrupts the soul, while generosity liberates. The greed of the rich consumes them; the only salvation for the rich is to help the needy.

A unique contribution of James 5 is its investigation into *why* the poor are poor. James' approach establishes a radical way of thinking about poverty that is still foreign to the Church today but is vital for us to learn. It involves seeing poverty as a systemic issue, recognizing the power imbalance between rich and poor, and ultimately, unmasking the injustice and violence at the heart of inequality. James argues that the poor are *made poor* by the rich; poverty is *not* accidental. Poverty is not the result of laziness but of injustice. The only moral failure is the corruption of the rich, not the desperation of the poor. James describes this in detail:

> Listen! The wages of the laborers who mowed your fields, which you kept back by fraud, cry out, and the cries of the harvesters have reached the ears of the Lord of hosts. You have lived on the earth in luxury and in pleasure; you have fattened your hearts in a day of slaughter. You have condemned and murdered the righteous one, who does not resist you.
>
> — JAMES 5:4-6

The rich like to claim they have earned riches, but James lifts the veil and demonstrates how riches come from injustice by exploiting the labor of the poor. That is how the rich acquire their wealth. He describes an agrarian society wherein the laborers do not receive the full value of their work but are taken advantage of by the rich, who profit off their toil and hardship. Thus, the rich become wealthy not by earning their gold but by exploiting the labor of others. Therefore, the very mechanism of their wealth is injustice and theft.

Furthermore, they know that the laborers have no other option. The rich exploit the systemic injustices of society to abuse the vulnerable and profit from their misery. It is a form of social violence. There is a power imbalance between the rich and the poor; the rich abuse their privileged position to increase their riches and suppress the rights of the poor. James identifies violence, theft, deception, and the exploitation of the vulnerable who have no other choice as the true source of the riches of the wealthy.

The situation is the same today. No one *earns* a billion dollars. It is only through the violence of a system that profits off the poor. Consider the exploitation of the so-called third world by the first. Those of us living in the West often fail to consider how our luxuries exist by exploiting and oppressing the global south. Our sugar, fruit, clothes, and consumer products are affordable *because* the rich take advantage of the poor who make them. Instead of paying a fair wage to workers in America, companies pay 1% of what they would pay here by paying poor workers in the third world. Our luxuries are soaked with the blood, sweat, and misery of the poor. This system of violence towards the vulnerable is the foundation for the enormous profits of the rich. The exploited poor have no choice but to accept whatever terms the rich offer them. Economic violence against the poor is the core of the capitalist system.[17] The neoliberal economist Milton Friedman recognized this and wrote, "The hidden hand of the market will not work without a hidden fist."[18] Capitalism relies on force.

James' reflections raise an essential point. It is not enough to help the poor with charity. We must also ask systemic questions about *why* they are poor and what keeps them bound to cycles of violence. In today's world, why have enormous increases in productivity and profits not resulted in a more liberated society? Why must people suffer from homelessness if millions of homes sit empty? We produce more with greater efficiency than ever before. We have the means to feed, clothe, house, and care for everyone. Modern agriculture produces enough food for ten billion people. So why do millions die every year from hunger? Why are we more productive than ever, yet we struggle to provide everyone the right to life? James' answer is worth taking seriously: the poor are poor because they are exploited and oppressed by the rich. "Is it not the rich who oppress you?" (James 2:6).

Another aspect of James' rebuke is his emphasis on the judgment of the Lord against injustice. Hope in the coming Kingdom includes hope in the rich being brought low and the poor, whom they have exploited, lifted from their misery. Christ often spoke of this eschatological reversal, "The first shall be last, and the last shall be first" (Mt. 19:30). This reversal has profound economic implications. The poor shall be exalted, and the rich will be brought to shame. Or, in Mary's words, the rich will go away empty while the poor will be fed (Lk. 1). Justice in the Kingdom looks like the condemnation of the rich and the blessing of the poor. Christian hope for Christ's eschatological Lordship is intimately bound to this reversal.

The Church today has failed to take the message of Jesus seriously. We commonly condemn the "lazy poor" but not the exploiting rich who oppress the poor. However, the Bible has no concept of the "undeserving" poor and often rebuked the unjust rich. We are obligated to help the poor—full stop. There are no conditions placed on this commandment. We often coddle the wealthy by softening Christ's words while proclaiming moralistic judgments to shame the poor. In contrast, James 5 and Luke 6 demonstrate that the gospel proclaims "woe" to the rich and "blessing" to the poor. May we proclaim *this* gospel again today.

5. Paul

In Paul's first letter to Timothy,[19] he stresses the importance of modest, inexpensive clothing (1 Tim. 2:8-10) and that bishops must not be in love with money (1 Tim. 3:3). At the center of both issues is the virtue of contentment. The rich never have enough. That is the downfall of greed; it is unending and self-destructive. The greedy man tries to improve himself by *having more* rather than being content with what he has and striving to develop a good character of faith, love, and hope. Thus, the rich hoard wealth while the righteous are rich in good works. This is the context of the most famous saying in the Bible regarding money, "The love of money is the root of all evil" (1 Tim. 6:10). The full passage is worth considering:

> Of course, there is great gain in godliness combined with contentment; for we brought nothing into the world, so that we can take nothing out of it; but if we have food and clothing, we will be content with these. But those who want to be rich fall into temptation and are trapped by many senseless and harmful desires that plunge people into ruin and destruction. For the love of money is the root of all kinds of evil, and in their eagerness to be rich some have wandered away from the faith and pierced themselves with many pains.
>
> But as for you, man of God, shun all this; pursue righteousness, godliness, faith, love, endurance, gentleness. Fight the good fight of the faith; take hold of the eternal life, to

which you were called and for which you made the good confession in the presence of many witnesses.

— 1 TIMOTHY 6:6-12

First, Paul juxtaposes "gain" with contentment. The pursuit of "gaining" riches is deemed noble by the world, yet Paul subverts this assumption to argue that true gains are found in the holiness of contentment. Seeking to be rich is a trap. Thus, there is far more value in the contentment of faith than in all the riches of the world. That is the true and godly "gain" we should pursue.

Paul then reflects on a familiar theme from wisdom literature: We came into the world naked, and we leave naked. Paul applies this to the meaninglessness of hoarded riches. The realization that we are "dust and to dust we shall return" makes hoarded riches an apparent absurdity. What good is it to hoard more wealth than we can spend in a thousand lifetimes when we cannot take any of it with us? We are but a breath, here a moment, then gone. What good is all the gold in the world when one corpse is just as poor as another? Or, as Jesus asked, "For what will it profit them to gain the whole world and forfeit their life" (Mk. 8:36)?

We only have one stomach. We only have one body to clothe, one head to put a roof over, and one life to live. Yet the rich hoard luxuries to adorn their every waking moment while millions live in poverty and degradation without daily bread. The problem with the world is not the supposed laziness of the poor but the insatiable greed of the very rich, who do not need their riches yet hoard it at the expense of the poor, many of whom die or die too soon because they do not have enough.

The Christian approach to money is simple: be content with enough. Anything hoarded in excess—that is, beyond subsistence living—belongs to the needy. This principle repeated throughout the Church Fathers, most notably in Basil, who argued that the extra bread in your pantry *belongs* to the hungry. The extra houses hoarded by the rich belong to the homeless who have no place to lay their head; the extra food and material goods thrown away or wasted because they cannot be sold for profit belong to the hungry and needy. Paul suggests that contentment is the guiding principle for how we should live. To be content is to accept subsistence living and give away what's left over. By definition, the rich sin by hoarding more than they need.

Many say the rich do not "owe" anything to the poor. But the Christian message says otherwise. The rich owe a debt to the poor *because* they are rich. By giving alms to the poor, the rich free themselves from a great stumbling block, threatening to destroy their mind and soul. Greed is a disease that consumes all those who make it their god. That is why Paul refers to the desire for riches as a senseless, harmful trap. Truly, it is easier for a camel to go through the eye of a needle than for a rich man to enter the Kingdom of God.

That is also why Paul tells Timothy to *shun* the pursuit of wealth. The word in Greek is aggressive. N. T. Wright translates it as "run away," as if to flee in terror.[20] Cyprian of Carthage of the third century vividly expounds on this point, writing, "Such wealth is to be avoided as an enemy, to be fled as a thief, to be feared by its possessors as a sword and poison."[21] The image evoked by Cyprian adds depth to Paul's point. Riches should be avoided like an enemy.

Thus, the pursuit of riches is unchristian. We either follow Christ or mammon. The two directions could not be more opposed to each other, which is Paul's point. To *flee* from something, one must be running towards something else, towards safety. The way of Christ is antithetical to the way of mammon.

We must flee from the love of money, which Paul calls the root of *all* evil. It is strange that theologians have not made more of this statement. We talk about the doctrine of original sin almost exclusively in spiritual terms. Yet Paul is direct in saying that the root of evil is the love of money. Thus, original sin has an unavoidable material dimension. Sin cannot be a purely spiritual failure if Paul's statement is taken seriously.

Today, the love of money is systematized under capitalism. To live in capitalism necessitates loving money because money is life. That is why capitalism itself is a system of evil, a social form of original sin, which must be overcome in Christ's name. If the root of evil is the love of money, then certainly, a systematic critique of capitalism is not only possible for the Christian faith but *necessary*.

Paul concludes the letter with a direct word to those already rich in this life:

> As for those who in the present age are rich, command them not to be haughty, or to set their hopes on the uncertainty of riches, but rather on God who richly provides us with everything for our enjoyment. They are to do good, to be rich in good works, generous, and ready to share, thus storing up for themselves the treasure of a good foundation for the future, so that they may take hold of the life that really is life.
>
> — 1 TIMOTHY 6:17-9

Hoarded riches are *unreal*. They are divorced from the life that truly matters. We often stand in awe at the extravagance of the rich and wonder what planet they live on. Indeed, they do not live in the real world. Their greed for riches ruins them. For the rich, to be human is to *have things*— better things, and more things—at the expense of their very soul.

Paul is commanding the rich to give up their arrogance *by giving up their riches* and being *rich in good works*. What does this mean other than to give extravagantly to the needy? And by doing so, to hazard their status as the rich? To become content with enough and to give away everything else that is superfluous? I think that is what Paul is getting at. Thus, far from codling the rich, he is prodding them to do good and be rich in Christ by giving away their excessive wealth to the needy. That is how they will flee from the love of money and follow Christ.

Those who turn Paul's words into an excuse to justify the riches of the wealthy are missing the point. The only way to become rich in good works is to share the riches one has with those who lack. This is a radical call for the rich to renounce their riches. It is a mistake to read Paul here as watering down Christ's difficult words to the rich young man: give up everything you own and follow Christ. I would argue Paul is making the same command, only saying it differently. One cannot be rich in good works and rich in hoarded material wealth; the two realities are antithetical.

Riches are dehumanizing. A person becomes a thing by hoarding things. The rich think owning stuff makes their lives real and true. But it is a false life, a shallow existence. We are not human *havings*, but human beings. Thus, the rich are humanized by generosity, by giving up all they own and becoming content with the simplicity of *enough*. When the rich abuse the poor, they harm themselves. Freedom comes, however, from renouncing mammon and following Christ by giving away their riches for the least of these. That is the model of Christ, who was rich and yet became poor for our sakes. To be a Christian is to walk that very same road. Thus, to follow Christ and remain rich is to renounce Christ and his radical way of solidarity with the poor and needy. It is to renounce the Kingdom of God, where the first are last, and the last are first. Therefore, a "rich Christian" is an oxymoron.

6. The Early Church

Having established the biblical foundations for an anti-mammon gospel, we now turn to the Early Church Fathers. Of course, the Bible's critique of unjust wealth has not been exhausted with this chapter. Indeed, we have barely touched the surface. But this brief survey is sufficient to set the stage for the witness of the Church Fathers, to which we now turn.

2

CAN THE RICH BE SAVED?

This question is an awkward one. Because we know, of course, that God is powerful to save. So why doubt the salvation of the wealthy? For the first Christians, it was rooted in two considerations. First, the origin of wealth is injustice, exploitation, and violence (physical or social). And second, mammon is a rival deity that must be rejected and hated by a Christian. Because of the impossibility of serving Christ and mammon, the Early Church wondered how a rich person could be a Christian and *remain* rich. The rich can be saved, but can they keep their riches after becoming a disciple of Christ, who commanded the rich to give their wealth to the needy?

Clement of Alexandria's answer is familiar, although he retains a radical edge. He concluded that, yes, the rich can be saved by grace. The rich are no different than any other sinner, accordingly. *But*—and this is key—the rich Christian must strive to become rich in *good works* and, therefore, must give away their wealth. Indeed, "almsgiving" was considered a prerequisite for the rich to be saved by some Fathers. Charity was not optional. Justo L. González summarizes Clement well, writing:

> Thus the full answer to Clement's question 'who is the rich to be saved?' is that those among the rich will be saved who measure their possessions by their real need, consider the rest superfluous, and give it to the needy.[1]

Thus, the rich prove their faith by giving their excess wealth to the needy; they do not hoard luxuries for themselves but store up riches in heaven, i.e., "good works" of righteousness. How does this relate to the nature of divine grace? Does this not turn salvation into a *work*?

Most Christians can recite Paul in Ephesians 2 that we are saved by grace through faith. But perhaps this concept alone, removed from a larger biblical context, has been overemphasized at the expense of ignoring salvation's demands on the individual and their community. Paul is right to stress that we are saved by grace through faith, but James is also correct in emphasizing that faith without works is dead (James 2). Both sides should be emphasized; one without the other can lead to serious theological and practical errors. The question about whether or not the rich can be saved, then, should be understood within this dynamic. Christ, of course, is powerful to save all sinners, the rich included. That was not denied by those asking the question. Instead, this question becomes vital because they take James' words regarding the *works* of faith seriously.

At the heart of this question is another: Is God's saving grace merely a one-and-done *transaction* or a lifelong *transformation*? The latter is preferred both theologically and biblically—despite the evangelical fallacy of reducing salvation to a "get out of hell free" card activated with a pre-scripted prayer. Thus, because salvation means transformation (i.e., sanctification), because it is not an empty transaction but a life-changing process, the question of the rich being saved does not downplay grace but actually heightens it. The question understands the true nature of grace.

In many regards, grace has become a commodity for evangelical Christianity, like any other commodity we can buy at the store. It is a commodity we purchase by saying a simple prayer. The commodification of grace is thus a result of modern capitalism infecting our theological thinking. Capitalism turns everything, even religious ideas, into commodities. But divine grace is no commodity. True grace is the grace we could never give ourselves, a costly grace that puts to death the old nature and raises us anew with Christ. Bonhoeffer's "cheap grace" is the grace we try to control like a commodity, while costly grace always leads to good works of love. The difference is between grace as a ticket to heaven vs. an initiation to following the way of Jesus Christ.

It is not grace if it leaves the sinner in the muck of their sin; true grace lifts the sinner out of their unholiness and into the righteousness of Christ. In other words, we must ask: Is it genuinely grace if it does not sanctify the person, leading them to follow Christ and forsake all other lords? Is not the most fundamental declaration of our faith "Jesus is Lord," which excludes service to any other master, most of all mammon? Can one honestly confess that Jesus is Lord while serving another master?

The rich can be saved. But the rich cannot be saved without being challenged to repentance by grace. Grace is not grace if it does not lead to transformation, and in the case of the rich, that looks like demanding good works of righteousness, namely, giving away their wealth. Put differently: The rich must be *liberated* from their slavery to mammon and given over to the slavery of Christ. The rich can do this by giving their wealth to the needy. The point is not that good works save, but that faith is dead without good works. That is made explicit in Christ's teachings on mammon, which established a clear either/or. Thus, at the root of this question is the presupposition that to *remain* rich is to remain un-sanctified, stubbornly. It is to reject the *effects* of grace. And that is why the question of the rich's salvation is potent.

To draw an analogy from history, we might ask another question: Can a member of the KKK be a Christian? Or would the love of Christ not command them to love their neighbor as themselves? Is it possible to be "saved" by Christ without walking the *way of Christ*? Jürgen Moltmann argues that it is not enough to talk only about the nature of Jesus Christ theologically; we must also be concerned with the *way* of Jesus Christ.[2] Thus, to be a Christian is not so much about professing a set of doctrinal creeds as it is *learning to walk Christ's way.* And Christ's way *excludes* hoarded riches, as we have seen from surveying the Scriptures. Thus, we must either follow the way of mammon or Christ.

So if the rich become Christians, they will not remain rich for long according to what it means to follow the way of Jesus Christ. Thus, the Early Church Fathers were skeptical of any rich person claiming Christ as their Lord. The expectation was for the rich to "put their money where their mouth is" by giving away their excess resources to the needy, proclaiming Jesus is Lord with their riches, not just their words.

Just as we today might be skeptical of any member of the KKK claiming to be Christian, the Early Church was suspicious of any rich person claiming Christ as their Lord. Of course, there were KKK members who claimed Christ—a large number, sadly, which speaks volumes about the shameful history of white supremacy in America (a subject for another book).[3] But it also says a lot about how powerful oppressors have co-opted the Christian faith to harm the vulnerable, to brutalize and murder the "least of these," all in the name of Christ. The Christian message is misused by those who justify the violent systems of oppression that affect the poor and weak today, namely, global capitalism and imperialism.

In this chapter, we will examine quotes relating to these two points. First, that riches are rooted in injustice and sin, and second, that following Christ means serving Christ alone by hating and rejecting mammon.

The way of death

 There are two ways, one of life and one of death, and there is a great difference between the two ways. [...] But the way of death is this[:] loving vain things, pursuing a recompense [repayment/compensation for damages], not pitying the poor man, not toiling for him that is oppressed with toil, not recognizing Him that made them, murderers of children, corrupters of the creatures of God, turning away from him that is in want, oppressing him that is afflicted, advocates of the wealthy, unjust judges of the poor, altogether sinful. May ye be delivered, my children, from all these things.[4]

— THE DIDACHE

Written sometime in the first or second century, the Didache is one of the earliest Christian texts outside the New Testament. The Early Church held it in such high esteem that a minority of Fathers—such as Clement of Alexandria and John of Damascus—considered it Scripture. It explains the "teaching of the Lord to the Gentiles by the twelve apostles." It is the oldest written Christian catechism (a summary exposition of doctrine). Thus, it is among the oldest sources outside of the New Testament for understanding what the first Christians believed and offers valuable insight into what early Christian communities thought about wealth and poverty.

The text describes two ways: the way of righteousness leading to life and the way of evil leading to death. It is patterned after Matthew's gospel, especially Christ's Sermon on the Mount (Mt. 5-7). The text has three parts: Christian ethics, rituals and practices, and Church organization. This first ethical section includes familiar commands like loving one's neighbor, blessing those that curse you, praying for your enemies, and turning the other cheek. The text summarizes Christian beliefs and practices for outsiders (i.e., Gentiles).

The anonymous author follows Jesus' either/or between God or mammon with a life/death schema. The point is clear: the way of mammon is irreconcilable with the way of Christ; the former is a way that leads to death, and the latter is a way to life.

There are several notable insights from this passage. Perhaps the most interesting—and a bit shocking—is that the text considers those who act as "advocates of the wealthy" to be on the way of death. In other words, it condemns apologists for the rich. In contrast, the way of life means siding with the poor, not the rich. Advocating for the wealthy and defending their interests is so common that it seems absurd today to suggest that this would be a sinful approach to the rich and poor—but that is what the Didache does.

This is instructive for those who think it is unfitting for a Christian to judge or condemn the wealthy today. The rich do not need protection—the poor do. This condemnation of advocating for the rich has radical implications for our situation today.

A modern example is the labor struggle. Workers standing alone are vulnerable, but together, they can collectively bargain for better working conditions and fairer wages, and to exercise more of a voice in their company, which profits off their labor. But when laborers unionize, strike, or struggle for their rights, vocal critics side with the powerful bosses against the workers. But the workers are the source of value—and thus profit—for the company. Without them, the company cannot operate.

I have worked various warehouse jobs, and from firsthand experience, can attest to the real risk manual laborers take every time they clock in. I have also worked in retail, an emotionally abusive job far more difficult than any office job I've ever had. I was lucky enough to leave the warehouse and storefront to pursue other opportunities, but many people will make a career out of either kind of work. The working conditions in a warehouse are dangerous and difficult, and the workers are vulnerable to injury. All it takes is a back or knee injury to be out of the job. And that is not to mention the long-term damage, such as chronic back pain or other health risks. Retail workers are seldom better off—their injuries are just better hidden. I can attest to the mental distress of working retail, which had lasting effects on my overall mental health for years after I left.

Apologists for capitalism often mention how much "risk" the capitalist takes when starting a company. But the truth is, their workers take far more significant risks every day. They risk not only their bodies and long-term health but sometimes their lives. That is not hyperbole. Recently, exploitative practices in a major US retailer directly led to the deaths of six people.[5] And for those who are only injured on the job, they often risk their family's financial security. And that is without mentioning the perpetual threat of sudden unemployment, which can be horrifically destabilizing. Large companies will report record profits yet lay off much of their labor force without explanation (though it is clear that the reason is to put more money in the pockets of wealthy shareholders). The capitalist risks only their capital—though sometimes it is not even theirs, and they can always declare bankruptcy—but workers risk far more.

The worker is vulnerable. The Didache does not have twenty-first-century labor conditions in mind, of course, but in an agrarian society, a very similar situation is the probable context of this rebuke of defending the rich. The rich were typically large land owners that hired day laborers for their harvests. Day laborers were among society's most vulnerable and exploited, often living below subsistence levels and thus vulnerable to abuse. And in that situation, they would be forced to accept whatever small wages they are offered—because the alternative was starvation. So, the context of this rebuke has direct implications for today. At the root of both issues is *exploitation.*

The difference between rich and poor is not material security or lack thereof. It is also an indicator of *social power.* The rich wield enormous social power over the poor. To defend their interests over that of the poor is to side with the powerful in their exploitation of the powerless. That dynamic is a way that leads to death both socially and physically. The Didache makes clear that a Christian must be a voice and defense of the poor and to rebuke the exploitation of the rich against the vulnerable.

There are seven times in the passage above where the text commands us to defend the poor against the rich. First, the Didache critiques the practice of recompense, which means seeking repayment. This likely refers to usury, wherein the rich lend to the poor at extortionist rates to profit off their misery. Today, usury is common; loan sharks and high-interest rates are still a burden on the poor, a practice that relies on exploitation. Or consider the student debt crisis in the United States, which often cripples the financial future of the disadvantaged. This command against usury defends the poor against the methods of the rich to exploit their vulnerability. We will talk about usury in chapter six, but for now, it is worth noting that usury is based on the exploitation of the powerful against the powerless and desperate.

Second, not pitying the poor leads to death. I do not think "pity" here should be read as simply an emotional response, as if it is okay to *feel* sad for the poor without *acting* to help them. It is not enough to feel sympathy for the destitute. Like the good Samaritan, we should do everything we can to help them in their plight.

Third, it is wrong not to labor with those that toil, that is, failing to take sides in situations of injustice. Poverty is a violent cycle that keeps the poor bound to their condition. The Christian way of life is to act in radical solidarity with the laborers exploited by the rich for profit. This has a direct implication for those who do not stand in solidarity with the vulnerable struggling for their rights, such as in the labor struggle.

Fourth, the Didache condemns turning away the needy. Giving to the needy is not *optional* for Christians, as we will see in chapter four. Failing to help the "least of these" is a failure to help Christ (Mt. 25). It is our obligation to help those in need.

Fifth, the Didache rebukes oppressing the afflicted. This is because God's concern for the oppressed is such a central theme in the Bible. But today, we have majored in the minors, such as minute differences in doctrine, while in the Bible, the main point is doing justice to the poor and needy, freeing the oppressed, and releasing the captives. Therefore, we must once again be a Church that takes the command seriously to be allies of the oppressed, to end their oppression.

Sixth, the Didache critiques being advocates of the wealthy, which we addressed above, and seventh, unjustly judging the poor. Thus, it is clear from all seven of these descriptions that not helping the poor is a way that leads to death. The way of death is the way of the rich, who hoard their wealth at the expense of the poor. The exploitation of the vulnerable means social death for those struggling to survive. The Christian message is antithetical to those who defend the rich and trample the poor. The gospel condemns the hyper-capitalist approach to life—wherein the only purpose is to make as much money as humanly possible—calling it a way leading to death.

Like a difficult walk on briars with bare feet

'And from the third mountain, which had thorns and briars, they that believed are such as these; some of them are wealthy and others are entangled in many business affairs. The briars are the wealthy, and the thorns are they that are mixed up in various business affairs. [...] Such men therefore shall hardly enter into the kingdom of God. For as it is difficult to walk on briars with bare feet, so also it is difficult for such men to enter the kingdom of God.[6]

— THE SHEPHERD OF HERMAS

The Shepherd of Hermas was another early text, written slightly later than the Didache but still quite early, probably mid-to-late second century. Irenaeus, Clement of Alexandria, Origen, and others considered it Scripture, and it was canonical Scripture for some regions before the fourth century. But even for those Fathers that didn't, the text was highly influential—indeed, it was one of the most quoted sources outside the Bible. The Shepherd records five visions, twelve commandments, and ten parables to instruct and guide the Christian life. A notable feature of the text is its frequent attention to the problem of riches.

The Shepherd uses the metaphor of a man walking barefoot over briars (prickly shrubs and thorns that cut deep into the foot) to describe how difficult it would be for the rich to enter the Kingdom of God. This is a vivid image with a clear message. It evokes intense, debilitating pain. And while it is not impossible to walk through briars, it is clearly difficult. Thus, the meaning is clear: the rich cannot *easily* enter the Kingdom but must give away what they own, which they will do with great difficulty because the rich are lovers of money. It would be like physically injuring themselves by walking on sharp thorns. That is the difficulty of the rich entering the Kingdom of God.

Jesus' metaphor is more radical: "Indeed, it is easier for a camel to go through the eye of a needle than for someone who is rich to enter the kingdom of God." Another translation puts it like this: "Walking the good road is a hard thing for the ones who have many possessions. It would be easier for a moose to squeeze through the eye of a beading needle."[7] This translation captures how the Kingdom is not a static place but a *way*, which is the point of the Didache's way of life/death imagery. It is not merely about entering "heaven" but about following the way of Christ. The rich would find it easier to fit a camel through a needle than walk in the discipleship of Christ and follow his way.

Commentaries on this passage have softened the hard saying by suggesting there was a gate in Jerusalem called the "eye of the needle," which camels could squeeze through if they knelt down. But there is no evidence of such a gate, and most scholars believe this myth was a later invention (likely by Anselm in the eleventh century).[8] Furthermore, the phrase appears in Jewish thought, suggesting it has the quality of an aphorism rather than referring to a physical location. The Babylonian Talmud talks about an elephant going through the eye of a needle. It thus points to an unthinkable possibility. In Jesus' use, the point is that it is unthinkable that the rich might walk in the way of the Kingdom. That is why his disciples cry out, "Then who can be saved?"

The Shepherd of Hermas' image captures one aspect missing from the eye of the needle aphorism. While it is often admitted that the grace of God can save the rich, it is one thing to say that grace will save the rich and another to suggest that it will be a process of extreme pain and difficulty. But that is what the Shepherd captures with this image of walking barefoot on briars. The Christians who try to walk the way of Christ *and* the way of mammon will suffer because of it.

Unless it be cut away

'But the white and round stones, which did not fit into the building, who are they, lady?' She answered and said to me, '[...] These are they that have faith, but have also riches of this world. When tribulation cometh, they deny their Lord by reason of their riches and their business affairs.' And I answered and said unto here, 'When then, lady, will they be useful for the building?' 'When,' she replied, 'their wealth, which leadeth their souls astray, shall be cut away, then will they be useful for God. For just as the round stones, unless it be cut away, and lose some portion of itself, cannot become square, so also they that are rich in this world, unless their riches be cut away, cannot become useful to the Lord.'[9]

— THE SHEPHERD OF HERMAS

In his third vision, the Shepherd describes a tower representing the eschatological Church. First he describes how the tower is made of square stones, but then he describes round stones and how these stones do not fit in the tower. An angel explains to the Shepherd what this means. The round stones represent the rich and their wealth. To contribute to the tower's construction—to be a part of the Church—the rich must cut away their riches just as a round stone must be cut to fit into a square hole. It is quite similar to saying you cannot fit a "square peg in a round hole."

With this image, the Shepherd exemplifies how first Christians might have answered the question, Can the rich be saved? His allegory implies that a substantial change, a cutting away, must take place in the life of the rich before they can fit into the Church. For the rich to be saved, they must give away their riches. Excessive wealth has no place in the Church. The Church should not conform to the rich but rather the rich to the Church. Riches are a barrier to Christian fellowship.

Today, the rich are often celebrated in our Churches. We have conformed to the ways of mammon and its religion, capitalism. I am thinking specifically of the prosperity gospel and its proponents, many of whom are rich. However, the capitalist ethic of riches as a blessing is antithetical to Christ's way. Riches are not a blessing but a *barrier* to holiness. The Shepherd reminds us today that the Church should not conform to the ways of mammon but must remain a prophetic witness to the command that we must hate mammon if we truly love God—that we cannot love both.

Job and the man named by what he loved

"There was a certain rich man." What seemed better to him was not really better. According to Solomon's words, "a good name is better than much wealth." The opposite seemed better to him: great wealth rather than a good name. So, he is named by what he loved; he is called "rich," not "holy" or "just." But the poor man, who had nothing in this world, is called by the simple name of "Lazarus." But, see how the Savior of all describes the characteristic qualities of the rich man. He says, "And he was clothed in purple and linen, and he feasted splendidly each day." He did not give the man's proper name, but said, "There was a certain man," to bring out the element of uncertainty by this common designation, and to stress the common, insulting element by the unclarity. But it is not so with the just. How is it? Scripture says, "There was a certain man in the land of Uz named Job." And, "There was a man in Jerusalem whose name was Simeon." Why? Because Scripture adds about Job, "And that man was blameless, without evil, just, truthful, and God-fearing; and he refrained from every evil deed." And about Simeon, "This man was just and reverent, and awaited the deliverance of Israel, and the Holy Spirit of God was with him." Job was also rich, but he did not pass his life in luxury and lack of compassion. His house stood open to every needy person by his loving will. He treated no one unjustly, but helped those who suffered unjustly; he furnished the things needed for life to widows and orphans. For, these are the just deeds of just rich men.[10]

— ORIGEN OF ALEXANDRIA (185-254)

Origen was an influential third-century theologian, biblical exegete, and scholar. He is known for writing the first systematic theology (*On First Principles*) and pioneering a method for biblical interpretation known as the allegorical reading. This quote is from a homily on Luke, and Origen is commenting on Jesus' parable of Lazarus and the Rich Man.

Origen brings up the example of Job to contrast with the rich man in Christ's parable. Some might object to the claim that all riches come from injustice by pointing out how the Bible has plenty of examples of righteous rich men, such as Job. How can the Bible say that Job was *both* rich and righteous if what I am arguing is true, that riches come from injustice?

Origen brilliantly suggests that the rich man is named after what he loves. He does not have an honorable name but is called by what he possesses. Origen contrasts the rich man with Job, who is called righteous. Why is he not named by his riches? It is because his riches were shared freely for the benefit of all. Job's house stood open for the poor and needy to come and be fed, to benefit from his riches.

That is why the rich man is unnamed and condemned by Christ's parable, yet Job is still remembered today as just and wise. The rich man is named according to his bondage, but Job is known for his generosity and thus as a faithful servant of the Lord. Accordingly, Job is *also* known for what he loves. His trials prove that Job loved God above all else. That is how Origen answers the question of Job's riches. Job did not live in luxury or without compassion; he used his wealth to help those in need. Mammon is the lord and master of the nameless rich man in Jesus' parable, but Job used his riches as a tool and was not mastered by mammon.

We often overlook the material implications of Job's story by reading it purely as a spiritual allegory. But the father of allegorical readings of the Bible —Origen—makes a strong case for reading Job's story in the context of mammon and Christ's warning to the rich. Job was tested to see if he served God or mammon. As a result, his riches were restored, and his righteousness was confirmed because he proved through suffering that he served only one God and Lord. And Job's house was open to those in need.

Exterminating the desire for more

> How then is it possible for the rich man to be saved? By possessing his goods in common with them that are in need, being such as Job was, and exterminating out of his soul the desire of more, and in no points going beyond real need. [...]
>
> And we therefore, if we should taste as we ought of spiritual fruits, shall thenceforth not even account the things present to be anything, being seized by the desire of the things to come as with some most noble intoxication.
>
> Let us taste of them, therefore, that we may both be delivered from the turmoil of the things present, and may attain the good things to come, by the grace and love towards man of our Lord Jesus Christ, to whom be the glory and the might, now and ever, and world without end. Amen.[11]

— JOHN CHRYSOSTOM (349-407)

John Chrysostom was a prolific fourth-century Father, saint, and archbishop of Constantinople. "Chrysostom" is an epithet meaning "golden-mouthed" in Greek, which aptly describes his talent for eloquent and powerful orations. He was also one of the fiercest critics of the rich and used his rhetorical talents to criticize the injustices of the powerful sharply. For that reason, he is the most quoted Father in this book.

Chrysostom also practiced what he preached. He was appointed as the bishop of Constantinople, an extremely rich city. One of his first acts was selling the luxury items that adorned the bishop's palace to feed the hungry.[12]

For John, the rich are saved by holding their excessive riches in common with the poor, helping the hungry, clothing the naked, and liberating the oppressed. The rich need a healing that only Christ can offer, a liberation from the bondage of greed and selfishness. Chrysostom stresses that riches beyond the point of "real need" should be given to the poor. That is a radical challenge for the rich. But it is also a challenge to us today in the privileged first world.

When we can give, we should. We talk about tithing ten percent of our income, but what if we thought about giving according to Chrysostom's challenge? Then we would strive to give *everything* above "real need." What that might look like in the modern world is perhaps something different than what Chrysostom describes since some saving is essential for survival. But there is a fine line between saving for survival and hoarding. The metric of giving anything that goes beyond "real need" is a challenging one. Most of all, it is a critique of the rich who live in such absurd luxury that they do not even have a concept of what "real need" looks like.

The remedy is to become intoxicated with the things to come, the Kingdom of God. Christian faith is forward-looking. It is rooted in a profound hope for new heaven and earth. This hope draws us forward, working today for a better tomorrow and trusting God will make all things new. Christian hope must not lead us to escapism or to ignore the needs of the poor and oppressed. Rather, our hope must lead to radical solidarity with the needy *because* of Christ's coming Kingdom. Jürgen Moltmann explains:

> Those who hope in Christ can no longer put up with reality as it is, but begin to suffer under it, to contradict it. Peace with God means conflict with the world, for the goad of the promised future stabs inexorably into the flesh of every unfulfilled present.[13]

Let us be so intoxicated by Kingdom come that we fight tirelessly for justice and righteousness on the earth here and now, refusing to give up on the least of these for the sake of Christ.

The sin of wealth

> And these things I say, not because riches are a sin: the sin is in not distributing them to the poor, and in the wrong use of them. For God made nothing evil but all things very

good; so that riches too are good; i.e. if they do not master their owners; if the wants [i.e., needs] of our neighbors be done away by them. For neither is that light good which instead of dissipating darkness rather makes it intense: nor should I call that [true] wealth, which instead of doing away poverty rather increases it. For the [truly] rich man seeks not to take from others but to help others: but he that seeks to receive from others is no longer [truly] rich, but is emphatically poor. So that it is not riches that are an evil, but the needy mind which turns wealth into poverty. [...] Do but consider; which of the two among all men is reckoned disgraceful, to beg of the rich or the poor. Every one, I suppose, sees it at once:—of the poor. Now this, if you mark it, is what the rich do; for they do not apply to those who are richer than themselves: whereas those who beg do so of the wealthy: for one beggar asks not alms of another, but of a rich man; but the rich man tears the poor in pieces.[14]

— JOHN CHRYSOSTOM (349-407)

What is the sin of the rich? It is not riches themselves. God blessed the earth with abundance and called it good. Riches become evil when hoarded. Hoard wealth is a sure sign that money is the lord over the one who hoards it. Helping the needy liberates those enslaved by mammon. Chrysostom observes that hoarded wealth is not true wealth because rather than doing away with poverty, it increases it. That is a common theme for Chrysostom, true riches vs. false riches. True riches are found in good works of righteousness, while false riches are defined by hoarded material abundance.

In the second part of the quote, Chrysostom asks, "Where do the rich get their wealth?" He contrasts their approach with the poor. The poor ask the rich for assistance, but the rich become rich by exploiting the poor. The rich are more disgraceful than beggars because they seek their wealth by "tear[ing] the poor in pieces," while the poor merely beg to survive. The rich exploit down while the poor beg upward. Who is more condemned? It is clear, for Chrysostom: the rich.

This point is instructive for us today. Chrysostom clearly distinguishes between righteous and unrighteous uses of the earth's abundance. It is righteously used when shared for the good of all and unrighteously used when hoarded for the private luxury of the few. But what is most instructive in this example is how Chrysostom interrogates the *source* of the luxury of the rich. He refused to accept that the rich have become rich by accident. Instead, the rich become rich by *exploiting* the poor and vulnerable. It is a powerful image: the rich tear the poor to pieces.

The sin of inequality is portrayed vividly in another sermon by Chrysostom:

> The gold bit on your horse, the gold circlet on the wrist of your slave, the gilding on your shoes, mean that you are robbing the orphan and starving the widow. When you have passed away, each passer-by who looks upon your great mansion will say, 'How many tears did it take to build that mansion; how many orphans were stripped; how many widows wronged; how many laborers deprived of their honest wages?' Even death itself will not deliver you from your accusers.[15]

This further illustrates the connection between the rich's hoarded wealth and the poor's misery. Notice how directly Chrysostom traces the luxury of the rich to robbing the orphan and starving the widow. Riches do not happen in isolation from the poor.

Thus, Chrysostom suggests that it is not enough to help the poor while also accepting that poverty is a naturally occurring event. Instead, we must interrogate the source of differentiating riches. For us today, that leads to the necessity of a socioeconomic analysis of the causes of poverty, which is a point we will return to in chapter eight. But for now, let Chrysostom's conclusion challenge us to reflect on the way the rich exploit the poor. There is an imbalance in the relationship. Today, it is common for us to criticize the poor who are just trying their best to survive, but we fail to criticize how the rich exploit the poor. If we follow Chrysostom's example, we must focus on the disgrace of the rich, not the desperation of the poor.

He exalts the low and humbles the mighty

> If riches were a good, God would not have seated the poor before His own vestibule. And if He admits rich people also, wonder not for He admits them not on this account, that they may continue [to be] rich, but that they may be delivered from their encumbrance.[16]

— JOHN CHRYSOSTOM (349-407)

Chrysostom frames the salvation of Christ as liberation from the encumbrance—burden—of wealth. Indeed, if the rich are saved, it will not be *because* of their riches but in spite of them. Furthermore, he argues that their salvation does not permit the rich to *remain* rich. If the rich are saved yet stay rich, they remain in sin. In other words, Christ's salvation does not validate their riches. The existence of a rich Christian does not mean God accepts differentiating riches.

Calvinist theology has sometimes made this mistake. Calvin's doctrine of election (unintentionally) led to the question, "What gives us the assurance of election?" With this arose the search for criteria, the marks of election. One possible sign is economic prosperity. Calvin did not argue for this, but riches eventually became a sign of election. For many today—especially American prosperity preaching—it is still true that riches are a sign of God's favor.

Chrysostom contradicts this idea and argues that if God accepts the rich into the Church, it is not so that they can remain rich or, worse yet, become richer still. No, it is so that they might be *liberated* from their riches. *That* is the Christian word to the rich, not that their riches are valid, but that they can be liberated from the burden of their wealth.

Chrysostom's first sentence is also critical of our assumptions today about the acceptability of wealth. He points out that the poor are seated in a place of honor. Thus, if riches are a net good for the soul, why would God set the poor in a place of honor in the Kingdom? Why are the weak and needy exalted in Mary's Magnificat? Why are the rich and powerful brought low and put to shame?

It is a mistake to assume riches are a sign of blessing. Instead, as Chrysostom notes, it is the opposite. Riches are a sign of the sin of the rich and also a testament to God's grace to save sinners, even the rich.

Christ's message challenges our assumptions. What appears like a blessing on the outside—riches—is sinful and condemned when viewed with the eyes of Christ. That is the nature of the Kingdom: that the first will be last and the last first.

Attacking the rich?

> I am often reproached for continually attacking the rich. Yes, because the rich are continually attacking the poor. But those I attack are not the rich as such, only those who misuse their wealth. I point out constantly that those I accuse are not the rich, but the rapacious; wealth is one thing, covetousness another. Learn to distinguish.[17]
>
> — JOHN CHRYSOSTOM (349-407)

An ideological preoccupation of many Christians today is "peace," but it is often a false peace. It is peace as an *ideal* rather than the *fruit* of justice. Without justice, peace is an illusion. Jürgen Moltmann writes, "Peace is not the absence of violence, but the presence of justice."[18] When peace means upholding the status quo, then it is oppressive. A familiar objection to the critique of the rich is that it is too hostile for the Christian faith. It is unfashionable in a liberal society to disrupt the norm, but when the norm is built on injustice, it is sinful to accept the status quo without protest. Without seeking an end to oppressive systems, peace is just a word. Blessed are the "peace*makers*," not the peace*keepers* (Mt. 5:9).

Chrysostom's sermons ostracized the rich. Rich courtiers claimed that Chrysostom "had closed the Churches to them" because when he preached "the eyes of all would turn upon them."[19] When he preached on wealth, it was not the repetition of cliches, as our preaching often is today; but rather, Chrysostom proclaimed a radical message that led to public shame for the rich. But it is essential to recognize that this was not done arbitrarily. Chrysostom preached so harshly against the rich because the rich attacked the poor.

An attack on the rich is not a *disruption* of peace but a step towards it. The rich oppress the poor daily by exploiting their misery and poverty. The poor are kept poor and beaten down continually by the greed of the rich and the systems of capitalist exploitation. Poverty is violence against the poor. Tax cuts for the rich, leading to budget cuts in social spending, are an act of class warfare. It is a mistake to call for "peace" when there is no peace for the poor, homeless, or disadvantaged under capitalism. One might argue that even Christ was crucified in the name of "peace" by the Roman Empire.[20] But Pax Romana—or today's Pax Americana—is never true peace. It is peace by oppression. The rich must be brought low, the powerful must be humbled, the lowly must be exalted, and good news must be proclaimed to the poor.

The bondage of riches or the freedom of the cross

> The gospel thunders forth its divine warning: "Ye cannot serve two masters," and does any one dare to make Christ a liar by serving at once both God and mammon? Repeatedly does He proclaim, "If any one will come after me let him deny himself and take up his cross and follow me." If I load myself with gold can I think that I am following Christ? Surely not. "He that saith he abideth in Him ought himself also so to walk even as He walked."[21]

— JEROME (347-420)

Can the Rich be Saved?

Jerome was a late fourth-century theologian and scholar known for his Latin translation of the Bible (the Vulgate) and many excellent commentaries. He also wrote powerful letters, offering practical and theological guidance for Christian faith and living. This quote is from a letter to the monk Heliodorus, composed around 373 or 374.

Jerome argues that a person loaded down with gold cannot follow Christ. Only a disciple that takes up Christ's cross is truly free. Jerome lived as a hermit in the wilderness for some time, and even while he lived in Rome, Jerome tried to live the ascetic life. He recognizes that the rich carry a weighty and all-consuming burden. But the burden of Christ is light and liberating. It is the liberty of servitude, the joy of self-giving love, even to the point of death. That is true freedom: to not hold on so tightly to this world but to love as Christ loved, to love selflessly and sacrifice freely for the needy and downtrodden.

Wealth is not neutral. It is impossible to serve both God and mammon. Either we love God and are consumed by God's love for all people, or we love mammon and are consumed by the tyranny of greed. These loves are irreconcilable. Great wealth is a sin because to obtain such wealth means giving oneself over to a false lord and god. That is the tyranny of mammon, which can be overcome only by the love of God that liberates human beings into the life that is truly life.

That leads to a surprising realization: The rich need liberation just as much as the poor need relief. Indeed, the question about the salvation of the rich is at once a question of their liberation from the bondage of mammon. The rich are enslaved by greed; they are slaves of mammon. To break out of their bondage, they must renounce their wealth and help the poor. That is their redemption. That also explains why many teachers in the Early Church considered almsgiving a redemptive act.[22] A heart given wholly to God cannot be rich materially but in good deeds, which means giving away one's excess wealth to those in need.

Sure to burn in hell

> Those of you, whose estates are so far flung that you do not know where they are, who sheathe your palaces in marble, who string your villas, one after another, estate by estate—what was ever lacking, I ask you, to that old man? You drink from jeweled cups, he from a natural stream. You sew gold thread into your robes, he wore clothes that not even the most exploited of your slaves would wear [...] Covered with the meanest dirt, Paul lies at rest, sure to rise again in glory. The

> stones of carefully constructed tombs rest on you, with all your riches—sure to burn in Hell.[23]
>
> — JEROME (347-420)

This radical critique is from Jerome's *Life of Paul the Hermit,* written while he was living in Syria (379). Jerome contrasts the lifestyle of Paul the Hermit (a third-century Egyptian hermit and saint) with the lifestyle of the rich, resulting in a bitter reproach against riches. While the rich have so many estates, they cannot remember them all; Paul the Hermit lacked nothing. While they drink from jeweled cups, he drinks from the river. While they wore gold clothes, Paul wore rags. But now, Paul is buried in the earth with nothing to adorn his grave, while their graves are decorated with sumptuous luxury. Yet Paul will rise into glory, while the rich will surely burn in hell with their riches.

Peter Brown notes that Jerome is practicing the art of satire with this and other statements against the rich. The point was to provoke the conscience of the rich and urge them to repentance. "Indeed, what Jerome wrote about upper-class Roman society had the delicious triviality of great satire. His unfailing pen picked on the vivid minutiae of the day-to-day life of the fashionable rich."[24]

This practice of satirizing the rich was used elsewhere by Jerome to great effect. For example, in a letter to Paula about an illuminated bible that was being produced by the rich at great cost, Jerome comments: "The parchment page is dyed deep in purple, the letters are a trickle of gold, the bound volumes are dressed in gems—and the naked Christ lies dying at the gate."[25] There is a beautiful sharpness to this critique.

An example of renunciation: Paulinas of Nola

> "There," Martin kept exclaiming, "there is someone to imitate." He held that our generation was blessed in possessing such an example. For Paulinus, a rich man with great possessions, by selling all and giving to the poor has illustrated Our Lord's saying [Mt. 19:21]. He has proved that what is impossible with man is possible with God [Mt. 19:26].[26]
>
> — SULPICIUS SEVERUS, *LIFE OF SAINT MARTIN*

Martin of Tours was a fourth-century bishop; Sulpicius Severus records his comments, which refer to Paulinas as someone worth imitating. So, who was Paulinus, and what did he do?

Paulinus of Nola was an extremely wealthy governor in Rome. Upon converting to Christianity, he renounced his vast riches in a stunning counter-cultural act of devotion to Christ and rejection of mammon. Peter Brown describes the radicalness of this:

> Paulinus [...] had passed through a spectacular conversion. He has abandoned an entire senatorial fortune. It was like the crash of an avalanche. For the first time, Christian ascetic teaching had touched a male member of the super-rich.[27]

Brown further comments that this conversion was truly about wealth. Paulinus "had, in no uncertain manner, turned away from wealth."[28] Or, as Augustine writes, "Our Paulinus [...] whom, from being rich as rich can be, made himself extremely poor."[29] While Brown further notes that this act of renunciation was not immediate,[30] it was nonetheless a stunning testimony to the Early Church's understanding of how the rich might follow the way of Christ.

This chapter has considered wealth and salvation in the Early Church. The example of Paulinus of Nola is a fitting conclusion because it demonstrates that this was not just a matter of teaching but of action. Many Church Fathers, such as Basil, also practiced renunciation, but Paulinus is a radical example of an elite aristocrat who renounced his enormous wealth for Christ. Martin of Tours says that for the rich to pass through the "eye of a needle" (Mt. 19:25)—for the rich to be saved—they should follow the example of Paulinus and give away their wealth. The first Christians took Christ's words to heart: God or mammon. There is no middle ground.

3

THE EARTH IS COMMON

The current level of food production yields enough to feed ten billion people annually.[1] Yet millions go hungry daily, and over a billion people are food insecure worldwide. This contradiction exists because *profit* rather than *human need* determines food production and distribution. The factors that go into food waste are more complex than that, of course, but it would be naive to overlook how subjecting food to the will of mammon might lead to hunger for those unable to pay. When essential needs become a commodity for profit, the poor are denied their God-given right to life. We *could* eliminate systemic hunger with current levels of technology, but because profit is the economic priority, hunger remains a constant misery for millions. Food—a necessity for all—has been given over to the tyranny of mammon.

World hunger is not an accident. It is a direct result of the hoarded riches of the wealthy. The rich have privatized for profit the common earth given by God for the benefit of all. That is why many of the Church Fathers condemned private property as an unrighteous use of God's earth. Justo L. González explains:

> [T]he main cause of hunger and want in the world is the unwillingness of the rich to share with those in need. Such unwillingness creates misery [...] The rich must realize first of all that what they have is not really theirs but God's. They cannot take it with them when they die. Indeed, the only wealth that survives death is that acquired through loving one's neighbor and through properly administering God's

gifts. [...] All that is not necessary is superfluous and therefore must not be retained as long as others lack the necessities of life. To do otherwise, to claim that one has exclusive right to something that another needs, is tantamount to theft and even homicide. These views all three Cappadocians share.[2]

When discussing hoarded riches, we must remember that we are talking about the very few hoarding for themselves enormous means of subsistence, without which many suffer and die. It is a sin of omission but a sin nonetheless. Jesus condemned those who failed to help the needy, often reserving some of his harshest words for those who could help but did not (Mt. 25).

That is why hoarded wealth is sinful and unjust and must be condemned by the Church again today. The Godly use of wealth is to share it with the needy, to hold it in common. As we have stressed, hoarded riches are sinful; shared wealth is a blessing. The Church's task today is to proclaim the godly use of property and to critique the ungodly accumulation of resources for private profit while millions suffer from lacking essential needs such as food, water, shelter, and medicine.

"The earth is the Lord's and the fullness thereof." This declaration from Psalms 24:1 summarizes the biblical doctrine of property. First, it stresses that all creation belongs to the Lord. Human ownership is under divine providence and contingent on God's will. No property is absolute; it is borrowed on loan, and the debt is the Lord's. Second, God has determined the correct use of property as holding what is essential for sustenance in common. We are stewards of the earth whose stewardship is contingent upon using it in a Godly way. God alone determines what the earth is for and to whom it belongs. Legality is thus secondary to ethical use or misuse of God's earth.

In other words, property is not ours to do anything we want. That may be the *legal* definition of property—since Roman law established the right of private property—but stewardship is contingent upon the *righteous use* of property, not upon an abstract claim to absolute ownership.

Because the earth is common, the righteous use of property is to satisfy human *needs*. Property rights are not absolute but relative to the sustenance of all creation. The law of need is higher than the legal claim to property. Charles Avila summarizes this well:

> The right to subsist on nature's bounty is a right common to all.
>
> *The most basic title to property is the title of need.* To this title all other titles are subordinate, and by this title the right of ownership is limited. Any individual right of ownership is limited by the equal rights of others.

> The only valid, legitimate, ethical view of property, then, is one that considers its purpose. The right which human arrangements may accord individuals to own material goods cannot be anything but a *means to achieve the end* of these material goods, namely, the sustenance of all.[3]

Ownership is invalid whenever property is misused, such as when the few hoard resources while the many suffer. Thus, inequality and privatization go against God's created order. That is why the Torah established the practice of debt cancelation and commanded care for the stranger, orphan, and widow.[4] The obligation of those with excess is to share with those who lack. The Christian doctrine of property rests on God's ownership of the earth and desire for it be held in common for the benefit of all. No legal definition of property is more foundational for a Christian than this.

The Church Fathers frequently referred to the commonality of the earth in their defense of the poor. It was almost a given for them that the best approach to life is to share what is essential. They called unjust the practice of hoarding resources while others suffer. Righteous stewardship of the earth entails prioritizing the needs of the poor and weak and holding all things in common for the benefit of the community rather than the private profits of the few. Many Church Fathers, such as Basil, practiced this by selling everything they owned and giving it to the poor. The communalism of Acts 2 and 4 did not end with the New Testament but was practiced by Christians for hundreds of years in monastic communities as they held everything in common.

The Fathers condemn private property in favor of common property. The root of this condemnation is God's ownership of the earth. The land is sustenance; to deny the poor the right to subsistence is genocidal. Those who privatize what God has made common practice injustice. Their greed is the cause of the poverty of the least of these. We might rightly call them murderers who stockpile the common earth for profit while millions who could have been fed from their hoarded property die from hunger.

A capitalist society *encourages* hoarding the earth's resources. It is an economic system defined by "private property" and rooted in the privatization of common lands. The result is that the poor suffer greatly under capitalism, many of whom die from hunger or malnutrition or preventable diseases that would have otherwise been avoided had the resources of the rich been shared commonly for all—especially those in the so-called third world. Therefore, the Christian Church should condemn the privatization of the earth's wealth for the luxuries of the few as ungodly; it is a *misuse* of creation.

Koinōnia

It is God himself who has brought our race to a *koinonia,* by sharing Himself, first of all, and by sending His Word (Logos) to all alike, and by making all things for all. Therefore everything is common, and the rich should not grasp a greater share. The expression, then, 'I own something and I have more than enough; why should I not enjoy it?' is not worthy of a human nor does it indicate any community feeling. The other expression does, however: 'I have something, why should I not share it with those in need?' Such a one is perfect, and fulfills the command: 'Thou shalt love thy neighbor as thyself.' [...] For I know quite well that God has given us the power to use; but only to the limit of that which is necessary; and that God also willed that the use be in common.[5]

— CLEMENT OF ALEXANDRIA (150-215)

Clement was a second-century father and theologian who taught at the influential Catechetical School of Alexandria (with Origen). This quote is from the second in Clement's trilogy of works, the *Paedagogus,* which dealt with Christian ethics. Clement also wrote a treatise that asked if the rich can be saved. This passage examines the nature of Christian fellowship (koinōnia).

Koinōnia is an important New Testament word that is often translated as "fellowship," as in Acts 2:42, "They devoted themselves to the apostles' teaching and fellowship." Here and elsewhere, the term describes what it meant to live as a disciple of Jesus Christ. But the word means more than just coming together as friends: "*koinonia* is much more than a feeling of fellowship; it involves sharing goods as well as feelings."[6] It is notable that today the word "fellowship" among Christians rarely involves sharing material goods, even though it was central to the first Christians. That is clear from how Acts 2 described their fellowship, "All who believed were together and had all things in common" (v. 44). Paul also used koinōnia in describing a contribution to the poor in Romans 15:26.

This suggests that the core of Christian love—the love of fellowship—includes sharing with the needy, feeding the hungry, clothing the naked, and helping the stranger. For Luke and Paul, koinōnia is the core of Christian fellowship and praxis, explicitly related to sharing in common what one has with the needy. That is what it meant to be in fellowship: to share one's burdens. Fellowship today has become simply a social program, but the usage of koinōnia in Scripture indicates that Christian fellowship is more than just a social club. Instead, the economic sharing of goods defines Christian fellowship. Indeed, it could be suggested that any fellowship without the koinōnia of shared material needs is not truly a *Christian* fellowship, as Paul and Luke described.

The *Epistle of Barnabas,* written shortly after the New Testament period (around 135) in the second century, also uses koinōnia to describe the practice of Christian sharing:

> Thou shalt communicate [practice koinōnia] in all things with thy neighbour; thou shalt not call things thine own; for if ye are partakers in common [koinonoí] of things which are incorruptible, how much more (should you be) of those things which are corruptible!⁷

— EPISTLE OF BARNABAS, 19.8

The disciples who follow Christ share in incorruptible salvation; how much more should we share that which is corruptible?

In the quote above, St. Clement uses koinōnia to connect this vision of Christian fellowship with the original order of creation: all things are a blessing from God to be shared in common for the good of all God's creatures. That leads to his conclusion that all things *are* common, yet the rich hoard for themselves what belongs to all creation. Thus, Clement argues that God has given us the power to use the material bounty of the earth, but only within a set limit: *necessity*. What is necessary for sustenance is ours, but what goes beyond our "daily bread" belongs to those without. That is at the heart of this connection between sharing in Christian fellowship and the commonality of the earth.

Thus, at its core, the Christian faith is devoted to distributing resources and wealth for the good of all. God has given human beings the power over resources, but within the limit of necessity and to share the excess. "God... willed that the use [of property] be in common." This does not mean a total denial of personal property but of sharing what goes beyond the daily essentials of sustenance. It articulates the difference between a Godly and ungodly use of wealth and the earth's resources.

It may be helpful to clarify the difference between personal wealth and communal resources, i.e., the modern discussion about *personal* and *private* property. In brief, these two types of property are distinguished by function. If the property is used for the consumption and survival of an individual or their family, it is personal property. In Clement's words, personal property fits the description of "necessity" rather than excess. Private property, on the other hand, serves a wholly different function. Private property is the ownership over large manufacturing centers or distribution channels, which *could* benefit the common good but are instead monopolized for private profit. A simple distinction could be between a bed where one or two people sleep at night versus a factory that manufactures thousands of beds daily. The former is personal property ("necessity"), while the latter is private property.

Bread is another example. The motif of "daily bread" in the Bible reminds us that so long as our necessities are taken care of, the excess belongs to the hungry. Thus, the bread in our pantry is personal property under the definition of "necessity." In contrast, a bread factory run for private profit is private property and thus no longer within the realm of necessity. The phenomenon of capitalism is that bread is *not* produced to meet a human need but to turn a profit. Its distribution is in the hands of the wealthy few that determine who eats their "daily bread" and who does not, i.e., those who have money and those who do not. Thus, the capitalist usurps God's providence and distributes the earth's goods for their benefit. They hoard for themselves for private profit what belongs to God and was given freely for the good of all creation. Christian teaching is opposed to the core values of the capitalist economy, which prioritizes profit over people. Thus, it is against private property.

These points are far from Clement's passage, of course. He would have no concept of private property as we know it today. But what he argues points toward this interpretation by distinguishing between necessity and excess. The logic of this implies that anything beyond "need" belongs to God and thus to all in common.

Greed is dehumanizing because it transforms human beings into human *havings*. Greed distorts how we were created to live. Koinōnia is the God-ordained way of being human and fulfilling our potential. We were created to be outward-centered, to love as God loves, and give freely to our neighbor in the spirit of koinōnia. Community, not individualism, is the aim of creation.

The Triune God is a community of persons, a life of self-giving love: Father, Son, and Holy Spirit. The rich distort the image of God in themselves by hoarding what God gives for all in common. Human beings made in the image of God are created to help the needy and love their neighbor as themselves. Anything less is a distortion of humanity, a dehumanizing sin.

It is absurd that one man lives in luxury while so many suffer in poverty

> God has given us the power to use our possessions, I admit, but only to the extent that is necessary: He wishes them to be in common. It is absurd that one man lives in luxury, while so

many suffer in poverty. How much more glorious it is to serve many than to live in luxury. How much more reasonable to spend money on human beings than on stones and gold! How much more useful to have friends as our ornamentation than lifeless decorations! Can possessing lands ever give more benefit to anyone than practicing kindness? [...]

Riches should be possessed in a becoming manner, shared generously, not mechanically or ostentatiously. [...]

Wealth, in fact, seems to me like a snake; it will twist around the hand and bite unless one knows how to grasp it properly, gangling it without danger by the point of the tail. In the same way, wealth, wriggling either in an experienced or inexperienced grasp, tends to cling to the hand and bite unless a person rises above it and uses it with discretion, so as to crush the beast by the charm of the Word and escape unharmed.[8]

— CLEMENT OF ALEXANDRIA (150-215)

This quote is from Clement's main work, *The Instructor*. He again argues that possessions are limited by necessity. González summarizes this point: "The measure of proper use is necessity. Just as the size of the foot determines the size of the shoe, so should the needs of the body determine what one possesses."[9] Outside of necessity, property becomes sinful. Property and possessions, like a snake, can be deadly if not held correctly.

God has ordained all things to exist for the common good of all. Creation is a gift from God out of love for humanity. It is a sin against God to hold the right to life on the earth exclusively, to hoard the earth's resources for oneself in the name of private profit while others suffer and cannot find enough to eat. That is the ethical side of the commonality of the earth. Because the earth is common, the Lord has arranged it so that all might have enough to eat and live freely on the earth. It is a sin to hoard the earth's resources into private hands while others suffer from lack, to live in luxury while the poor die of hunger. The imbalance of resources between the rich and poor is in and of itself a sign of the sinfulness of the rich. They grasp more than their fair share and thus steal from God by hoarding what belongs to the poor.

Abundance is not the problem but differentiating wealth. Thomas Sankara echoes this sentiment, "We must choose either champagne for a few or safe drinking water for all." The choice is between prioritizing needs or luxuries. Sankara—the first president of Burkina Faso, who overthrew the oppressive French colonial rule—took courageous action for the benefit of his people. He did not just talk about helping the poor; he worked tirelessly to improve their lives.

Under Sankara's leadership, Burkina Faso experienced Africa's most successful literacy campaign, which raised literacy from 13% to 73% in just four years. His public health policies led to vaccinating 2.5 million children against meningitis, yellow fever, and measles—saving the lives of an estimated 50,000 children annually. In addition, he sold the government's fleet of Mercedes cars and made the cheapest car at the time (Renault 5) the official government vehicle. He also lowered the presidential salary because it would be unjust for the president to live in luxury while his country struggled to survive. Overall, Sankara's policies sought to improve people's lives by building schools, healthcare centers, and water reservoirs. He not only spoke about the goal of clean water for all but actively worked to build a better future for his people.[10]

Sankara's example illustrates what can be accomplished when we prioritize the needs of all over the luxuries of the few. That should also be the economic goal of the Christian faith—not to support a capitalist system that gives luxuries to the few but to prioritize the needs of the masses. Differentiating wealth is the heart of capitalism, but it is unacceptable to Christian ethics.

The rich are consumed by a "ravening and satanical lust" that consumes and dehumanizes them. Their lust for money is illogical. When the primary objective of an economic system is to satisfy the greed of the rich, then it is a fundamentally irrational and inhumane system. Poverty does not exist because we lack the ability to feed the poor but because we are unable to satisfy the greed of the rich.

Thus, the rich must be saved *from* wealth and the poor *from* oppression. Those are the two sides to liberation. The hoarded wealth of the rich is a disease for their soul, an alienating power, a rival god, an idol. And like all idols, it lives off the blood of those who serve it. But mammon is a demonic false god. The rich must be saved from their slavery to mammon. How? The answer is simple: by sharing their wealth. The point is not charity but radical repentance. Hold all excess riches in common for the sake of the poor. The point is justice—to hold all things in common. That is how the rich will be saved from the tyranny of mammon and the poor will be liberated from oppression. Repent and renounce mammon, share excess riches with the poor, live with "enough" by not trusting in hoarded riches, and follow Christ instead of money. The champagne lifestyle of the wealthy is unjust and will remain unjust so long as there are people who do not have clean drinking water.

All things in common except our wives

 Family possessions, which generally destroy brotherhood among you, create fraternal bonds among us. One in mind and soul, we do not hesitate to share our earthly goods with one another. All things are common among us but our wives.[11]

— TERTULLIAN (155-240)

Tertullian was a second-century apologist who defended the reasonableness of Christian faith and refuted popular heresies such as Gnosticism. This text is from his *Apology*, written to refute those who criticized Christian practices and beliefs. The "you" in this quote is thus the pagan unbeliever, and Tertullian distinguishes between their approach to possessions and the Christian approach.

This defense reveals two remarkable things about the early Christian community. First, it suggests that common ownership was a Christian practice that lasted beyond the first community in Acts 2 and 4. This practice was regular enough among Christians that Tertullian would need to defend it from pagan objections. Thus, Tertullian argues that holding possessions in common did not lead to strife and jealousy, as it does with the pagans, but that it led to deeper bonds as in a family. Christians were of one mind and soul and thus shared what they owned freely and without hesitation.

Second, it is remarkable that Christian generosity and common ownership practices would need to be defended against the claim of sharing their wives. Pagan rumors about Christian practices were widespread in second-century Rome. Some pagans even speculated that Christians practiced cannibalism during the Lord's Supper, while others thought their communal fellowship entailed sharing wives. The fact that Tertullian's defense of Christian practices had to clarify this point indicates how seriously the first believers took the command to share all things in common.

This objection has an interesting modern parallel. Marx had to offer a rebuttal against the claim that communists have a policy of communal wives or women.[12] But that was merely a slanderous rumor used to discredit socialism. Likewise, Tertullian had to defend the Christian practice of koinōnia against this objection. Apparently, anyone talking about common ownership —Christian or socialist—faces this objection. It is fascinating to find this objection in both Marx and Tertullian. For our purposes, this demonstrates how much the early Christian teaching on possessions shares with modern socialism.

Justice: piety and equality

> The two veins of justice are piety and equality; all justice springs from these fountains. While piety forms its source and origin, equity provides all its energy and method. [...] The whole force of justice lies in the fact that it makes equal everyone who comes into this human condition on equal terms [...] This is the greatest and truest fruit of riches: not to use wealth for one's own personal pleasure, but for the welfare of many; and not for one's own immediate enjoyment, but for justice, which alone endures.[13]
>
> — LACTANTIUS (240-320)

Lactantius was a third and fourth-century Christian writer and apologist from Northern Africa who served as an advisor to Emperor Constantine and a tutor for Constantine's son, Crispus. His most important work is *The Divine Institutes,* which is where this quote is from. The *Institutes* defend the Christian faith and criticize the pagan beliefs and practices of Rome. The work contrasts the pagan practice of reciprocity and patronage, common in Rome at the time, with the Christian approach to justice, which is directed not toward the rich and well-connected but toward the poor and needy.[14]

Lactantius links the love of God (piety) with justice, which is marked chiefly by equality. The origin of justice is the love and knowledge of God, but the method, the way justice works, is through equality. The proper use of wealth, then, is the welfare of many. To know God is to do justice, which means concretely doing justice for the poor and vulnerable.

A wise administration of society's wealth would follow a similar approach, prioritizing the welfare of the many over the private enjoyment of the few. But capitalism reverses this. Notice that equality is defined by Lactantius by this prioritization of the needy. Under capitalism, equality is blank and empty. It is the equality of oppressors who have equal rights to oppress as the poor have to be oppressed. Equality as an ideal without *justice* for the poor is an empty slogan. The rich will use this facade of equality to abuse the vulnerable. But the proper use of equality is to use riches for the welfare of all.

The commonality of the earth does not mean that everyone has equal access to exploit the earth's resources. Rather, it means that society should ensure that all have equal *access* to the common resources of creation. That means prioritizing the needs of the hungry over the luxuries of the rich. That is true equality and the Christian definition of justice. Preference for the poor and their needs is true equality not a contradiction of equality.

Greed has made it a right for the few

> God has order all things to be produced so that there should be food in common for all, and that the earth should be the common possession of all. Nature, therefore, has produced a common right for all, but greed has made it a right for a few.[15]
>
> — AMBROSE OF MILAN (340-397)

Ambrose was a fourth-century theologian, statesman, and bishop of Milan. Ambrose was known as an outspoken critic of the rich and defender of the poor, who recognized the social interdependence of each. According to Peter Brown, Ambrose "spoke as an advocate of the oppressed poor."[16] And he did so despite being a relatively rich man from the aristocratic class of society.[17] However, after he was ordained, Ambrose gave all his property to the Church and the poor.[18] Thus, he preached a powerful message against the rich and practiced it with good works.

Ambrose recognized greed as a threat to society. Ambrose thus emphasized that common sharing benefited *both* the rich and the poor. That is why some have argued that Ambrose's social ethics represent an example of proto-socialism within the Church[19]—as this quote demonstrates.

This quote is from Ambrose's *Duties of the Clergy*, written to advise the leaders of the Church on how to behave and lead their community. Ambrose argues that God has arranged the world so that all things might be used to meet the needs of all. The earth is not a commodity but a gift. God gave it for the good of all. The divine order of creation prioritizes the needs of all above the greed of the few. Ambrose here directly names two things that must be common, food and the earth (land). Greed has made these common gifts the exclusive right of the few. Thus, the privatization of necessities is a sin.

The logic for this is clear. If God created for the good of all, then those who greedily hoard for themselves the resources of the earth are guilty of sinning against their fellow creatures who lack essential needs. For one to have excess, another must suffer from a lack of essentials. The divine order of creation is disrupted by greed. That is why Ambrose considered greed a threat to society, not just the poor. Thus, it is in the best interest of all—rich and poor alike—to share the bounty of creation.

Many centuries later, Thomas Aquinas also recognized this distinction, writing, "In cases of need, all things are common property. There is no sin in taking private property when need has made it common."[20] This adds an important distinction. The commonality of the earth does not mean everything must be shared, including personal items. Personal ownership is not a sin unless it comes at the expense of meeting the needs of all humanity. Until everyone has enough to eat, clean water to drink, shelter, medical care, and other necessities, it is an injustice for the rich to hoard these things for private profit. Those things that supply needs should be held in common, while personal property is permissible so long as it does not hinder the needs of the poor.

What right have you to monopolize the soil?

> You rich, how far will you push your frenzied greed? 'Are you alone to dwell on the earth?' [Isa. 5:8.] You cast out men who are fellow-creatures and claim all creation as your own. Why? Earth at its beginning was for all in common, it was meant for rich and poor alike; what right have you to monopolize the soil?[21]
>
> — AMBROSE OF MILAN (340-397)

This quote is from Ambrose's *On Naboth*. The story of Naboth is found in 1 Kings 21. He was a Jezreelite who owned a vineyard beside King Ahab. One day, Ahab commanded Naboth to give him his vineyard "for a vegetable garden" (1 Kings 21:2). But the vineyard was Naboth's ancestral inheritance, and he refused sell it. That saddened Ahab—even though he is already rich, his covetousness was not content with his vast wealth and requires what others have. His wife, Jezebel, sees his distress and plots to kill Naboth after a show trial. After Naboth is stoned to death, Ahab takes possession of his vineyard.

It is a story that illustrates the abuse of the poor by the rich and powerful. Ambrose uses this to say that the same abuse happens every day when the rich exploit the poor, stealing what rightfully belongs to them as a free give of God. The common earth is given to all, the birthright of all creatures, but the rich, in their greed, seek to monopolize it for themselves. Ambrose powerfully suggests that "every day some Naboth is put to death, every day the poor are murdered."[22]

Ambrose is also challenging the supposed "right" of the rich and powerful to monopolize the soil for personal gain. Ahab did not *need* the vineyard. He wanted it for a garden. But it was very likely the only source of sustenance and income for Naboth. Thus, the story illustrates a common tendency among the rich to exploit the poor, taking for luxury what the poor rely on for sustenance.

Today, the rich still privatize the essentials of human existence but at a much larger scale. They have made food, water, shelter, and medical care a private means of enrichment. The Ahabs of this world—those with power and privilege—still exploit the Naboths, who are defenseless against their abuse.

When the COVID-19 pandemic first hit the United States, there was a panic-induced toilet paper shortage. As a result, some crafty individuals went out of their way to buy up all the toilet paper to sell it at a higher price on the streets. A few of these price gougers were arrested or fined, and most condemned their actions. In times of dire need, hoarding resources for profit is widely considered shameful by society.

Now apply that same principle to another essential for human survival: shelter. Large capital investors buy up houses and apartments to manufacture demand and charge high rates to people who have no choice *but* to rent from them or live on the streets. When more than half of the city is owned by capital investors, who do not even live there, the citizens suffer. They hoard essentials for profit. Like the toilet paper hoarders, housing "investors" do not create value—they do not build the homes, even if they fund them by paying someone else to build them—but instead, they force higher prices by monopolizing something everyone needs to survive.

The same is true about any industry that manufactures scarcity for profit. A few large companies now control most of what we consume, operating near-monopolies of essential products and services. When a handful of corporations produce 90% of what you buy, it can no longer be called a "free market." It is a dictatorship of the few over the many. Furthermore, their greed has manufactured a disposable consumerism culture, rapidly destroying the planet.

Ambrose cites Isaiah 5:8 to profound effect. Do the rich live on the earth by themselves? Because they certainly act as if they are the only ones with the right to earth's abundance. It is almost as if this is *their* world, and we all have to pay to live in it. But the earth is the Lord's and the fullness thereof. They have no right to monopolize what God has given all in common.

Against private property

> For [the philosophers] say that the first duty of justice is not to harm anyone unless provoked by injury; but this is voided by the authority of the gospel (cf. Luke 9:55). [...] Next, they deem it a duty of justice to consider the things that are common, that is, those what are public property, as public property indeed, and those that are private as private. But the

> latter term is not according to nature, for nature has brought forth all things for all in common. Thus God has created everything in such a way that all things be possessed in common. Nature therefore is the mother of common right, usurpation of private right.[23]
>
> — AMBROSE OF MILAN (340-397)

Justice, according to the Bible, is not passive but active. In contrast, the Socratic philosophers defined justice as doing no harm, as the absence of conflict. Many today still assume that definition. But justice means doing good for the least of these. Justice looks like loving our neighbor as ourselves. Thus, the individualistic notion of doing no harm to others is not enough for a Christian. It is not enough to refrain from injustice; we are called to do good works of righteousness.

Ambrose applies this concept of justice to private and common property. The problem with a passive definition of justice is that it supports the status quo without considering whether or not it is an unjust situation. Legality is not the same as justice. Defenders of private property hide behind legality, but divine justice condemns hoarded wealth. If the status quo is unjust, then the righteous should act to change it. Passivity is unjust in situations of oppression.

God created nature for all in common. Therefore, the right of all to hold the bounty of the earth commonly is original, while private property is usurpation. A usurper is someone who illegitimately claims by force what belongs to others. Thus, Ambrose calls usurpation the right of private property because it is rooted in the original injustice of taking what God made common for the private hoards of the few. For Ambrose, private property is injustice; justice is common property.

The earth is the Lord's; those who claim it as their possession blaspheme against God. What would it look like today to prophetically stand and declare God's ownership of the earth, to condemn those who abuse nature for profit and destroy the environment as blasphemers? The environmental crisis is easily the greatest existential threat facing humanity today. But it is not merely a human issue; it is also a theological problem. Our abuse of the earth is a sin against the creator.

A prophetic Christian response to the ecological crisis should include these points. First, the earth is the Lord's and belongs to all in common. This permits a more radical critique of society. Instead of focusing on recycling more or using electric cars, this radical critique leads to a fundamental rethinking of property laws.

Second, because a sin against creation is a sin against God, the Church should hold accountable those who have privatized the earth. If an oil baron attends Church and is not the recipient of a word of rebuke, then the Church has failed to proclaim the Word of God that day.

Third, the Church should focus on systemic issues at the root of the ecological crisis, not merely symptomatic issues. Ambrose's point in this passage leads to the potential for a radical critique of capitalism and its role in the ecological crisis. Chico Mendes, an outspoken defender of the Amazon rainforest who was later martyred for his passionate activism, summarized this point well: "Ecology without class struggle is gardening." Without a systemic critique of capitalism, our theological response to the ecological crisis is severely lacking.

Ambrose does not have the ecological crisis in mind, of course. But his critique can help us recognize the absurdity of something we take for granted today. We do not flinch at owning land, but it would have shocked Fathers like Ambrose to learn that every corner of the earth has been claimed for profit. Except for government-owned lands, there is not an inch of land that has not been privatized. But the Bible declares that the earth is the Lord's. Today, the ecological crisis has exposed the damage of privatization, of cutting down the forests, poisoning the rivers, and burning oil into the atmosphere. In such an extreme situation of sin against the earth and the Lord of the earth, we need to reclaim Ambrose's radical approach.

Let us therefore abstain from the possession of private property

Those who wish to make room for the Lord must find pleasure not in private, but in common property [...] Re-double your charity. For, on account of the things which each one of us possesses singly, wars exist, hatreds, discords, strifes among human beings, tumults, dissensions, scandals, sins, injustices, and murders. On what account? On account of those things which each of us possess singly. Do we fight over the things we possess in common? We inhale this air in common with others, we all see the sun in common. Blessed therefore are those who make room for the Lord, so as not to take pleasure in private property. [...]

Let us therefore abstain from the possession of private property—or from the love of it, if we cannot abstain from possession—and let us make room for the Lord [...] In property which each possess privately, each necessarily becomes proud [...] The flesh of the rich person pushes out against the flesh of the poor person—as if that [rich] flesh had brought

> anything with it when it was born, or will take anything with it when it dies.[24]
>
> — AUGUSTINE OF HIPPO (354-430)

Augustine was a fourth-century Father, theologian, and one of the most influential writers in Christian history. But a lesser-known passion of Augustine's life was his desire to develop a communal form of living among his friends. For a while, his experiment succeeded. His commune was radical in how it treated all property as common. Even clothing was shared by those in his community.[25]

Augustine's commune was an influential experiment that shaped the future trajectory of monasticism. For Augustine, the monastery was a "glimpse of the future." He explains, "The abandonment of private wealth was a first step toward the future. It pointed the way to a radically new world in which the private itself would fade away."[26] Thus, because the Kingdom of God will be a society without private wealth, where all things are common, the monastery should model that future here and now. This idea reflects Christ's parable about the Kingdom as yeast (Mt. 13:33). Monastic living is a foretaste of the future, yeast among the world that will cause it to hasten the arrival of that future.

Augustine describes his experiment:

> We had all but decided to withdraw from the mass of men and to live a life of philosophical detachment. [...] [W]e would pool all our belongings, creating a single household fund, so that in open fellowship no one would own this or that, but the contributions of each there would be common property, the whole of it for each, and all of it shared by all of us.[27]

It was a small experiment, not Augustine's ideal for society, but this experiment highlights an under-examined aspect of Augustine's teachings: his critique of private property.

One of the reasons for this critique is that private property leads to social unrest, such as war, murder, and injustice. The root of all this sin is the claim of some to privately own what God has given for the benefit of all. Augustine's remedy is to renounce private property—or at least the love of it—and "make room for the Lord" by holding common property.

Second, Augustine emphasizes that rich people become proud because of their property. Yet they were not born with property and cannot take it with them. It is much better to share property than to hoard it privately. Thus, private property causes the rich to oppress the poor and act unjustly. Only common property can lead to humility and justice.

Finally, the main reason is that private property will not exist in the Kingdom of God. As Christians, we pray for the Kingdom to come "on earth as it is in heaven." The Kingdom is not somewhere we go when we die; it is a reality we anticipate and await in the present. We anticipate the future reign of God by rejecting private property and striving to hold all things in common. That is why the first Christians practiced this early common ownership in Acts 2 and 4. They were anticipating the immediate arrival of the reign of God. That is still our hope and our anticipation.

A Christian apologist for private property must perform some wild mental gymnastics to justify their position. If there will be no private ownership in the Kingdom, then what is the reason for claiming that God has ordained private property and thus, capitalism? Christianity is not about validating the systems of this world in the name of God, such as capitalism. On the contrary, the Christian faith stands in perpetual revolt against every existing order in the name of the Kingdom of Christ which we anticipate and await eagerly. A Christian lives unreconciled to this world because our home is the world to come. That means no political, social, or economic system can be baptized in the name of Christ.

Privation as sin

> Let each man question himself regarding his soul, to learn to hate in it a private feeling [...] and to love in it that communion and society of which it is said, 'They had but one soul and one heart outstretched to God' (Acts 4:32).[28]
>
> — AUGUSTINE OF HIPPO (354-430)

Augustine calls Christians to examine their affections. Do we love privation or communion? Do we cling to a system that prioritizes private ownership, or do we hope and strive for a world where all things are common, and no one is in need? He suggests we must love the latter and hate the former.

This gets to an interesting aspect of Augustine's theology. According to Peter Brown, Augustine's concept of sin centers around the idea that *privation* is sin. Even though his idea of sin is arguably the most influential for the Western Church, this aspect has been overlooked and neglected. Brown explains:

> Augustine put forward an act of 'privation' as lying at the very root of the fallen human condition. The victory of the private over the public good was not something that had happened in the distant past, at the end of a Golden Age [...]. It was the template for all sins—from the first sin of Adam up to the present.[29]

The fall of Adam was an act of rebellion—that insight is well-established. But Augustine further suggests that rebellion is an act of private self-interest against the common good. Because "God was the common good of all," Adam's rebellion was an act of privation, prioritizing self-interest above common interest.[30] That is how Augustine arrives at this definition of sin as privation.

Accordingly, this explains why the monks commonly owned clothing in Augustine's commune. He prioritized public good over private will to such an extent that his communal experiment demanded the total renunciation of private ownership—*even of clothing.*

The above quote is from a letter which continues, "So, indeed, is your very soul not your own; it is also that of all your brothers [...] the One Soul of Christ."[31] Earlier in this chapter, we looked at a similar quote from the Epistle of Barnabas. The point is that, as Christians, we share in common the spiritual life of Christ, and therefore, it is no issue to share the material things of this life.

For Brown, Augustine's position is far more radical than most interpreters have permitted. Indeed, "He was bent on the erasure of the private itself. Unwealth must become no wealth at all."[32] The French Augustine scholar Goulven Madec even went so far as calling this "the spiritual communism" of Augustine.[33] And while Augustine's concept of private property differs from ours, he was interacting with the Roman concept of property, which is the foundation of ours.[34] Roman property laws remain the model for most countries today, and so his critique of privation has direct implications for our situation.

To each according to need

> There are, then, many who, going beyond the use of what is necessary, turn poverty into an occasion for profit and a source for disgraceful pleasures; hence those who have charge of the poor must form a common treasury and with wise

administration, distribute to each one according to his needs.³⁵

— BASIL OF CAESAREA (329-379)

Basil was a fourth-century theologian and bishop of Caesarea known for his passionate defense of Nicene Christianity and his critique of Arianism. Basil is also remembered for his robust defense of the poor and critique of wealth. He helped establish what is sometimes called the first hospital, which was also a house for the poor, a food pantry, and a monastery—*the Basiliad*. The facilities also provided clothing and shelter, free of charge, for the poor in Caesarea as well as travelers in need. The Basiliad was a monastic community that did not remove itself from society but recognized its role as servants of the poor and needy—disproving the common notion that monasticism meant escapism. Basil was a theologian and Father who practiced what he preached.

This quote comes from a homily on Psalm 14, and it bears remarkable similarity to another famous saying from Karl Marx. The principle of distribution according to need has been familiar to modern socialists ever since Marx's phrase, "From each according to his [or her] ability, to each according to his [or her] need."³⁶ For Marx, this describes the end goal of communism. Likewise, Basil describes the ideal form of administration in terms quite similar to Marx's famous description. The reasons for this convergence are apparent. Christianity and socialism share many ethical concerns, including holding all things in common, prioritizing the needs of the poor over the luxuries of the rich, and striving toward a just and equitable society for all.

We often forget that the first socialists were religious, even if later revolutionaries were not.³⁷ The overlapping ethics of Christianity and socialism is often overlooked by the critics of both. But the origin of modern socialism—while finding its fullest expression in Marx and Engels—can be traced to the religious utopianism of Thomas More, the peasants' revolt of Thomas Müntzer, and even the first Christian community of Acts 2 and 4. Given the anti-mammon impulse of the Bible and the concepts explained in this chapter, it seems natural this would be the case.

Those quick to reject the central impulse of modern socialism fail to see that it shares this goal with the Christian faith. According to Basil, "wise administration" means distributing resources according to need, not greed. The priority of the many's needs over the few's luxuries is central to the Christian confession in the commonality of the earth. It is a radical, revolutionary aspiration that the Church has neglected. But this principle of wise administration situates the gospel in closer partnership with socialist revolutionaries than with capitalist profiteers.

Fidel Castro—whatever else we might think of him as a political thinker

—was undoubtedly correct when he said, "There are 10,000 times more coincidences between Christianity and communism than between Christianity and capitalism."[38] Even Pope Francis has admitted to the similarities, saying in a recent interview, "The communists stole some of our Christian values."[39]

In chapter nine, we will directly examine the contribution and difficulty of Marxism. But it is worth noting the remarkable agreement between Basil and Marx in their description of ideal administration: to distribute each according to need.

All things common to all

> Therefore the creatures in need should be made equal to the one who has a larger share, and that which is lacking should be filled by what has abundance. This is the law mercy gives men in regard to the needy [...] Mercy is a voluntary sorrow that joins itself to the suffering of others [...] Mercy is the loving disposition towards those who suffer distress. For as unkindness and cruelty have their origin in hate, so mercy springs from love, without which it could not exist [...] Mercy is intensified charity. Hence a man of such dispositions of soul is truly blessed, since he has reached the summit of virtue [...]
>
> For all things would be common to all, and man's life as a citizen would be marked by complete equality before the law, since the person who was responsible for the government would of his own free will be on a level with the rest.[40]
>
> — GREGORY OF NYSSA (335-395)

Gregory of Nyssa was the younger brother of Basil, and together with Gregory of Nazianzus, the three are known as the Cappadocian Fathers. Also, their elder sister, Macrina the Younger, rightly belongs among the Cappadocians. All four were significant figures in the fourth-century Church, and their contributions to theology remain influential. Gregory was the bishop of Nyssa and an outspoken critic of slavery. Indeed, he was likely the first Christian theologian to condemn slavery explicitly; J. Kameron Carter refers to Gregory as "a fourth century abolitionist intellectual."[41] Gregory was a brilliant theologian and a social reformer far ahead of his time.

In addition to his critique of slavery, Gregory's homily on the beatitudes, from which this quote is taken, proclaims the radical Christian vision of sharing all things in common. A familiar theme in the Bible is the importance of prioritizing the poor and needy over those with an abundance. Here Gregory of Nyssa stresses equality and highlights how Christian mercy demands solidarity with those in need. It is not a Christian attitude that says, "I do not need to concern myself with the suffering of the poor." Instead, the way of Christ is to enter into solidarity with the least of these, to suffer what they suffer, and to struggle with them for liberation.

Interestingly, Gregory discusses this in the context of equality before the law. Unfortunately, the hoarded riches of the wealthy negate this equality through brides, lobbying, and the corruptive nature of their power in society to direct production. Thus, differentiating wealth will always be at odds with true equality before the law. An ideal state of society would be one in which every person has true equality, but that will be impossible when a select few hoard the riches and power of society for themselves and actively work to protect their interest accordingly.

Slavery

> You condemn a person to slavery whose nature is free and independent, and in doing so you lay down a law in opposition to God, overturning the natural law established by Him. For you subject to the yoke of slavery one who was created precisely to be a master of the earth, and who was ordained to rule by the creator, as if you were deliberately attacking and fighting against the divine command [...] What price did you put on reason? How [much money] did you pay as a fair price for the image of God? For how [much money] have you sold the nature specially formed by God? God said, 'Let us make man in our image and likeness.'[42]
>
> — GREGORY OF NYSSA (335-395)

Gregory's critique of slavery is important in its own right as a profound example of Christian social imagination. But for our purposes here,[43] we might apply this logic more directly to the economic conditions that lead to poverty for many and luxuries for the few, i.e., modern wage-labor. The foundation of his argument is that the right to life is God's gift, and all human beings are made in God's image. Therefore, only God has the power over life and death, and every act of enslaving or oppressing an image of God (a human being) is committed against God.

The right to life does not belong to the bosses who hire laborers and pay them barely enough to survive. The right to life belongs to God alone, as a gift given commonly to all, yet the rich claim it as *their* exclusive right. They call themselves "job" providers—after first monopolizing all the earth's resources for private profit and thus forcing laborers to sell their labor in the production process. The choice is between selling one's labor or starvation, which is no real choice. The right to life has been bought and privatized by the rich, and the poor have been made the slaves of mammon.

Gregory's prophetic question reverberates to us today. In a world where the majority of humanity must toil for the private profit of the few, we should critically interrogate the rich: How much did you pay for the image of God? The dehumanization of modern capitalism, turning human beings into working machines and alienated producers, is a sin against the image of God in each person. The rich have no right to degrade the poor with such hostility, yet that is done daily through the standard cycles of poverty, homelessness, hunger, and unemployment. God has given the resources of this earth for all in common, yet the rich have made it their private source of profit, monopolizing as a class what belongs solely to God. The Church today must stand up and say, "The earth is the Lord's and the fullness thereof!" Only then will we be able to distribute the abundance of God's earth for the good of all God's children equitably.

Just as the sun is common

> All things, in fact, are God's. When then he calls and chooses to take things away from us, let us not, like ungrateful servants, flee away from him and steal our Master's goods. Your soul is not yours, much less are your riches your own. How is it then that you spend on what is unnecessary the things that are not yours? Do you not know that we will soon be on trial if we use them badly? But since they are not ours but our Master's, we should spend them for our fellow-servants [...]
>
> Say not then: 'I am but spending my own, and of my own I live a voluptuous life.' It is not your own, but belongs to others. 'Others', I say, because such is your own choice: for God's will is that those things should be yours which have been entrusted to you on behalf of your brethren. Now these things which are not your own become yours, if you spend them on others. But if you spend them on yourself unsparingly, your own things become no longer yours. For since you use them cruelly and say that it is fair to spend your own things entirely for your exclusive enjoyment, I say they are no

longer yours. For they are common to you and your fellow-servants, just as the sun is common, and the air, the earth, and all the rest [...] So also regarding wealth, if you enjoy it alone, you have lost it, for you will not reap its reward. But if you possess it jointly with the rest, then will it be more your own, and then will you reap the benefit of it.[44]

— JOHN CHRYSOSTOM (349-407)

Chrysostom is commenting on 1 Corinthians 3:18-9, wherein Paul discusses the wisdom of this world as foolishness to God. The Early Church's stress on the commonality of the earth would likely seem naive to capitalist economists, but the wisdom of God is foolishness to the world.

Chrysostom then makes a powerful argument: Privately hoarding the common wealth of creation is as absurd as trying to privatize the sun. Just as we cannot imagine the absurdity of hoarding the sun's light for private profit, we should reject the absurdity of privatizing the common earth, given for the good of all by our creator. The earth belongs to the Lord. The air, earth, and sun belong to all God's creatures from the abundance of God's love for being. The problem with capitalism is that it has normalized the rich's absurd pursuit of privatization. To enjoy wealth alone is to lose it; only common ownership fulfills the divine order of creation. The Christian witness must once again call capitalism and privatization what it is: sin.

An episode of the TV show "The Simpsons" is a suitable parable of the insatiable greed of the rich and their desire to privatize all things. The episode was called "Who Shot Mr. Burns? (Part One)," and it is generally considered one of the show's best. The plot is simple: Mr. Burns, who owns the nuclear power plant, is looking for a way to increase profits. So he has a devious idea: block out the sun with a massive machine, which then requires the who town to use more power and thus increase his profits at the plant.

The rest of the episode is not worth restating (though, as one might guess from the title and absurdity of the premise, the town becomes quite angry, and someone shoots Mr. Burns). But it is a funny example of how far the capitalist class will go to increase their profits. By blocking the sun, Mr. Burns has privatized light itself. It is a fictional example of a tendency that is the *modus operandi* of capitalism: privatization.

Chrysostom rightly calls this approach to God's earth absurd. Just as the sun and the air are common, God has given all things commonly for the benefit of all. Those privatizing the earth and its resources are as delusional as Mr. Burns.

Just one stomach to fill, not ten

What, too, of the earth, is not this left common to all? 'No,' he saith. How sayest thou so? tell me. 'Because the rich man, even in the city, having gotten himself several plethra [unit of measurement], raises up long fences round them; and in the country cuts off for himself many portions.' What then? When he cuts them off, does he alone enjoy them? By no means, though he should contend for it ever so earnestly. [...] And his enjoyment of the earth is no more than thine; for sure he fills not ten stomachs, and thou only one.[45]

— JOHN CHRYSOSTOM (349-407)

The hoarded abundance of the rich is wasteful. The rich forget they only have one body to clothe and one stomach to feed. Yet the rich hoard houses, cars, and luxuries for private use, greedily taking what could feed, clothe, or house many. The rich have only one life, one body, and one stomach, but hoard privately enough for hundreds if not thousands of people. When the wealthiest eight men on the planet hoard more wealth than 50% of the remaining population, they act insanely and with great evil in their hearts. By monopolizing the poor's goods, they store for themselves judgment. The voices of the poor and oppressed will witness against them on the final day.

Chrysostom's point is potent. It is even more relevant today, with far greater levels of inequality than in his time. The 1% hoard enough resources to feed millions of hungry stomachs despite having only one. They amass for themselves more wealth than can be feasibly spent in a thousand lifetimes, even with the most luxurious spending habits. The insanity of this economically, politically, and socially, not to mention ethically and spiritually, should be obvious. The claim that these rich billionaires deserve their money misses the point. They hoard wealth at the expense of the poor and needy, who suffer and die from a lack of essentials. It is a sin against God and a crime against humanity to accumulate such abundance.

Mine and thine

For 'mine' and 'thine'—those chilly words which introduce innumerable wars into the world—should be eliminated from that holy Church [...] The poor would not envy the rich, because there would be no rich. Neither would the poor be despised by the rich, for there would be no poor. All things would be in common.⁴⁶

— JOHN CHRYSOSTOM (349-407)

Returning to the commonality of the earth is a path to peace. Privation is a path to war. World history has demonstrated this well. Most wars have been fought over land and wealth. Private property is perhaps the original injustice of modernity; without justice, there can be no peace.

The childish cries of "mine" and "thine" are absurd when all creation is recognized as a gift from God. Chrysostom imagines a world beyond rich and poor, where all things are held in common. It may be a utopian hope, but creative imagination is necessary for the struggle for a better tomorrow. If we have no vision for a better world, we will resign ourselves to this unjust order. Be realistic, yes, but do not give up hope. Gramsci prescribes, "Pessimism of the intellect, optimism of the will." Another world is possible.

The rich monopolize for themselves the common gift of God

Those who neither make after others' goods nor bestow their own are to be admonished to take it well to heart that the earth they come from is common to all and brings forth nurture for all alike. Idly then do men hold themselves innocent when they monopolize for themselves the common gift of God. In not giving what they destroy all the starving poor whose means to relief they store at home. When we furnish the destitute with any necessity we render them what is theirs, not bestow on them what is ours; we pay the debt of justice rather than perform the works of mercy [...] Of Dives in the gospel we do not read that he snatched the goods of others but that he used his own unfruitfully; and avenging hell receive him at death not because he did anything unlawful but because he gave himself up utterly and inordinately to the enjoyment of what was lawful.⁴⁷

— GREGORY THE GREAT (540-604)

Gregory the Great—also known as Pope Gregory I—was a sixth-century bishop of Rome known for his missionary efforts to the Anglo-Saxons in Britain. This quote comes from the 22nd Admonition of Gregory's *Pastoral Rule,* a guide for pastors and leaders in the Church. The passage here reiterates this chapter's main point: that the earth is common. Therefore, giving to the poor is justice, not mercy, and God's judgment is upon those who do not use wealth fruitfully by helping the needy.

The rich monopolize what God has given in common and then blame the poor for their own suffering. The parable of the rich man and Lazarus demonstrates that tendency. Gregory stresses that the rich man tried to excuse himself by thinking he did nothing wrong to Lazarus, but Jesus' parable shows that the rich man sinned by *not* helping the poor.

Today, it is supposed that the rich "earned" their luxuries while the poor equally "earned" their misery. But that is blasphemy against the God who created this earth for the benefit of all, rich and poor alike. By hoarding the resources of the earth, the rich steal from the poor, and ultimately, they steal from the Lord to whom the earth belongs. They sin by failing to help the needy.

That final point brings us to the next chapter, which is closely connected to this one. Because the earth is common, hoarded wealth is *theft* from the poor and needy. Those who hoard more than their fair share have robbed the needy and the hungry of their God-given right to subsistence, to share in the common gift of life.

4

HOARDED WEALTH IS THEFT

Since the earth is the Lord's and given for the good of all, differentiating wealth is an injustice to the divine order of creation. Hoarded wealth is an attempt to "play god" and monopolize the earth. Thus, in the material sense, justice looks like restoring God's good order so that the earth's abundance is held in common and wisely distributed according to need. That explains why many Church Fathers understood almsgiving as an act of *justice*, not simply an act of *mercy* as we think today. This shift in perspective is vital for understanding how the Church should engage with poverty and riches.

There are two common objections to socialism's approach to helping the poor. The first suggests that Christian giving is *voluntary*, and therefore, government programs that turn giving into an obligation contradict personal freedom. The second objection blames poverty on the laziness of the poor rather than the exploitation of the rich. It thus suggests that poverty is simply a matter of individual choices. But the Church Fathers can help us break out of these two errors.

The first objection overlooks how the Bible talks about giving as an *obligation*, not a personal choice. Furthermore, it ignores the systemic nature of poverty, which can be overcome only by systemic changes, not personal remedies. The second objection fails similarly by overlooking how the Bible talks about our debt to those in need through the language of caring for our neighbor and being our brother's keeper. God has made the poor our burden. Their plight is also ours.

So the first change that has to be made in our thinking is to reject the idea that helping the poor is voluntary for a Christian. We cannot pursue the way of Christ and also the way of mammon. So we might say that helping the poor is "optional" in the same sense that being a Christian is an option; yet if one decides to follow Christ, that entails helping those Christ calls his own. Good works of justice are non-negotiable; faith without works is dead. Helping the poor and needy is the duty of every Christian. Understanding charity as *justice* is a perpetual reminder that *not acting* is just as sinful as directly doing evil to the poor.

Furthermore, the desire to defend personal freedoms by rejecting systemic solutions misunderstands what freedom means for a Christian. The liberty of Christ is freedom *from* evil, which includes the freedom *for* good. Paul warns, "For freedom Christ has set us free. Stand firm, therefore, and do not submit again to a yoke of slavery" (Gal. 5:1). The freedom of Christ is thus not *absolute* freedom to do "whatever we want." Instead, it is freedom *for* good works, freedom *for* justice, mercy, and love. We often wrongly think of freedom as an abstract negation of bondage. But the New Testament's concept of freedom is *slavery to Christ*. It is being yoked together with Christ in the work of the Kingdom. Thus, the individualistic concept of "freedom" is not the same freedom we have in Christ. We are free *for good works*. That means we are unfree whenever we refuse to do good works in the name of abstract "freedom."

Another mindset we must overcome is how we think about poverty as the result of individual choices. We often treat poverty as the poor's fault, a burden they are solely responsible for and thus must bear alone. But the poor are *our* burden because they are Christ's burden. God is the defender of the weak and needy. When Cain asked God, "Am I my brother's keeper?" (Gen. 4:9), the implication was clear: Yes, we are responsible for others. Individualistic self-preservation is a fruit of mammon; concern for our neighbor is the fruit of Christ.

Jesus tells the parable of the Good Samaritan in response to a question similar to Cain's: "Who is my neighbor?" Answer: whoever is in need is your neighbor and thus your burden to help. The core of Christ's social teaching is well-known, "Love your neighbor as yourself." But what good is love for the needy without material generosity, such as food, clothing, shelter, and money?

The Church Fathers understood love to mean more than empty "feelings" of warmth. Roman A. Montero explains, "Love for the early Christians was not an abstract feeling, it was realized in the forming of real economic relationships."[1] Thus, love that does not lead to good works of justice is not love in the Christian sense of the word. Christian love looks like Jesus laying down his life for those loved by God; love is an action.

Furthermore, the parable of the Sheep and Goats identifies God with the needy. Whoever does not help the least of these does not help Christ. Thus, we must stress that the poor are the burden of the rich and those with more than enough. Those with full bellies owe a debt to the hungry. Those with a closet full of clothes owe a debt to the naked. Those with much owe a debt to those with little. That is justice and the fruit of love.

The story of the blind man in John 9 is instructive for this context:

> As he walked along, he saw a man blind from birth. His disciples asked him, "Rabbi, who sinned, this man or his parents, that he was born blind?" Jesus answered, "Neither this man nor his parents sinned; he was born blind so that God's works might be revealed in him. We must work the works of him who sent me while it is day; night is coming when no one can work. As long as I am in the world, I am the light of the world."
>
> — JOHN 9:1-5

We often ask the same question regarding the plight of the poor today. We speculate, "What did the poor do to *deserve* poverty? Was it their fault or their parents (their upbringing)?" However, we seldom stop to think of the complex socioeconomic realities of poverty, that the poor are not poor by *choice* but often because of the exploitation of the rich (directly or indirectly).[2]

Notice that Christ refuses to play the victim-blaming game. The Pharisees tried to shame the victim. But Christ ignores this underlying motivation entirely—as we must again today—because it is not what matters. Rather, the priority is to *help*. Instead of asking what the blind man did to deserve his condition, Christ simply healed him. So today, our duty is not to shame the poor but to help.

A frequent theme in the Church Fathers is the debt those with excess owe to those without. All those with abundant wealth beyond their daily necessities *owe a debt to the needy*. Thus, the hungry are the burden of those with extra food, the naked of the clothed, and the poor of the rich. This is the yoke of Christ. Therefore, we owe a debt of justice to the least of these, for Christ's sake.

This reflects the systemic nature of poverty, which demands systemic solutions. Those with excess owe a debt to the needy, and we cannot wait for the greedy to get around to making good on that debt. Instead, we should strive to create systems that distribute the earth's resources according to need (i.e., socialism).

Of course, it *is* essential to ask why the poor are poor—but only when our motivation is not to shame them but to liberate them from their cycles of poverty. When we approach a man in his plight, what is our obligation? It is not to judge him from afar and place further shame on his already dehumanized condition. Instead, it is to help, to do the work of the Father. That is what Christ does by healing the blind man.

How does this justify the claim that "hoarded wealth is theft?" For the Fathers, the existence of inequality points to theft and injustice because of how they understood creation as God's give to be shared commonly. Thus, the hoarded riches of the wealth are theft from the poor. Their riches are not their own but belong to the Lord, and the righteous distribution of wealth is to each according to need. That means the rich sin against God's order of creation and are guilty of theft. We will explore these interconnected points in this chapter.

Hoarded abundance is sin; shared abundance is righteousness

> Now then hear me and be at peace among yourselves, and have regard one to another, and assist one another; and do not partake of the creatures of God alone in abundance, but share them also with those that are in want. For some men through their much eating bring weakness on the flesh, and injure their flesh; whereas the flesh of those who have nought to eat is injured by their not having sufficient nourishment, and their body is ruined. This exclusiveness therefore is hurtful to you that have and do not share with them that are in want. Look ye to the judgment that cometh. Ye then that have more than enough, seek out them that are hungry, while the tower is still unfinished; for after the tower is finished, ye will desire to do good, and will find no place for it. Look ye therefore, ye that exult in your wealth, lest they that are in want shall moan, and their moaning shall go up unto the Lord, and ye with your [abundance of] good things be shut outside the door of the tower.[3]

— THE SHEPHERD OF HERMAS

This quote is from the Shepherd's third vision. It emphasizes the importance of helping the needy and even suggests that those who hoard more than their share do harm to themselves. The Shepherd then directly suggests that the duty of those with more than enough to eat is to *seek out the hungry*. This is an active form of assistance, not a passive one. That makes the command to feed the hungry more actionable. There is no excuse for not helping the needy. Just as Christ sought out the lost, the rich and those with excess should seek out the needy and help them.

We explained the meaning of "the tower" in chapter two. It refers to the eschatological Church, which God is building on earth. But it also refers to the Kingdom of God that is still coming. Thus, the reference means that those with excess should do good before the eschaton, the coming reign of God. The point is that those who hoard wealth will be shut out of the tower, while those who give freely to the needy will be included. This warning retains the New Testament sense of urgency for the coming reign of God.

Those who have more than enough yet fail to seek out the hungry and feed them, to seek out the naked and clothe them, and pursue the prisoner and bring them comfort—and Christ will judge them. Christ's parable of the Sheep and Goats suggests that all are obligated to seek after the "least of these" and help. We cannot claim innocence. Thus, the Shepherd stresses that helping the needy is an *obligation,* not a suggestion.

No "undeserving" needy

> You must not try to distinguish between the deserving and the undeserving. You may easily make a mistake, and as the matter is in doubt, it is better to benefit the undeserving than, in avoiding this, to miss the good. We are told not to judge.[4]
>
> — CLEMENT OF ALEXANDRIA (150-215)

This quote is from Clement's treatise, *Concerning the Salvation of the Rich*. We are called to help the needy—period. There is nothing ambiguous about it. That much is clear from Clement's argument. He is criticizing those who try to excuse themselves from giving by judging the worthiness of those in need. The point is that we are not called the categorize the needy into worthy and unworthy; we are called to help.

The Christian does not judge whether or not the poor "deserve" our help; the Christian helps. Why have we permitted this idea to flourish that the poor must be deserving before we can fulfill Christ's command to help the needy? We become fixated on how the poor use their money, condescendingly teaching them how to manage a budget as if that is why they are poor and not the oppression of the rich (which is the biblical view, as we saw in James 5).

But that is a double standard. We do not show the same concern for the rich. Why do we not interrogate the rich for hoarding multiple mansions and unused luxurious estates, while thousands are unhoused in the same city?

Clement's reminder is simple: we are not permitted to judge the poor. We are obligated to help. It is actually us who misuse what we have been given when we fail to help the needy.

There is no Christian justification for questioning whether or not the poor will use what they are given wisely. Being pragmatic about limited resources is one thing, but it should always be within the context of actively giving, not an excuse not to give. When Christian charities require moral prerequisites such as sobriety or force the needy to listen to a sermon before they help them, they restrict the love of God. These resources are not ours but belong to God. We fail to be good stewards by gatekeeping God's loving-kindness toward the least of these.

We freely and generously give because God first gave freely and generously to us. It is not our place to play God and examine the motives of people's hearts. Our place is to help. God gave to us without asking about our use or misuse of divine grace. So, we should not judge the poor as an excuse not to share what belongs to the needy. It is not our wealth but theirs that we are holding back. God will decide what is in their heart. It is not for us to judge.

If you don't, they die

> Give to the blind, the sick, the lame and the destitute: if you don't, they die. Men may have no use for them, but God has: he keeps them alive, gives them breath and honours them with light. Cherish them as much as you can, and sustain their souls with humanity so that they do not die. Anyone who can help a dying man but doesn't is his murderer.[5]
>
> — LACTANTIUS (240-320)

This quote demonstrates that the problem of hoarded wealth is not an abstract one. It has real implications for actual human beings. Lactantius drives this home with a brutal realization: all those who can help the hungry but do not are guilty of their suffering, even their death. It is murder, therefore, to hoard the resources of this earth for private luxuries while millions starve and perish from unmet needs on a planet that produces more than enough food to feed everyone.

Inequality is not just an economic problem; it is a moral one. It is murderous to hoard so much abundance—abundant food, medicine, and clean water—while so many suffer and die. Capitalism prioritizes accumulation above all else. But when a pile of gold is more valuable than a person, we have strayed far away from God's system of value and are in the hands of demonic mammon.

But one person is worth more to God than all the money in the world—just one. Therefore, the Church must loudly proclaim human dignity in the face of this inhumane system of capitalist exploitation. Every starving person is a perpetual horror. Every homeless man or woman is a silent scream against a speculative housing market that prioritizes a return on investment above human dignity. May we never become desensitized by these horrors, and may our sadness lead us to radical, prophetic resistance against the systems of injustice that cause them.

The bread in your hoard belongs to the hungry

'I am wronging no one,' you say, 'I hold fast to my own, that is all.' Your own! Who gave it to you to bring into life with you? You are like the man who takes a seat in a theater and then keeps out newcomers, claiming as his own what is there for the use of everyone. Such are the rich; they seize what belongs to all and then claim the right of possession to monopolize it; if everyone took for himself enough to meet his own wants and gave up the rest to those who needed it, there would be no rich and no poor. [...] Why are you rich and another poor? [...] Who is the covetous man? One for whom plenty is not enough! Who is the defrauder? One who takes away that which belongs to everyone! And are you not covetous, are you not a defrauder, when you keep for private use what you were given for distribution? When some one strips a man of his clothes we call him a thief. And one who might clothe the naked and does not—should not he be given the same name? The bread in your hoard belongs to the hungry; the cloak in your wardrobe belongs to the naked; the shoes you let rot belong to the barefoot; the money in your vaults belongs to the destitute; All you might help and do not —to all these you are doing wrong.[6]

— BASIL OF CAESAREA (329-379)

This quote is from Basil's sixth homily, which was preached during a time of famine in Caesarea. In 368, drought and famine lead to a deadly food shortage throughout the region. Basil's homily is directly addressing those who hoard grain while others starved. But it addresses a larger point beyond this context. He stresses how the hoarded resources of the rich are unjust because the refusal to help the needy is a misuse of God's creation. All things belong to God, and those who hoard riches for themselves owe a debt to the needy. The excess bread they hoard belongs to the hungry.

Basil's image of a theater aptly describes how the rich became wealthy. They have claimed the "right" to privatize God's gift for all. Either because they arrived first or by force have pushed out all competition, the rich privatize the earth's land, labor, and resources for profit. Historically, the example of colonialism demonstrates on a large scale how the wealthy enriched themselves by force. The first world did not become rich because of its work ethic but because their ancestors pillaged and brutalized the land and resources of the third world—and this continues today through financial imperialism.

Those hoarding the earth's wealth are like an audience member claiming all the theater seats. God gave the earth for all, yet they profit off monopolizing the planet. The focus of Basil's critique is against hoarding, and these examples demonstrate how this might be applied today. Even those who claim they have somehow "earned" what they own are in error. As Basil makes clear, it is ultimately from God that all blessings derive. Therefore, it is offensive to God as the creator and giver of life to hoard what God gave for all. These material riches do not belong to the rich, even if it would be possible for their riches to arise from just means (which is doubtful). Ultimately, it belongs to God, who wills for these things to be held in common. Only common ownership can ensure prioritizing the needs of the many over the luxuries of the few.

We are just as responsible for those we could help but do not help as we might be for any direct harm we do. For example, we are complicit in the starvation and misery of the hungry by failing to feed them. Basil does not mince words: You commit an injustice whenever you are capable of helping the needy but choose not to. That is why hoarded wealth is such an evil; to accumulate excessive piles of wealth while millions suffer and die from unmet needs is a great sin. It is murder by inaction, by failing to help. Basil does not hold back in this radical judgment.

Whoever loves his neighbor as himself owns no more than them

> Care for the poor absorbs all available resources. [...] So whoever loves his neighbor as himself owns no more than his neighbor does. But you have a great fortune. How can this be, unless you have put your own interests before those of others? [...] I know many people who fast, pray, groan, and do any kind of pious work that doesn't affect their pockets, but at the

> same time they give nothing to the needy. What good are their merits? The Kingdom of heaven is closed to them. Every time I go into the home of one of these foolish rich people, resplendent with ornaments, I notice that for its owner there is nothing more precious than visible goods, which deck him out according to his pleasure, but that he despises his soul. I wonder then what great benefit this silver furniture and ivory chairs can be producing while all these hoarded riches are not passed to the poor, who in their multitudes cry in misery at the gates of rich men's houses.[7]
>
> — BASIL OF CAESAREA (329-379)

This quote is from Basil's seventh homily, which directly addresses the rich. He discusses their obligation to love their neighbor as themselves, writing, "It is thus evident that you are far from fulfilling the commandment." Why is it evident? Because Jesus' words to the Rich Young Ruler show what the obligation of love means for the rich: to give away all one's possessions. That is why Basil says the love of the poor consumes all of one's resources and that whoever truly loves their neighbor as themselves does not have more than them. Basil argues, "For the more you abound in wealth, the more you lack in love." Love is proven by action.

Love is not an empty emotion: love demands justice. Thus, Basil stresses that to love our neighbors means caring for their material needs. Whoever loves their neighbor does not have more than them, especially if they live in luxury while their neighbor suffers and starves. Unfortunately, the abstract sentiments of love that dominate the Church fail to live up to this radical definition. Love is a verb.

God demonstrated this in Jesus as an example for us to follow. Christ did not want the blessed riches and comfort of the Triune life without us. Indeed, creation and redemption mean God did not will to be God without human beings. Instead, as Paul writes, Christ emptied himself and became poor for our sakes (Phil. 2:7). That is God's extravagant love for us.

God became one with the poor and sinful so that we might participate in the wealth of the divine life. Irenaeus understood this with his famous phrase, "God became man so that man might become God." God became one with our poverty so we might share in God's riches. That is also the way of Christian discipleship. We should become needy with our neighbors who suffer from lack. Christ showed the way of love, which is the way of radical solidarity with the least of these. It is the way of the cross.

The point here is not to glorify poverty. But to suggest that Christian love refuses to coexist with inequality. Love that is true love will act for the good of those who have less. Love demands more than the law. The law says do not steal, but love says, "I refuse to have excess and live in luxury while another suffers from lack." We often excuse ourselves as Christians because we think according to the law of "do not" instead of the way of love.

The Good Samaritan parable is a good illustration of what love does. Love is not self-justifying like the priest or the Levite, who crossed over to the other side. The law of "do not" let them off the hook. The suffering of the man was of no concern to them. But Jesus rebukes this way of thinking. Instead, he praises the Samaritan who out of love and concern for the neighbor, goes out of his way to help the downtrodden, taking his burden upon himself.

Many Christians look at a homeless beggar, a hungry child, or a desperate drug addict and say, "That is not my problem." And they cross to the other side of the road. But the teachings of Jesus are clear on this matter: the misery of another human being *is* our problem. It is an *obligation* to help. We sometimes talk about the free choice to serve the poor or not, but this framing is all wrong. Love does not choose who to help or when to help. Love helps when there is a need. That is what love does. It is costly, inconvenient, and difficult, but it is the way of Christ.

In economic terms, I have often heard Christians criticize social programs such as welfare and public housing as an overreach of the state and interference in the private business of individuals. The logic here is that it is wrong for the state to force taxpayers to help the needy by funding these programs (but somehow, it isn't wrong to use those funds to pay for endless war and militarization). Instead, the poor should help themselves, or private individuals should have the choice to help who they want to through private charities. But the minute a social program is suggested, the very same Christians who hear about the Good Samaritan parable in Church on Sunday reject anything that turns charity into an obligation.

Perhaps it is because we have "privatized" the duty of love, making it a personal choice to help or not to help. If we return to the radical approach of Jesus and the Early Church, however, we should not begin with the individual choice to give. Instead, we should start with the obligation of love: if anyone has less, it is my obligation to help.

Furthermore, what is the best way to help? Publicly funded support systems are more equitable, sustainable, consistent, and cost-effective than private charities. Private charities are a band-aid solution to systemic issues like poverty, hunger, homelessness, and debt. The logic of love seeks the most effective way to help combat systemic inequality and ensure that no neighbor goes hungry, homeless, or without medical care. A private charity will never be able to meet those needs as efficiently, systemically, or sustainably as publicly funded programs.

On building bigger barns

> The wealth you handle belongs to others; consider it accordingly. Not for long will it delight you; soon it will slip from you and be gone, and you will be asked to give a proper account of it all. Yet, you keep it all locked up behind tightly sealed doors, and the thought of it keeps you awake at night; you take counsel about it within yourself, and your counsellor is a fool! 'What can I do?' How easy it would have been to say: 'I will fill the souls of the hungry; I will open my barns; I will invite all the poor. I will be like Joseph in his charitable summons; I will speak generous words—All you who have need of loaves, come to me; each shall have his fill from God's bounty, which flows forth for everyone.' But this is not your way; no indeed, you grudge others their needs; you contrive evil schemes within your soul; you are not concerned how to distribute to each in accordance with his need but rather how to get everything yourself and to prevent anyone else from using it.[8]
>
> — BASIL OF CAESAREA (329-379)

Basil discusses Jesus' parable of the rich man's barns. Christ tells of a man whose crops yielded an abundant harvest. However, instead of distributing the excess to the needy, he hoarded it by building a larger barn. He then dies and is condemned by God for his injustice. The parable concludes, "This is how it will be with whoever stores up things for themselves but is not rich toward God" (Lk. 12:21). How could the man become rich in God? The implication would have been clear to Jesus' Jewish audience. The Torah commands them to help the poor and needy.

The Jews have a word for the obligatory nature of giving: *tzedakah*. It means "righteousness" and describes the ethical obligation of the Torah to help those in need. The word directly contrasts with "charity" because it points to an obligatory call to give not a spontaneous one. Jesus' listeners would have understood the rich man's sin as a betrayal of tzedakah.

Furthermore, Peter Brown describes the cultural setting of the parable of the man who builds bigger barns instead of helping the needy:

> Those who could store up surplus of the harvest by gathering it into their granaries were the ones who could take advantage, every year, of this rise in prices. Further harvest shocks

might turn the regular sale of grain into a 'killing' in times of shortage. Not surprisingly, therefore, granaries emerge as the economic villains of the ancient world.[9]

Jesus' words in Luke would have echoed this cultural mood, but there is an important difference: Jesus' parable *validates* the anger of the masses because he suggests that God judges and condemns the one who hoards more than their fair share. Thus, granaries are not just culturally and socially condemned but theologically. God is against this practice of accumulating excess wealth while the community suffers.

Hoarded wealth becomes capital, which is then leveraged against the masses, abusing their vulnerability for profit. Similar to how granaries were used to profit off of shortage, the market is designed to privilege those with capital and penalize those without. For example, in times of economic crisis (every 5-10 years under capitalism), the poor suffer while the rich consolidate their interests and use their capital to buy more property at lower prices. The rich have built larger and larger granaries, and the result has been greater misery for the masses. But Christ's parable is clear: God condemns those who use the suffering of the poor to turn a profit.

Basil follows this interpretation by stressing that the hoarded grain in the rich man's barn belonged to those without enough to eat. So today, excess wealth is not ours to hoard but belongs to the needy. We are quick to work out schemes to keep what belongs to the needy for ourselves. But we are condemned by Christ's words. We should share with the needy, not build bigger barns for hoarding. that is true both personally and economically. A popular saying expresses this well: "When you have more than you need, build a bigger table, not a higher fence."

That everything may be gold

Everything is gold in your eyes and fantasy; gold is your dream at night and your waking care.[10] As a raving madman does not see things themselves but imagines things in his diseased fancy, so also your greed-possessed soul sees gold and silver everywhere. The sight of gold is dearer to you than the sight of the very sun itself. Your prayer is that everything may be changed to gold, and your schemes are aimed on bringing this about.[11]

— BASIL OF CAESAREA (329-379)

What is a person worth? Just one image-bearer is worth more than all the money in the world. Yet daily, the rich chase money and trample over the human beings made in God's image who suffer from hunger, sleep homeless on our city streets, and live in poverty. That is the pathological obsession of the rich, summed up with a word: *more!*

The rich sell the well-being of living persons for dead capital. So long as profits go up, there is no human price too high for the rich to increase their hoarded wealth—even if it means the suffering and misery of millions. Basil's observation is strikingly similar to the political theorist Michael Parenti's description of capitalism. Parenti writes:

> The essence of capitalism is to turn nature into commodities and commodities into capital. The live green earth is transformed into dead gold bricks, with luxury items for the few and toxic slag heaps for the many. The glittering mansion overlooks a vast sprawl of shanty towns, wherein a desperate, demoralized humanity is kept in line with drugs, television, and armed force.[12]

Capitalism wants to turn everything into a commodity. The efforts to privatize water by companies like Nestlé is a current example of taking a common resource essential to life and turning it into a commodity.[13] As Basil astutely realized about the rich, "[Their] prayer is that everything may be changed to gold." But we cannot eat gold nor drink cash.

The threat of climate change makes this more than just a metaphor, as capitalism races towards catastrophic environmental conditions with no signs of slowing. Apocalypse can be monetized, which is what the rich are doing by continuing to push the earth toward collapse. But what good is gold if the planet becomes uninhabitable—if we do not have clean water, the oceans are polluted beyond repair, and the ice sheets melt? The love of mammon is not *rational*. It is like a *raving madman*, diseased and possessed by greed. The rich are delusional. Their blindness may lead to the end of life on this planet—all in the name of profit.

Murderer

> The most miserable of deaths is, no doubt that by starvation […] Now, what punishment should not be inflicted upon the one who passes by such a body? What cruelty can surpass that? How can we not count someone like that among the fiercest of beasts and consider that person as a sacrilegious one

and a murderer? The person who can cure such an infirmity and refuses one's medicine because of avarice, can with reason be condemned as a murderer.[14]

— BASIL OF CAESAREA (329-379)

This is from Basil's eighth homily on the famine at Caesarea. He does not mince words: those who can help the starving but choose not to are guilty of murder. Indeed, anytime the rich can help the needy yet choose not to, they become complicit in the death of the less fortunate, whether it comes from hunger, malnutrition-related diseases, exposure, or any other premature death caused by poverty. The rich do not exist in an accidental relationship with the poor; those with excess are indebted to those without. The blood of the poor covers the hands of the rich and all those who refuse to help the needy.

Friedrich Engels powerfully described a similar situation in the nineteenth century. Engels discusses the systemic causes of premature death in the industrial world. He calls this "social murder," and it is an apt phrase for what Basil describes regarding those who hoard in a time a famine. Engels writes:

> When one individual inflicts bodily injury upon another such that death results, we call the deed manslaughter; when the assailant knew in advance that the injury would be fatal, we call his deed murder. But when society places hundreds of proletarians [i.e., the working class poor] in such a position that they inevitably meet a too early and an unnatural death, one which is quite as much a death by violence as that by the sword or bullet; when it deprives thousands of the necessaries of life, places them under conditions in which they cannot live – forces them, through the strong arm of the law, to remain in such conditions until that death ensues which is the inevitable consequence – knows that these thousands of victims must perish, and yet permits these conditions to remain, its deed is murder just as surely as the deed of the single individual; disguised, malicious murder, murder against which none can defend himself, which does not seem what it is, because no man sees the murderer, because the death of the victim seems a natural one, since the offense is more one of omission than of commission. But murder it remains.[15]

While Engels' observation has a modern context, it is remarkable how similar it is to Basil's. The sin of omission described by both is one in which the rich use their power and wealth to create the conditions for the poverty, misery, and death of the poor and working class. Thus, the rich are guilty of "social murder" because of their indifference to the suffering of the poor—all those who can help the needy and do not are guilty. Furthermore, Engels' point heightens Basil's by suggesting that in our times, those who permit unfair labor conditions to shorten the life expectancy of the working poor, who use their power to oppress the weak and vulnerable, are also guilty of social murder. Both are grasping at the mechanism of systemic injustice and its effect upon the most vulnerable in society. We do not often think of this as social murder, but an analysis of poverty and harsh working conditions unveils the truth.

Engels' description highlights the power dynamic of capitalism. The rich are not merely better off financially. Their wealth means social power. And what do the rich use their power for? They use it to increase their wealth. Thus, the misery of the poor is a result of this power imbalance. The capitalist class uses social power to repress wages, restrict benefits, and increase prices. Yet we call this a "free" market. But it is merely the freedom of the rich to exploit the poor.

This power dynamic is at work in the deaths of the hungry, misery of the homeless, and insecurity of those who lack medical care (due to cost or inaccessibility). In all these situations, profiteers are guilty of social murder.

The sixth-century theologian and pope Gregory the Great also argued that those who fail to help while being able to help are guilty of murder:

> In vain do they think themselves innocent who appropriate to their own use alone those goods which God gave in common; by not giving to others that which they themselves receive, they become homicides and murderers, inasmuch as in keeping for themselves those things which would alleviate the sufferings of the poor, we may say that every day they cause the death of as many persons as they might have fed and did not. When, therefore, we offer the means of living to the indigent, we do not give them anything of ours, but that which of right belongs to them. It is less a work of mercy which is performed than the payment of a debt.[16]

There are 20 million unnecessary deaths *every year* because of capitalism. Eight million die from lack of unclean water, over seven and a half million die from hunger on a planet that produces enough to feed ten billion, three million die from curable disease, and another half a million die from malaria.[17] These are *preventable* deaths. Any system that prioritizes the private profits of a few individuals above these needless deaths is inhumane and evil. That system is called capitalism. The power to change it is in the hands of the masses, who must stand up and resist capitalism for the good of all. It is not enough to move money from the rich to the poor (charity). The only way to end these injustices is to change the power imbalance between the rich and poor by overthrowing the system. That means working for a world beyond capitalism.

Hoarded wealth is not only theft. In times of extreme inequality, it is also *murder*.

On the Love of the Poor

> How can we enjoy pleasures amidst the calamities of our brethren? May God preserve me from being rich while they are indigent, from enjoying robust health if I do not try to cure their diseases, from eating good food, clothing myself well and resting in my home if I do not share with them a piece of my bread and give them, in the measure of my abilities, part of my clothes and if I do not welcome them into my home.[18]
>
> You, who are strong, help those who are weak; you, who are rich, assist those who are poor. You who have not stumbled raise up those who have fallen and are afflicted; you who are full of spirit, comfort those who are discouraged; you, who enjoy prosperity, aid those who suffer adversities.[19]
>
> — GREGORY OF NAZIANZUS (329-389)

Gregory of Nazianzus was a fourth-century Cappadocian Father and Archbishop of Constantinople who was famous for his orations. His rhetorical preaching was powerful, as these two quotes demonstrate, and his theological contributions were vast. These two quotes come from a short treatise, *On the Love of the Poor*.

The first quote reveals an essential component of our obligation to help the poor. Gregory asks, "How can we enjoy pleasures amidst the calamities of our brethren?" The question reflects a call to *solidarity*. We should strive to live in such a way that our lives are bound to the lives of the least of these; whatever is done to them is our burden, too. Solidarity means linking our situation with the needy. If they suffer, we suffer.

Solidarity as a virtue has been lost today. But it is vital for our individualistic society. We are driven by self-interest. But solidarity was an important Christian principle before it was ever a socialist one. The love of God compels us to follow the way of Christ beyond ourselves and our concerns and enter into the situation of those in need. Just as Christ became poor for our sakes, we are obligated to stand with those in need, consider their plight our own, and struggle with them in their difficulties. This solidarity is theologically rooted in God's solidarity with human beings in Jesus Christ.

Someone once asked the third-century desert Father Abba Agathon how "sincere love for one's neighbor might be made manifest," and he responded: "Love is to find a leper, to take his body, and gladly to give him your own."[20] Agathon practiced solidarity, as early writers recounted how "Many times he was seen wandering in a sheet wrapped around his naked body, because he had given his clothing away in an act of charity."[21] That is the radical nature of Christian solidarity.

While we may not go to such extremes as Abba Agathon, the principle remains important. When we think about the poor, we cannot consider their plight as something external to our own. Instead, we should strive for the kind of love that stands in such radical solidarity with the poor that every attack on their situation is responded to as if it were an attack on ourselves. And then we should refuse to have more than the poorest among us, to live in unjust luxury while they suffer. Just as Christ took up the status of the poor, becoming poor for our sakes, we should consider ourselves one with the needy. That is the way of Jesus Christ, to run away from the isolation of luxury and join the community of the poor. Their plight is ours.

Give the poor their due

> Not from your own do you bestow upon the poor man, but you make return from what is his. For what has been given as common for the use of all, you appropriate to yourself alone. The earth belongs to all, not to the rich; but fewer are they who do not use what belongs to all than those who do. Therefore you are paying a debt, you are not bestowing what is not due. Hence Scripture says to you: 'If a poor man speak to thee, lend him thy ear without grudging; give him his due and let him have patient and friendly answer' (Ecclus. 4:8).[22]
>
> — AMBROSE OF MILAN (340-397)

Ambrose helpfully connects the theme of this chapter with the previous one. Because the earth is common and created for the good of all, it is *justice*, not charity, to give to the needy. The rights of the poor are robbed by the rich in their mad effort to monopolize God's earth. González explains, "In general,

Ambrose apparently believes that almost all methods of acquiring wealth are unjust."[23] The presence of differentiating wealth is a sign of injustice. Ambrose thinks giving to the needy is justice, not charity. It corrects an injustice rather than merely expressing generosity.

The substance of the law of Christ is not a negative, "do not sin," but a positive, "do right by your neighbor." Or, do unto the least of these as unto Christ himself. Thus, Christ's law *obligates* us to do good and serve the needy. Mammon says, "What's mine is mine. I do not owe anyone." Christ says, "Those in need are your burden; failing to act is to condemn yourself." Christ's commandment that we show mercy to the least of these is the same as the anti-mammon mandate; to do good and to reject mammon go hand in hand.

Hoarded wealth is theft

> It is the bread of the poor which you are holding back; it is the clothes of the naked which you are hoarding; it is the relief and liberation of the wretched which you are thwarting by burying your money away.[24]
>
> — AMBROSE OF MILAN (340-397)

The problem with hoarded wealth is not so much that it is sinful to be greedy, but because hoarding while others suffer means the poor are condemned to misery and death. By hoarding, the rich deny the poor the right to *life* by denying them the *means to live*. That power belongs only to God, who alone controls life and death. The rich position themselves in God's place when they wield the power of deciding who lives—those who can afford to live—and who dies. Their hoarded wealth is theft. Justo L. González comments, "Private property, whereby some can keep the produce of the land from others, is, as Ambrose would say, the result of usurpation—words that come close to the modern socialist dictum that private property is theft." [25]

Who are the rich to deny the poor what God has given them by grace? But that is what the rich do by hoarding private luxuries: they deny the poor their God-given right to life. The hoarded wealth of the rich is theft from the poor.

Justice, not charity

> You are not making a gift of your possessions to the poor person. You are handing over to him what is his.[26]

— AMBROSE OF MILAN (340-397)

The wealthiest people in the world today cannot hide behind *merit* to justify their wealth. They accumulate more than they could ever spend while millions of people starve. And that is a great sin. Those massive storehouses of wealth do not belong to the greedy rich but to the needy poor.

That is why philanthropy by the rich is often just a facade constructed to present a good public image and hide the injustice of their wealth. We sometimes think, "Look how generous they are to help the needy!" But if we follow Ambrose's lead, we might instead declare a word of rebuke to the unjust rich: "Woe to the rich! They have returned only a small portion of what belongs to the poor while hoarding the rest for their private luxuries. How sinful of them to think they might appease the poor with token gestures while sitting on their stolen surplus. God knows their injustice and will do right by the poor."

There is more honor in the widow's mite than all the flash and ceremony of the rich, who give only a token to the poor—whom they oppress—while holding back the lion share of what belongs to the needy.

Woe to the one who can save so many lives from death, but does not!

> The poor begs you for money and gets none. There is a human being seeking bread, and your horses chew gold in their bits. You rejoice in your precious adornments, while others have nothing to eat. A harsh judgement awaits you, oh rich! The people are hungry and you close your granaries. The people cry and you show your jewels. Woe to one who can save so many lives from death, and does not![27]
>
> — AMBROSE OF MILAN (340-397)

Luxury on the one hand and misery on the other—that is the problem of wealth. In Ambrose's time, this disparity was less extreme than ours, where a handful of billionaires hoard more wealth than half the human race combined. They live in unimaginable luxury while millions starve. John Chrysostom makes a similar remark, "Countless poor people have to go hungry so that you can wear a single ruby."[28] There is a human cost to the luxury of the rich. Every yacht is a village that might have been saved from starvation, but the greedy rich let them die.

If Chrysostom and Ambrose's situation led to these words of rebuke against the rich, how much more should the Church today condemn the wealthy? It is not about hating the rich as persons, but it is about recognizing that their hoarded luxuries could feed millions yet they choose not to help the starving, homeless, desperate masses every day.

Capitalism justifies this situation with endless excuses and apologetics. But it is unjustifiable to God. The existence of a billionaire is not a neutral phenomenon in society. On the contrary, a billionaire represents a situation that is unfathomably inhumane in that they are someone who can save the lives of millions yet does not. Woe to the rich! Woe to the billionaires who can help but do not! A harsh judgment awaits, indeed. God has not forgotten the cries of starving children, of desperate beggars, who could have been helped but were not.

Robbery

> Strictly speaking, the rich man [Lk. 16:19-31] has not committed an act of injustice against Lazarus, since he did not rob him of his possessions. His sin consisted rather in not giving part of his own possessions. [...]
>
> This is robbery: not to share one's resources. Perhaps what I am saying astonishes you. Yet be not astonished. For I shall offer you the testimony of the Sacred Scriptures, which say that not only to rob others' property, but also not to share your own with others, is robbery and greediness and theft. [...]
>
> Reproaching the Jews through the mouth of the prophet, God says: 'The earth has produced its fruits but you have not brought in tithes, and robbery of the poor dwells in your house' [Mal. 3:10]. [...] He says this in order to make it clear to the rich that what they possess belongs to the poor [...] whatever the source. Elsewhere God also says: 'Do not rob the poor man of his livelihood' [Sir. 4:1]. A robbery is taking and keeping what is not one's own. These texts therefore teach that if we refuse to give alms, we will be punished in the same way as robbers.[29]
>
> — JOHN CHRYSOSTOM (349-407)

Chrysostom discusses Christ's parable of the rich man and Lazarus, which is the biblical basis of the claim that *not* giving is a sin and injustice. The rich man is condemned because he did not help Lazarus, who begged daily at his gate. Jesus describes the rich man as one "dressed in purple and fine linen and who feasted sumptuously every day," while Lazarus lay at his gate longing "to satisfy his hunger with what fell from the rich man's table" (Lk. 16:19-20).

The parable is a powerful condemnation of inequality. But notice who is at fault. It is not Lazarus begging at the gate. Today, we are often quick to judge the poor and homeless, looking for every reason why they deserve to be in their miserable situation. But Jesus does not place any blame on Lazarus. Instead, Jesus condemns the rich man for failing to help.

Not feeding the hungry is a sin of omission. That is why many of the Early Church Fathers considered hoarded wealth (and inequality) *theft*. Christ's parable leads directly to this conclusion: inequality is a great injustice, and the rich stand condemned. Thus, Chrysostom argues that the rich who can help the needy but choose not to are guilty of robbery.

Today, it is common to suggest that the rich deserve their wealth. But it does not matter where their wealth comes from, for Chrysostom, because it belongs to the poor. We are quick to justify inequality under capitalism as the reward of hard work. But no matter what means the rich used to obtain their riches, the excess belongs to the poor.

In most situations, the rich do not even earn their wealth through their efforts. Rarely—if ever—is wealth acquired without the help of the poor. Think of a wealthy CEO of a large company. They do not gain riches by working hard; instead, they hire others to work for them.

Consider an example: Did Steve Jobs invent the iPhone? He certainly pushed for the idea and made it possible. But did he build it? Did he design the software? Did he physically put together its components? Did he manufacture it? Indeed, he did none of these things. Instead, he hired others to do that. Without their efforts, he would not have been successful. While Steve Jobs leadership was necessary, it should not be confused with the actual work of designing, building, and producing a commodity. The people who make the iPhone are not the same who profit from it; they labor namelessly in the factories and offices for relatively little money. Yet, *they* produce the value for one of the wealthiest companies on the planet. Without the misery of the poor, the wealth of the rich would be unthinkable.

The poor are not poor by accident but are made destitute by the exploitation of the rich. Thus, the rich do not *earn* their wealth. And accordingly, they owe a debt to the poor, not just in principle but in actuality. Without the toil of the poor, the rich could not become rich. Therefore, to claim that the rich deserve their wealth because they have earned it is unrealistic and false. It is not charity for the rich to give to the poor but justice.

Elsewhere, Chrysostom writes:

> The rich are in possession of the goods of the poor, even if they have acquired them honestly or inherited them legally.[30]

Chrysostom rejects the claim to legality in favor of a higher authority, God's lordship. God ordained the earth to be held in common for the benefit of the whole human race, yet the rich sin against God by claiming what God has given to the poor and needy. The excuse that the rich earned their wealth honestly or legally is just that, an excuse that does not hold water against God's lordship over all. The Church today must not conform to the ways of the capitalist world, which protects the rights of the rich to profit off the misery of the poor. Instead, the Church must stand up and be a voice for the voiceless poor and declare once again that their riches are unjust and sinful. "Legality" is one thing, but the Word of God is another.

To grow rich without injustice is impossible

If wealth is a good but is increased by greed, the greedier one is, the better the possessor must be. But is not this plainly a self-contradiction? But suppose the wealth is not gained wrongfully. But how is this possible? So destructive a passion is greed, that to grow rich without injustice is impossible. [...] But what if, you say, a man succeeded to his father's inheritance? Then he received what had been gathered by injustice. [...] some one must probably have unjustly taken and enjoyed the goods of others.[31]

— JOHN CHRYSOSTOM (349-407)

This quote is from a series of homilies on 1 Timothy. Earlier in the homily, Chrysostom argues, "The wealth is not a possession; it is not property, it is a loan for us."[32] This is a familiar theme for Chrysostom. Everything belongs to God. The rich monopolize what only God can claim as property. Chrysostom stresses that "We are all sojourners" who cannot take riches with us. The idea of owning wealth is absurd because we cannot take any of it with us when we die. True wealth, however, is the good work of almsgiving. That leads to the claim that it is *impossible* to grow rich without injustice. Because all things belong to God, hoarded wealth can only be obtained unjustly by taking what belongs to another.

Furthermore, Chrysostom stresses that *greed* makes the pursuit of riches impossible without injustice. Therefore, it is impossible to be exceedingly rich without being overcome by the sin of greed. Thus, all riches come from injustice. Either one has stolen what belongs to another by God's wise administration of the common earth, or greed has consumed the soul; in either case, injustice is the root of differentiating wealth. Notice, again, how Chrysostom refuses to allow any just means of obtaining riches, even inheritance. Whatever the source of hoarded wealth, it is sinful.

In the 1987 movie "Wall Street," Michael Douglas' character, Gordon Gekko, famously declares, "Greed, for lack of a better word, is good." The movie unveils the secret, unspoken core of the capitalist system. It is a system that praises greed and renounces humility and self-sacrifice. That is why Chrysostom rejects the familiar claim—repeated still today—that it is good to be rich. The origin of extraordinary riches is always sin, whether greed, theft, or violence. It is impossible to amass great hoards of gold without injustice. Chrysostom's focus on greed brings this reality into the context of a wealthy person's soul. Thus, the origins of wealth are derived from personal sin and are rooted in social injustice. Vast hoards of money in the hands of the few are detrimental to society and the soul alike.

Origin of riches is injustice

Tell me, then, from where do you get your riches? From whom did you receive it and from whom did he receive who transmits it to you? 'From my father and he from my grandfather.' But can you, going back through many generations show that the riches were justly acquired? No, you cannot. The root and origin of them must have been injustice. Why? Because God in the beginning made not one man rich and another man poor. Nor did he afterwards take and show to one treasures of gold, and deny the other the rich of searching for it. Rather, he left the earth free to all alike. How come then, if it is common, you have acres and acres of land, while your neighbor has not a portion of it? 'My father transmitted them to me' you say. But whom did he receive them from? 'From my grandfather.' But you must go back and find the original answer. [...]

'But if I do no evil, even though I do not do good, it is not bad,' you retort. True. But is not this an evil, that you alone should enjoy what is common? Is not 'the earth God's and the fullness thereof?' If then our possessions belong to one common Lord, they belong also to our fellow-servants. The possessions of the Lord are all common. [...] We share them equally. [...]

Observe further now concerning things that are common, there is no contention, but everything is peaceful. But as soon as someone attempts to possess himself of anything to make it

> his own, then contention is introduced, as if nature itself protests against the fact that, whereas God brings us together in every way, we are eager to divide and separate ourselves by appropriating things, using those cold words 'mine and yours.' Then struggles and hatred arise. But where this does not happen, no strife or struggles appear.
>
> Hence we should conclude that common sharing is more convenient and more agreeable to our nature.[33]
>
> — JOHN CHRYSOSTOM (349-407)

This quote is also from Chrysostom's homily on 1 Timothy. First, Chrysostom is not content with accepting inequality but asks why the rich are rich, and the poor are poor. In chapter eight, I will argue that this approach is vital for us again today. To faithfully proclaim the anti-mammon message of Jesus today, we need a socioeconomic analysis of capitalism.

Second, the commonality of the earth is the basis of this critique. Because the world belongs to God and is given for all in common, inequality is an injustice. God did not create the world with some rich and others poor. Thus, for some to be rich while others are poor, there must be an act of injustice done by the rich against the poor. Chrysostom recognized what was later termed "primitive accumulation" by economists. Primitive accumulation entails a history of violence, theft, and injustice. To accumulate great wealth is to act unjustly towards the poor because God gave the earth for all in common in the beginning.

And Chrysostom does not merely criticize the root of wealth but its continued existence as injustice. It is not just that someone's parents or grandparents unjustly acquired their riches, but that they, by having so much while others have so little, also continue to perpetrate that original injustice. Thus, it is not merely that the rich once committed an injustice years ago but that still to this day, wherever there is one who is exceedingly rich while others suffer from a lack of essentials, the injustice continues. Therefore, no one is without excuse.

Third, Chrysostom portrays an idyllic situation wherein all things are held in common, and there is peace. That refers to the community of Acts 2 and 4, but more importantly, it looks ahead to the Kingdom of God. Thus, we strive to make the Kingdom come here and now by seeking to hold all things in common with those in need, not hoarding for ourselves more than our "daily bread," and thus, to live at peace. But to expect to live at peace in a situation of injustice is a fantasy.

Those who claim that we, as Christians, must be at peace with both the oppressor and the oppressed have failed to understand what Chrysostom saw, namely, that the rich have their wealth through injustice and sin, through oppressing the poor. Peace between all is possible only when exploitation and oppression cease. We here and now must strive to make earth look like heaven, as Christ taught us to pray, "Thy Kingdom come, thy will be done, on earth as it is in heaven." Let us act today to make that a reality by sharing with those in need and calling to repentance the rich who hoard the earth's resources unjustly, which God has given for all in common.

Finally, the last sentence contradicts what capitalist apologists have argued repeatedly, namely, that socialism is incompatible with human nature. Some argue that capitalism, which prioritizes greed and selfishness, expresses our essential nature. But Chrysostom contradicts this. Instead, common sharing is more true to our nature than greed.

This "human nature" argument also fails to recognize how economic factors often determine how human beings act within society. For example, an economic system that relies on greed will lead to the impression that such greed is essential to human nature. But it is just as likely that capitalism has encouraged this greed. And in the same way, a system that prioritizes the common good of all, i.e., socialism, would promote a feeling of solidarity and common sharing, which Chrysostom considers more true to our nature.

Neither point contradicts the reality of sin, but ignoring the economic and cultural factors that emphasize different aspects of human nature is naive. Human nature is not fixed in time but changes with each given situation. Capitalism has encouraged greed, and capitalist apologists mistakenly argue that greed is the sum of human nature. That would be like feeding one's children a steady diet of junk food and then thinking their hunger for junk food is essential to their nature, not the symptom of the conditions created by choosing to feed them only junk food.

On justice and riches

> Assisting the needy is justice.[34]
>
> Riches are neither real nor are they yours.[35]
>
> The Superfluities of the rich are the necessaries of the poor. They who possess superfluities, possess the goods of others.[36]
>
> God commands sharing not as being from the property of them whom He commands, but as being from His own property.[37]

— AUGUSTINE OF HIPPO (354-430)

In these short lines, Augustine captures the core idea of this chapter: Giving to the poor is justice. The surplus we share with the poor does not belong to us; the abundance of the rich belongs to the poor. Hoarded riches are theft from those in need. We are not called to give when we feel like it but out of obligation to those without their daily bread.

These points demonstrate the radicalness of the Early Church on the question of wealth and poverty. They did not see riches in the way we do; instead, for one to hoard an abundance of resources meant the starvation of many. And that is rightly called sin and injustice.

5

CONTENTMENT AND THE SIN OF LUXURY

The cult of mammon turns human beings into consumers whose worth depends on their ability to purchase things. To be, under capitalism, is to consume. The mantra of every shopping mall is this: I buy; therefore, I am. Mammon corrupts the soul and turns human beings into "human havings." Marx correctly observed that a human being under capitalism lives in a state of alienation. He writes, "The less you *are,* the less you express your own life, the more you *have,* i.e., the greater is your *alienated* life, the greater is the store of your estranged being."[1] Humans are no longer defined by the content of their character but by their material possessions.

The way of Christ rejects the treadmill of having more as the ultimate end of existence. The goal is to *be* more: more generous, kind, loving, and Christ-like. These attributes are exceedingly more valuable than all the world's riches. Mammon pursues a cheap substitute for the true treasure of knowing and following Christ. It replaces good works of love with material goods. That is a parallel commonly drawn in Scripture and by the Fathers: reject the *false* riches of this earth and pursue the *true* wealth of good works.

This situation also calls us to return to the Christian message of radical contentment. To be *content* with enough is a revolutionary act in a world of rampant consumerism. Thus, one of the fruits of a soul that has renounced mammon to follow Christ is contentment with enough and generosity with what's left over. Therefore, the Christian witness must reject mammon and its attempt to define human worth according to having rather than being. That is the aim of this chapter, to reflect on the Christian commitment to contentment, to our "daily bread." In this, we reflect on the rejection of luxury by the Church Fathers.

James 2 condemns Christians living in luxury. Indeed, most passages that commend "modesty" have less to do with sexually modest clothing and more with economic modesty. In the Roman world, status was displayed by the clothes a person wore. There is an astonishing story in the Early Church of a woman who funded the building of a basilica entirely with the jewelry she wore.[2] It is clear from this example that what James had in mind with modest clothing was luxurious and expensive clothing, which was a sign of status. The problem was not sexual immodesty but the sin of luxury.

Indeed, it was considered a contradiction for a Christian to live in luxury. Then, modest clothing is best interpreted to mean modesty in riches, not just sexuality. But the health and wealth gospel today has made luxury something desirable, a goal for all Christians. Consider how some celebrity pastors see no issue in wearing designer clothing on stage yet will condemn immodest clothing without any hint of irony. The quotes in this chapter illustrate that to live in luxury is to go another way, to follow mammon and not Christ.

The way of Jesus Christ is not one of luxury but of solidarity with the poor. Thus, for some to live in extreme luxury while others suffer, starve, and die from unmet needs is a travesty and an embarrassment to the gospel. And most of all, it is a sin. Thus, we are to live in contentment without striving to have more than our neighbors. Modern capitalism's "rat race" is not a suitable path for Christians today. Instead, the way of solidarity with the least of these is the righteous path. To not care for the least of these is to neglect Christ. And one can hardly be called a follower of Christ if they do not care for Christ in the faces of the poor.

The mad pursuit

> I do not wish to rule. I do not long to be rich [...] I have renounced the mad pursuit of glory.[3]
>
> — TATIAN (120-180)

Tatian was a second-century Syrian theologian known for harmonizing the four gospels into a biblical paraphrase called the Diatessaron, which was used as the standard gospel text for the Syriac-speaking Churches until the fifth century. He is also known for critiquing paganism in *Address to the Greeks*, which is where this quote is from. He is addressing the vanity of pagans that pursue riches and glory, calling it a "mad" pursuit.

This renunciation is an essential first step in recalibrating our hearts to the way of Jesus. It is necessary to undo the capitalistic, health-and-wealth mentalities of the world that have infected the Church. We must boldly renounce the desire to be rich and famous—daily, if necessary. Social media has made this difficult. Our culture will frequently impress upon us the desire for wealth, but it is a "mad pursuit" unfitting to the Christian way.

Flee from wicked luxury

> 'Be temperate as to what is evil, and do it not; but be not temperate as to what is good, but do it. For if thou be temperate as to what is good, so as not to do it, thou committest a great sin; but if thous be temperate as to what is evil, so as not to do it, thou doest great righteousness. Be temperate therefore in abstaining from all wickedness, and do that which is good.' 'What kinds of wickedness, Sir,' say I, 'are they from which we must be temperate and abstain?' 'Listen,' saith he;' from adultery and fornication, from the lawlessness of drunkenness, from wicked luxury, from many viands [rich foods] and the costliness of riches, and vaunting and haughtiness and pride, and from falsehood and evil-speaking and hypocrisy, malice and all blasphemy. These works are the most wicked of all in the life of men.⁴
>
> — THE SHEPHERD OF HERMAS

The Shepherd of Hermas compares luxury with adultery as if greed is as grievous and destructive as fornication. This is a fascinating example of how the Early Church understood luxury as a sin on par with adultery. The Shepherd warns against haughtiness and pride, but not only the inner form of these; he also warns against rich food, excess drink, and costly expenditures. Those who argue that the problem with riches is *only* a matter of the *heart* will do well to hear what the Shepherd says. He calls both the heart-issue (idolatry) and material luxury sin.

Today, the Church has retained a puritanical approach to sexual desire but has neglected the command to flee from wicked luxury. Yet these are sins rooted in the same covetous heart. The Shepherd argues here that hoarded wealth is as sinful as marital unfaithfulness and that we must flee from both with equal tenacity. Thus, we must teach against luxury as fiercely as adultery. Some pastors have lost their jobs for cheating on their wives, but the same Churches readily accept leaders who hoard great wealth for themselves. That shows how far we have come from the original teachings of the Church on wealth.

The Shepherd encourages us today to flee from luxury and be radical in doing what is good. It is a "great sin" to fail to do good when able. Luxury is *wicked* and must be resisted. But notice how we are not given a list of "do nots" but are spurred on to be vigilant in doing good.

Every luxury is foolish

'Of what sort, Sir,' say I, 'are the works of the evil desire, which hand men over to death?' [...] 'Before all is desire for the wife or husband of another, and for extravagance of wealth, and for many needless dainties, and for drinks and other luxuries, many and foolish. For every luxury is foolish and vain for the servants of God. These desires then are evil, and bring death to the servants of God. For this evil desire is a daughter of the devil. Ye must, therefore, abstain from the evil desires, that so abstaining ye may live unto God.⁵

— THE SHEPHERD OF HERMAS

We again see a parallel being drawn between coveting our neighbor's wife and pursuing luxury. For the first Christians, this was a familiar comparison. To pursue great riches meant acting like an adulterer and being unfaithful to the way of Christ. Thus, the path of the Christian faith *includes* fidelity to the poor. It is impossible to be at once faithful to the poor and selfishly pursue great riches. Faithfulness to the poor *is* faithfulness to Christ.

It is foolish to pursue luxury. To hoard wealth is to steal what belongs to another. The world was given to all in common. Luxury is the sin of coveting what belongs rightly to the poor and needy, who lack their essential material needs without it. We do not often connect our desire for luxury with its effect on the needy, but we should. Every "Yes" to something is also a "No" to something else. Every "Yes" to luxury is a "No" to the needy, but it is also a "No" to Christ (Mt. 25:31-46).

No one should lead a luxurious life

Now, [Christ] has not merely related to us a story respecting a poor man and a rich one; but He has taught us, in the first place, that no one should lead a luxurious life, nor, living in worldly pleasures and perpetual feastings, should be the slave of his lusts, and forget God.⁶

— IRENAEUS OF LYONS (130-202)

Irenaeus was a second-century theologian and bishop of Lyons best known for his book, *Against Heresies,* which refuted the gnostic heresy. This quote is from that work, and it is an early example of how the first Christians understood themselves as walking a path that excluded luxury.

Accordingly, Irenaeus argues that a Christian living in luxury is an oxymoron, that is, an impossible contradiction. Furthermore, Irenaeus stresses that the way of luxury is antithetical to the way of Jesus Christ. In this text, he is commenting on the parable of Lazarus and the rich man. He recognized that it was not merely a story about respecting the poor; rather, it warns against the danger of living in luxury, of pursuing mammon over God.

It is monstrous to live in luxury

It is monstrous for one to live in luxury, while many are in want. How much more glorious is it to do good to many, than to live sumptuously [luxuriously]!⁷

— CLEMENT OF ALEXANDRIA (150-215)

Blessings are multiplied by sharing, but hoarded luxuries spoil abundance. Clement contrasts living for personal hedonism through luxury with the glory of doing good works, namely, giving alms to the poor and needy. It is glorious to share wealth; monstrous to hoard while others suffer.

Capitalism is a system that hoards the luxuries of society for the few while leaving the masses desperate for daily bread. When half of the planet's wealth and resources are accumulated and monopolized by a handful of individuals, it displays a level of atrocity far beyond anything Clement might have imagined when he said these words.

But that is what capitalism does by design. It leads to greater and greater consolidation of wealth into fewer and fewer hands thanks to market competition, monopolization, and capital accumulation, wherein larger companies routinely acquire or put smaller companies out of business. Thus, capitalism always tends towards monopolization, placing the few vast hoards of wealth and luxuries into the hands while stripping the masses of their necessities.⁸ We need an economic system that prioritizes the needs of the many over the luxury of the few. Anything else is monstrous.

Physical need is the measure of possessions

> Just as the foot is the measure of the sandal, so the physical needs of each are the measure of what one should possess. Whatever is excessive—the things they call adornments, but the trappings of the rich are not adornments—are a burden for the body... Scripture declares that really 'his own riches are the redemption of the soul of man' (Prov. 13:8), that is, if a man is rich, he will obtain salvation by sharing his wealth.[9]
>
> — CLEMENT OF ALEXANDRIA (150-215)

Clement's point is that money is good within a limit, but outside of that limit, it is unrighteous. The limit is set by physical need. Does a rich person genuinely *need* a dozen mansions around the world? Do they need designer clothing? Does a mansion provide shelter better than a humble single-family home? Does their luxury food satisfy hunger better than common meals? Sinful riches begin where need ends.

Greed is infinite, while material need is finite. Capitalism has made greed, not need, its central drive. Thus, the economy is subject to an impossible demand for more and more while millions starve without having enough to eat. Because we cannot satisfy the greed of the rich, the poor suffer. A humane system would prioritize the needs of all over the luxuries of the few. Unfortunately, the very opposite is true for capitalism today.

There is nothing inherently wrong with nice things or luxury items. It is a gift from God to enjoy the bounty of this earth. But it becomes sinful and inhumane when luxuries are hoarded at the expense of the necessities of the masses. It is differentiating wealth that is condemned, not God's abundant earth. The earth is good and wonderful, but it has been privatized for the benefit of the few. Until everyone's needs are met, luxuries are absurd and destructive. But the rich can be liberated from this pathological greed by giving the poor everything they own in excess.

Choose one

> Since we are different from them [the pagans], it befits us to give up not our life for money but money for our life, either by voluntary charity or by the patient endurance of loss.[10]
>
> — TERTULLIAN (160-240)

This quote is from Tertullian's *On Patience*. He contrasts the practice of pagans, who "set worldly goods before their life" by engaging in dangerous yet lucrative careers such as military service and working as sea merchants. These pagans thus risk their lives for money. In contrast, the Christian gives up their money for their life. This follows a larger argument exhorting Christians to be indifferent toward earthly goods because "our Lord himself [...] did not own any worldly riches. He always justifies the poor and condemns the rich."[11] Thus, because Jesus did not seek wealth, the followers of Christ should not either.

The pursuit of mammon is, by nature, alienating. It leads us to sacrifice our life for money. But we must, instead, sacrifice our money for our life, living simply for the sake of the gospel. That includes contentment with "enough" and renouncing the mad pursuit of riches. Because, in reality, wealth comes at a cost, and that cost is irreplaceable. Those who seek wealth trade what cannot be gained back for a lump of lifeless gold; they trade their life and the time they were given to serve God and each other for a pile of riches.

The psychologist Eric Fromm once captured the poverty of this approach, writing, "If I am what I have and if what I have is lost, who then am I? Nobody but a defeated, deflated, pathetic testimony to a wrong way of living."[12] When our lives are identified with *having stuff*, then our lives are filled with anxiety and fear. Instead, Fromm argues that we must focus on being, not having: "If I am who I am and not what I have, nobody can deprive me of or threaten my security and my sense of identity."[13]

This psychological approach reflects something essential about the Christian faith, especially its critique of idolatry. The Fathers say that *idolatry* also leads to self-alienation, this anxiety of having rather than the security of being. Only when God is the ground and power of being, will we find the true life.

Ultimately, those who spend their lives pursuing wealth, thinking it will add great joy to their lives, end up with neither their life nor their riches. All people die, rich and poor, and the rich have made the irrational decision to trade their lives for something transitory; the graves of the rich and poor are the same. No matter how beautifully adorned they may be, in each coffin sits a rotting corpse. So we should not trade our lives for money but money for our lives. If we have less but are rich in the works of God, then we are rich in what truly matters.

Daily bread

> For this reason we are enjoined to ask what is sufficient for the preservation of the substance of the body: not luxury, but food, which restores what the body loses, and prevents death by hunger; not tables to inflame and drive on to pleasures, nor such things as make the body wax wanton against the soul; but bread, and that, too, not for a great number of years, but what is sufficient for us to-day.[14]
>
> — HIPPOLYTUS OF ROME (170-235)

Hippolytus was a second-century theologian. Little is known for certain about Hippolytus except that he was an important teacher in Rome who wrote several influential theological and biblical works. This quote is from his commentary on Matthew 6:3, "Give us this day our daily bread." Hippolytus argues that Christ tells us to pray for our "daily bread," not for luxuries. The Lord's Prayer orients our Christian expectations for life. The way of Christ does not entail luxury but a simple life of being content with enough.

How perverse and distorted it is for those today to pray for riches in the Church, to promise believers that God will make them rich. We must be content with our daily bread and learn to live at peace with what God has promised. The priority of a Christian is to have enough so they will not be a burden to others. Then they will be free to help the poor and needy, preach the good news, and hasten God's coming Kingdom.

Luxury is inimical to holiness.

> [M]any things were called unclean, not as being condemned in themselves, but that the Jews might be restrained to the service of one God; because frugality and moderation in appetite were becoming to those who were chosen for this purpose. And such moderation is always found to be approximate to religion, nay, so to speak, rather related and akin to it; for luxury is inimical to holiness.[15]
>
> — NOVATIAN (220-258)

Novatian was a controversial third-century theologian who acted as an antipope in opposition to Pope Cornelius. Accordingly, Novatian was later excommunicated, and his followers created a schismatic Church known for refusing the readmission of those who had lapsed from faith and worshiped idols after baptism. While Novatianism was condemned as a heresy, Novatian was a notable scholar and theologian despite the heretical condemnation of his followers. This quote comes from a text by Novatian that discusses Jewish dietary restrictions.

Novatian calls luxury *inimical* to holiness. "Inimical" is an archaic word used to describe how luxuries *hinder* holiness. Another way of saying this would be that luxuries obstruct the path to holiness. Thus, Novatian indicates that the problem with wealth is that it leads to another God, but it is an idol standing in the way of serving the Lord. Therefore, riches are antithetical to the life of faith. To live in luxury is to live away from holiness and reverence. It is an oxymoron to serve God and live in luxury.

Novatian is discussing this in connection with the ban on meats in the Levitical law and the doctrine that Christians are no longer under this law. Accordingly, he asks, if we are free from the prohibition of certain meats, are Christians also free to live in luxury? He answers with a clear "No," writing: "But, on the ground that liberty in meats is granted to us, there is no permission of luxury, there is no taking away of continence and fasting: for these things greatly become the faithful."[16] Thus, there is no option for luxury for those who follow Christ. To be faithful to God's way that leads to life is to renounce vain luxuries and pursue justice for the least of these.

Starve the greed of mammon

> Therefore I say to you: Fast from evil-doing; discipline yourselves from covetousness; abstain from unjust profits; starve your greed for mammon, keep in your houses no snatched and stolen treasure. What use is it to keep meat out of your mouth if you wound your brother or sister by evil doing? What advantage is it to forgo what is your own if you seize unjustly what belongs to the poor? [...]
>
> Let Isaiah too set forth the actions of a pure and sincere fast: "Loosen every bond of injustice, set the oppressed free, untie the knots of covenants made by force. Share your bread with the hungry; bring the poor and homeless into your house. When you see the naked, cover them; and do not despise your own flesh" [Isa. 56:6–7].[17]
>
> — GREGORY OF NYSSA (330-395)

Today we think of fasting purely in terms of refraining from food. But fasting can also mean starving greed, jealousy, envy, and lust, as Gregory argues in this example. Furthermore, fasting is not merely refraining from doing wrong but also has a positive dimension: feasting on good works. Gregory points to Isaiah's definition of fasting, which involves liberating the oppressed from their injustice, feeding the hungry, housing the homeless, and helping the poor.

The ritual of fasting is an essential practice for Christians, but it is often limited when we confine fasting to food and not practicing a fast that starves mammon and injustice. Fasting is a powerful act on the personal level (fasting from greed and the desire for mindless consumption) and social level (starving mammon's power over the poor and needy). Let us fast from the greed of mammon and learn to do good.

God's dear poor

God himself is the prime author of beneficence, the rich and generous provider of all that we need. But we, who are taught in every letter of the Scripture to imitate our Lord and Maker —as much as the mortal may imitate the divine and immortal —we snatch everything to our own enjoyment, assigning some things to ourselves to live upon, hoarding the rest for our heirs. Merciless as we are, we care nothing for the unfortunate, we give no kindly thought to the poor. We see a fellow human with no bread to eat, no food to sustain life itself; yet far from hastening to help, far from offering that person a rescue, we leave him like a once sturdy plant to wither unwatered pitifully away under a scorching sun—and this even if we have wealth to overflowing and might let the channels of our abundance run forth to comfort many. [...]

You, therefore, who have been created rational beings, endowed with mind to expound and interpret divine things, do not be enticed by what is only transitory. Strive to win those things which never forsake their holder. Live with restraint; do not think everything your own, but reserve a part for God's dear poor. All things belong to God, our common Father. We are all of the same stock, all brothers and sisters. And when people are siblings, the best and most equitable thing is that they should inherit in equal portions. The second best is that even if one or two take the greater part, the others should have at least their own share. But if one man should

> seek to be absolute possessor of all, refusing even a third or a fifth to his siblings, then he is a cruel tyrant, a savage with whom there can be no dealing, an insatiate beast gloatingly shutting its jaws over the meal it will not share. Or rather he is more ruthless than any beast; wolf does not drive wolf from the prey, and a pack of dogs will tear the same carcass; this man in his insatiable greed will not admit one fellow creature to a share in his riches.[18]
>
> — GREGORY OF NYSSA (330-395)

Gregory calls us to love God's "dear poor" and practice that love by sharing with the needy. Those who can help but refuse to share are merciless beasts, unwilling to act kindly toward the needy.

Gregory refers to the common humanity of all for this argument. Because God is "our common Father," we are all brothers and sisters who should share. Even if there remains some imbalance between us, at the very least we should share what we have with our brothers and sisters in need. In contrast, the rich seek to be "possessor[s] of all" and consume everything as their property. But they are a cruel tyrant and unjust.

The most perfect Christianity

> This is the rule of the most perfect Christianity, its most exact definition, its highest point, namely, the seeking of the common good. [...] For nothing can so make a man an imitator of Christ as caring for his neighbors.[19]
>
> — GREGORY OF NYSSA (330-395)

For Gregory, the epitome of being a Christian is not doctrinal agreement, sacramental reverence, or moral superiority. Instead, a Christian is identified by their love for the poor, concretely expressed by caring for their needs. We cannot strive for luxury without sinning against our neighbors. Thus, the Christian life must be defined existentially according to the good works of the faithful.

A story about an Amish man explains this point well. Someone asks the man if he is a Christian. The man points to his neighbor's house and says, "To answer that question, you'll have to ask my neighbor." That profoundly reflects Christ's word on loving our neighbor as ourselves, which he then followed up with the Good Samaritan story. It also reflects Christ's claim that his disciples will be "known by their love" (John 13:35). This definition of Christian faith is perhaps more helpful than whether or not we profess *belief* in Jesus. Instead, we should ask if our love declares our faith more than our words. That is the most perfect expression of Christianity, to love our neighbor.

Hoarded wealth is a curse and accusation

Why do you choose to be rich through covetousness? To hoard up gold and silver for others and innumerable curses and accusations for yourself? The poor man whom you have defrauded is suffering anguish because of the lack of the necessities of life, and is lamenting, and drawing down upon you the curses of thousands. He may go about the market place in the evening and not knowing where he is going to spend the night. How can the unhappy fellow sleep, with pangs in the belly, tortured by hunger, while it is freezing and the rain coming down on him? And while you are coming home from the bath, clean and dandy, dressed in soft clothes, full of contentment and happiness, and hastening to sit down to splendidly prepared dinners, he is driven everywhere about the market place by cold and hunger, with his head hung low and his hands outstretched. The poor man does not even have the courage to ask for the necessary food from one so well fed and so well rested, and often has to withdraw covered with insults.

When therefore, you have returned home, when you lie down on your couch, when the lights around your house shine bright, when your table is well prepared and plentiful, at that time remember that poor miserable man wandering about like dogs in the alleys, in darkness and in mire, and from these alleys he goes back, not to his house, his wife, or his bed, but to a pile of straw, like those dogs which we hear baying all through the night. And you, if you see but a drop of water falling from the ceiling, you would throw the whole house in confusion calling for the slaves and disturbing everything, while he, laid in rags, and straw, and dirt, has to bear the bitter cold.[20]

— GREGORY OF NYSSA (330-395)

The rich go home to their luxury while the poor barely survive poverty. The wealthy today do not have to interact with the poor—"out of sight, out of mind." But God has not forgotten them; God is their defender. Therefore, the rich will be held accountable for the misery of the poor.

The poor are *made* poor by the exploitation of the rich. The logic of Gregory's words is that this inequality is because of their luxury. The root of this unjust system is the desire to live in luxury and never be content with enough. Notice how Gregory begins by asking why the rich *choose* to become rich through covetousness. The origins of their wealth are injustice and sin, and the daily reality of their hoarded wealth is found in the accusations of the poor. Indeed, they are judged daily for failing the help the needy, who must suffer and sleep in degradation while enjoying their luxuries.

Today, the global north lives in relative luxury while the global south is plagued by poverty, malnutrition, and social unrest. It is naive to see this as accidental. On the contrary, the luxury of the first world is directly related to the poverty of the third world. Those living in the first world should be conscious of this reality—not so that we feel guilty for a situation we did not directly cause. But rather, to be aware of it and act to end the inequality by fighting against the system that caused it: capitalism and imperialism. We are like the man in Gregory's parable if we do not go out of our way to hear the cries of the poor and hungry in the global south. But their cries are the cries of Christ.

The people are starving

> The poor man seeks money and has it not; a man asks for bread, and your horse champs gold under his teeth. And precious ornaments delight you, although others do not have grain… The people are starving, and you sloe your barns; the people weep bitterly, and you toy with your jeweled ring [...] The jewel in your ring could preserve the lives of the whole people.[21]
>
> — AMBROSE OF MILAN (340-397)

The people are suffering while the rich feast on luxury; they have no ears to hear the cries of the poor. Even their horses are adorned with gold, and the vulnerable die from hunger. This contradiction is sinful. The jewelry of the rich could save the lives of countless poor. And every day they refuse to help the needy is a day of judgment upon their ill-begotten riches.

In chapter four, we discussed Engels' concept of "social murder," and this quote from Ambrose returns to that idea. It is essential to see that luxury is not accidental. It does not exist in isolation from poverty. Instead, luxury is sinful precisely because it comes at the expense of misery for the poor and needy. That is Ambrose's point. The poor are starving while the rich fill their barns with excess food; the destitute weep while the rich clothe themselves in luxurious jewelry and clothing.

Today, every mansion is a sin against the poor, homeless, and hungry who are denied basic resources for survival *because* of the insatiable greed for luxury among the rich. God gave the abundance of the earth for the good of all, not for the private enjoyment of the few. And every day the rich lavishly live in luxury, they a sin against the image of God in the poor and starving. Indeed, the poor are starving, and we must be attentive to their cries.

You butcher your own soul

> Now do not tell me, that you do not worship an image of gold, but make this clear to me, that you do not do those things which gold bids you. For there be different kinds of idolatry, and one holds mammon lord, and another his belly his god, and a third some other most baneful lust. But, "you do not sacrifice oxen to them as the Gentiles do." Nay, but what is far worse, you butcher your own soul. [...] I therefore exhort you to lay to heart the exceeding unseemliness hereof, and to flee from idolatry.[22]
>
> — JOHN CHRYSOSTOM (349-407)

Idolatry leads to self-alienation; it is destructive to seek after the whole world and lose one's soul. Marx discussed the phenomenon of "alienation" as an unavoidable reality under capitalism. A system that prioritizes the love of mammon above all else leads to the spiritual, emotional, and physical abuse of the self in the name of this idol. Idolatry always leads to dehumanization.

Chrysostom criticizes those who think idolatry is no longer a problem. Unfortunately, the same assumption is common today. We do not think we are idolatrous because we no longer sacrifice animals to gods or keep statues in our homes. But Chrysostom stresses that, while we do not butcher animals, *we butcher our own souls* for the sake of mammon. That is the "unseemliness" of greed.

Every day, we wake up and serve mammon. That is an unavoidable feature of capitalism. And, if we are not careful, it can become an idol for us today. Money is, of course, a necessity for survival. But until we resist the cult of mammon, we will likely fall prey to the idolatry of wealth. This danger is especially acute for those of us in the first world with its privileges and temptations. But the gospel proclaims liberty to the captives and sight to the blind. May we see capitalism for what it is: the idolatry of mammon. And may we receive the liberty that only Christ can give. We serve either God or mammon.

Where mammon is, Christ is not

Free both thyself from thy bonds, and the poor man from his hunger. Why rivetest thou fast the chains of thy sins? Some one saith, How? When thou wearest gold whilst another is perishing, when thou, to get thee vainglory, takest so much gold, whilst another hast not even what to eat, hast thou not wedged fast thy sins? Put Christ about thee, and not gold; where mammon is, there Christ is not, where Christ is, there mammon is not. [...]

Clothe thee in alms; clothe thee in benevolence; clothe thee in modesty, humbleness. These are all more precious than gold; these make even the beautiful yet more comely; these make even the ill formed to be well formed.[23]

— JOHN CHRYSOSTOM (349-407)

Luxury suffocates our devotion to Christ. Where mammon is, Christ is not; where Christ is, mammon is not. Chrysostom does not allow any grey area. It is black-and-white: mammon or Christ. Clothing ourselves in Christ means rejecting the mad pursuit of luxury and gold. It was clear to Chrysostom that a Christian cannot be clothed in gold and Christ.

Paul writes in Romans 13:14, "Instead, put on the Lord Jesus Christ, and make no provision for the flesh, to gratify its desires." Other translations capture the military motif behind Paul's words: "Let Christ Jesus himself be the armour that you wear" (New English Bible); "Let us be Christ's men from head to foot" (Phillips Modern English). The image is not passive but active. The temptations of the sinful world must be *resisted*, like a war. So, too, must the temptations of mammon. It is a war: either Christ is Lord or mammon. There are no neutral bystanders in this battle.

Let us not admire wealth

 Wherefore, I exhort you, let us despise the many; or rather let us desire neither praises, nor possessions, nor wealth, nor deem poverty any evil. For poverty is to us a teacher of prudence, and endurance, and all true wisdom. Thus Lazarus lived in poverty, and received a crown; Jacob desired to get bread only; and Joseph was in the extreme of poverty, being not merely a slave, but also a prisoner; and on this account we admire him the more, and we do not so much praise him when he distributed the corn, as when he dwelt in the dungeon; not when he wore the diadem, but when the chain; not when he sat upon the throne, but when he was plotted against and sold. Considering then all these things, and the crowns twined for us after the conflicts, let us admire not wealth, and honor, and luxury, and power, but poverty, and the chain, and bonds, and endurance in the cause of virtue. For the end of those things is full of troubles and confusion, and their lot is bound up with this present life; but the fruit of these, heaven, and the good things in the heavens, which neither eye hath seen, nor ear heard; which may we all obtain, through the grace and lovingkindness of our Lord Jesus Christ, to whom be glory for ever. Amen.[24]

— JOHN CHRYSOSTOM (349-407)

Today, we admire the wealthy; we call them successful and intelligent because of their wealth. But that is not success in God's eyes. Those who deserve our admiration are those who suffer honorably: the martyrs of faith, the courageous activists of justice, and the vulnerable victims of capitalism. Our world's "heroes" are not the Kingdom's heroes. According to John's Apocalypse, the unnamed martyrs will receive honor and praise in God's Kingdom, while the rich and powerful will be brought to shame (Rev. 20). The first will be last; the last will be first.

What does it mean to admire poverty? Does this idolize poverty, sanitizing it in the process? No, poverty remains a brutal reality of existence. Chrysostom's point is that we should admire poverty in the eschatological sense—not by desiring the suffering of poverty but because of the belief that the first will be last and the last first. Moreover, he does not idolize suffering but admonishes the endurance of those who suffer for a righteous cause. The point is not to idolize poverty and suffering but to turn our hearts toward Jesus Christ, who became poor for our sake.

For us today, the point is to cultivate a Christian mind. That is the meaning of repentance, to change one's mind. The mind of Christ sees in the poor the promise of the Kingdom of God. The rich will be brought low, and the powerful will be condemned. But the last will be first. That is the radical proclamation of Kingdom come. To admire the poor means to adopt these eyes, the eyes that see the promise in a mustard seed (Lk. 13:18-9).

Owning things

> Everyone wants to be happy, but only those who act justly will be happy. I don't understand how those who do evil can hope to be happy. How? By owning money, silver and gold, land, houses and slaves, by the pomp of this world and worldly honor, which is fickle and transitory? They seek to find happiness by owning things.[25]
>
> — JOHN CHRYSOSTOM (349-407)

As cited above, Marx famously argued that under capitalism, a person's ambitions are too wrapped up in *owning things* that they miss the point of *becoming* more fully human. The two pursuits are antithetical. The more we have, the less we are. Thus, a person who lacks a certain quality will not work on themselves to improve but will try to fill the gap in their character by buying things. Likewise, an unhappy person will not seek after true happiness through self-reflection and community but merely through the fleeting happiness of buying newer and better things. Owning things becomes the way of being human, but it is an alienated and dehumanized *existence*, not a *life*.

Under capitalism, we do not aspire to become generous, kind, loving persons but to own a larger house, nicer cars, and better things. We answer the question, "What do you want to be when you grow up?" with a job description rather than one of character. That is a manifestation of the tyranny of mammon, which infects all aspects of life, killing life itself by suffocating it under the weight of meaningless stuff. Consumerism today is the greatest proof of this reality. Mammon is a tyrannical cult of empty stuff, desperately trying to fill the void and become more human by owning rather than being more.

6

USURY

Usury is the practice of lending money at interest. It is sometimes defined as unethically taking *excessive* interest on a loan, typically to the detriment of the poor and disadvantaged. But the Bible does not discriminate between "good" and "bad" interest rates; the Bible condemns *any* interest from a loan. Exodus 22:25 establishes this prohibition, "If you lend money to my people, to the poor among you, you shall not deal with them as a creditor; you shall not exact interest from them." Other passages banning usury include Leviticus 25:36-37, Deuteronomy 23:20-21, Ezekiel 18:17, 22:12, Nehemiah 5:7, and Psalm 15:5.

Why is the Bible against usury? It is because of God's lordship over the earth, the commonality of creation, and God's special concern for the poor. Usury takes what belongs only to God—time itself—and turns it into a tool for exploiting the poor. Thomas of Chobham, a Medieval theologian, explains, "The usurer sells nothing to the borrower that belongs to him. He sells only time, which belongs to God. He cannot, therefore, make a profit from selling someone else's property."[1] The rich leverage their hoarded wealth to exploit the poor, who often have no choice but to go into debt if they want to survive. Thus, like the attempt to monopolize land, God condemns using time to oppress the poor.

The first council of Nicaea banned clergy from the practice of usury. This was expanded later to include all believers, leading to the decision at Lateran III that usurers could not receive the sacraments and were denied a Christian burial. The Council of Vienne of 1311 condemned the practice as heresy. Many subsequent councils and declarations have denounced usury, such as the Synod of Elvira, the Council of Arles, the First Council of Carthage, the declarations of Leo the Great, and the Council of Aix. Murray Lee Eiland summarizes the situation well, "Every Church Father and every ecclesiastical council that addressed the topic of usury before the 16th century condemned the practice."[2]

The Church has a long history of condemning usury, but it began to fade with the Reformation. The Reformers—Calvin in particular—opened up the possibility of an acceptable form of usury. Unfortunately, that decision has led to disastrous results with the modern debt crisis. To Calvin's credit, he did attempt to limit usury to a reasonable interest rate. Still, the transition from a hardline ban on usury to a more flexible approach opened the floodgates in ways he could not have anticipated. The results have been catastrophic; in 2021, the average American was nearly $100,000 in debt.[3]

The Church today has neglected this long tradition of condemning usury. As a result, many in the Church are wholly unaware of it—or they find it archaic and irrelevant. But as the debt burden increasingly defines our age, it is time to rediscover and revitalize this ban. As capitalism becomes increasingly financialized (i.e., by moving away from production towards financial circulation and imperialism), debt has become a primary means of exploiting and oppressing the poor, both as individuals and as the richer nations exploit the poorer nations through debt. The Church today must take sides with the poor by standing against usury.

Unrighteous mammon

> 'Make to yourselves friends from the mammon of unrighteousness that when it shall fail, they may receive you into the eternal habitations' (Lk. 16:9). Thus he declares that all possessions are by nature unrighteous, when a man possess them for personal advantage as being entirely his own, and does not bring them into the common stock for those in need; but that from this unrighteousness it is possible to perform a deed that is righteous and saving, namely, to give relief to one of those who have an eternal habitation with the father.[4]
>
> — CLEMENT OF ALEXANDRIA (150-215)

This verse in Luke is sometimes used defend the possession of mammon as a necessary evil. But in this quote, from Clement's treatise *On the Salvation of the Rich*, he comes to a different conclusion. First, all possessions beyond necessity are deemed unrighteous. Second, anything used for personal gain and not brought into the "common stock" to help the needy is unrighteous. But how does Clement interpret the meaning of making friends with unrighteous mammon? It is by using mammon in a righteous and saving way, namely, by giving relief to the needy.

How does this relate to usury? Usury turns wealth into a tool for oppressing the poor for personal advantage. That is the opposite of what Clement calls a righteous use of mammon. For example, usury loans to the poor at interest, which abuses their vulnerable position. What is being described here are two different approaches to using wealth. Usury seeks personal gain, while the righteous use wealth to help the needy. Both look like they are helping the needy because they give excess wealth to the poor. But the usurer gives with conditions while the righteous give freely.

The question for us today is how we use our wealth. We cannot avoid wealth. The question is this: Do we concede to the ways of mammon and thus use wealth for personal gain, or do we live righteously and thus use wealth to help the poor?

Apologists for capitalism agree that mammon is a necessary evil. But they think the Bible's prohibition of usury is outdated and irrelevant to modernity. Why not expect a return on one's investment? What's so wrong with that? But as Clement recognized, there is no compromising with mammon. It is all or nothing. Either mammon is used righteously (and thus given to help the needy) or unrighteously used for private gain. In other words, the only *righteous* use of mammon is to get rid of it by only holding what is necessary for subsistence while giving the excess to the needy.

Usury gives excess wealth to the needy in return for profit. Christ's words in Luke about making friends with unrighteous mammon are not an excuse to justify this misuse of wealth. Rather, the point is that unrighteous mammon can be used righteously by aiding those in need.

This approach reminds me of the common childhood game called "hot potato." The object of the game is to hold onto the "potato" (usually a ball or some other round object) for as little as possible before quickly passing it along to the next person. A song plays, and the child with the potato in their hand when the tune ends loses. Similarly, that is what it means to make friends with unrighteous mammon. It is a bit like the game hot potato. The point of this phrase is not to justify hoarding wealth but to use it properly by giving it away as quickly as possible.

Jesus' words about unrighteous mammon come as a conclusion to his parable about a dishonest manager who forgives the debt of the master's debtors. It is an enigmatic parable, but the eschatological overtones are clear from verse eleven, which clarifies the point, "If then you have not been faithful with the dishonest wealth, who will entrust to you the true riches?"

Clement's reading of this passage argues that the proper use of unrighteous mammon is not for personal gain. How do we act faithfully with mammon? While money is unavoidable, the proper use of it is not to exploit the needy (which is what usury does) but to help them and forgive their debts. That is what the dishonest manager does with his master's wealth. The master of this world is unrighteous mammon, and we must subvert the use of mammon by shrewdly forgiving debts. The forgiveness of debts here means liberation. That is what Christ has done by liberating those oppressed by the burden of an immovable debt. Likewise, to make friends by means of unrighteous mammon means to forgive and liberate those in bondage by using wealth to help the needy.

Preferential option for the poor

> Our feast explains itself by its name. The Greeks call it *agapè*, i.e., affection. Whatever it costs, our outlay in the name of piety is gain, since with the good things of the feast we benefit the needy [...] But as it is with God himself, a peculiar respect is shown to the lowly.⁵
>
> — TERTULLIAN (160-240)

This quote is from Tertullian's great work, *The Apology*, and here he defends the Christian practice of "love feasts" and contrasts them with pagan practices. Love feasts were feasts for the poor, demonstrating the Christian priority of caring for the needs of the destitute. Tertullian highlights how these feasts contradicted and subverted the logic of pagan feasts, which typically showed honor and respect to the powerful and elite, not the lowly.

Pagan feasts required the commoners to give patronage to the rich and powerful. But Christian love feasts were the opposite of pagan feasts. The community did not gather to honor the rich with their feasts but to honor the poor. All were invited to the feast, but there were special warnings against the rich taking more than their fair share so that the poor would not go away hungry (1 Corinthians 11:21).

The love feasts also inverted the system of usury and directly subverted its aims. These feasts did not abuse the poor for profit but prioritized their rights by giving special attention to their needs. Usurers abuse the vulnerability of the poor by making them objects of exploitation rather than subjects to be included and cared for. Thus, both practices—usury and love feasts—are directed toward the poor, but only one is godly.

In this sense, it is possible to understand the Church's love feasts as a subversive witness designed to challenge the normalized abuse of the poor through usury and patronage. These feasts directly contradicted a culture that honored the rich and humiliated the poor. Today, we should follow the example of the first Christians by refusing to become desensitized to the way our culture humiliates the poor. And we should then do everything in our power to subvert and challenge a system that abuses the vulnerable for profit, that is, capitalism.

Their neediness is not your source of enrichment

> If you are a Christian, why do you scheme to have your idle money bear a return and make the need of your brother, for whom Christ died, the sources of your enrichment?[6]
>
> — HILARY OF POITIERS (315-367)

Hilary was a fourth-century theologian and bishop known for his robust critique of Arianism, earning him the title "Athanasius of the West." His *De Trinitate* was a major contribution to Trinitarian theology. This quote comes from his commentary on the Psalms, particularly Psalm 14, and it describes the sin of usury as an abuse of the needy.

Hilary is correct to recognize that usury makes the neediness of the poor a source of enrichment. The poor are no longer persons to be loved but objects to be exploited and used. That is the effect of mammon: Everyone is subject to the mad desire for accumulation, for more and more wealth. It is inhumane at its core. It uses people to obtain things rather than things for the sake of people. That is also the bankruptcy of the capitalist system. It prioritizes the accumulation of a dead, lifeless thing called "capital" over the living needs of the poor and hungry masses created in God's image.

Hilary's question has relevance for us today. There are many Christians who have no problem profiting off the vulnerability of others. Usury itself is not the primary temptation today. Instead, think about Christians who become landlords over hundreds of properties in impoverished neighborhoods. Is that not a kind of usury, an approach that profits from the misery of the poor? Even Adam Smith, the great capitalist economist, recognized that landlords are leeches on society.[7] They contribute nothing yet earn a return from the hard work of their tenants. Landlords "love to reap where they never sowed, and demand a rent even for its natural produce."[8]

The same logic behind usury is involved in landlordism: the one with capital invests and demands a return with interest; the hard work of the poor then becomes a source of profit for the rich. Landlords do not provide housing. They hoard and only share with the demand of a return.

To be clear: if a grandma rents out an extra property to retire, that is not necessarily immoral. But the problem is when investors buy up hundreds and thousands of properties. But the point here is to suggest that Hilary's question could be directed against those Christians who are large landlords and exploit the poor for profit. Of course, there are other modern examples, but this example will perhaps bring home the issue of usury for us today. The Christian use of excess wealth is not for personal gain but to help the needy.

There is a Jewish proverb that says: "Before every person walks an angel announcing, 'Behold, the image of God.'" The chief sin of usury is that the image of God on earth is defiled and degraded in the idolatrous greed for wealth, where riches weigh more than the image of God. The Church today must re-affirm the dignity of human beings and resist the mammon cult. Before every homeless person, there walks an angel declaring: "Behold, the image of God!" That angel is a perpetual witness against the idolatry of capitalism and its sin against the image of God.

Inhumanity

For in truth it is the last pitch of inhumanity that one man, in need of the bare necessities of life, should be compelled to borrow, and another, not satisfied with the principal, should seek to make gain and profit for himself out of the calamities of the poor […] [The lover of money] sees before him a man under stress of necessity bent to the ground in supplication. He sees him hesitating at no act, no words, of humiliation. He sees him suffering undeserved misfortune, but he is merciless. He does not reckon that he is a fellow-creature […]

[The poor] came seeking an ally, and he found a foe. He was looking for medicine, and he lighted on poison. You ought to have comforted him in his distress, but in your attempt to grow fruit on the waste you are aggravating his necessity. Just as well might a physician go in to his patients, and instead of restoring them to health, rob them of the little strength they might have left. This is the way in which you try to profit by the misery of the wretched. Just as farmers pray for rain to make their fields fatter, so you are anxious for men's need and indigence, that your money may make more. You forget that the addition which you are making to your sins is larger than the increase to your wealth which you are reckoning on getting for your usury. [...]

Learn from both Old and New Testament what is profitable for you, and so depart hence with good hope to your Lord; in Him you will receive the interest of your good deeds, —in Jesus Christ our Lord to Whom be glory and might for ever and ever, Amen.[9]

— BASIL OF CAESAREA (329-379)

As a farmer prays for rain for his crops, the usurer hopes for the misery of the poor for their profits. But a profession that *benefits* from the calamities of others is not honorable. It is sinful and inhumane to desire the shipwreck of others to turn a profit. The situation is one of pure exploitation and oppression.

Basil concludes with an interesting reversal: usurers should seek interest from good deeds. Instead of exploiting the poor, they should give freely to them without expecting anything in return (as Christ commanded in Mt. 5: 42). In this way, they will invest in good works and reap interest from Christ. As Proverbs 19:17 says, "Whoever is kind to the poor lends to the Lord, and will be repaid in full." Those who seek riches by exploiting the poor miss out on a much greater reward.

There is an anecdotal story from the Early Church about a saint put in charge of a rich man's wealth. The saint is in charge of a building project. The rich man wants an earthly palace dedicated to his honor. So what does the saint do? He goes out and distributes *all* of the rich man's money to the poor. He reports to the rich man that his palace is being built. Eventually, the rich man discovers what is really happening and is furious about what the saint has done. He demands an explanation. The saint explains that he has actually made the best investment the rich man could ever hope to make because he has exchanged what is temporal for what is eternal.[10]

The story raises some strange connotations, such as why the rich man is rewarded for what the saint did with his money, but it is nonetheless indicative of how the Early Church thought about giving to the poor. They did not seek out anything in return because the expectation was that God would reward their good works in the age to come.

The usurer exploits the poor and insults God by seeking interest from the misery of the poor. But God calls us to give freely to all those in need without any expectation because we know that God is the defender of the poor and will repay any kindness. Whatever is done to the least of these is done unto God. Thus, the exploitation of the poor is an injustice to Christ himself. Theologically, Christ's solidarity with the poor is the foundation of the ban on usury. It is not only an economic consideration but also a theological one. God has sided with the poor in their misery. To exploit the poor in their vulnerable state is to oppress Christ; to help them is to help Christ. Thus, the Christian with excess must help those who do not have enough, for Christ's sake.

Those who hoard excessive wealth and refuse to help the poor are only heaping up judgment for themselves. Mammon is like a brood of vipers, according to the thirteenth-century theologian Gregory Palmas, who writes:

> The man who lends at interest is eager to grow rich with sins rather than money, destroying both the borrower's livelihood and his own soul. For interest payments are like a brood of vipers nesting in the bosom of those who love money, foreshadowing the fact that such men will not escape from the unsleeping worms threatened for the age to come. If one of them were to say, however, "As you do not allow me to receive interest, I shall keep my surplus money by me, and shall not offer it to those who need to borrow," he should be aware that he is holding the mothers of those vipers in his breast, who will also be for him the mothers of those unsleeping worms.[11]

Those who grasp too tightly to mammon will be harmed, but those who give freely to the needy will be saved. Hoarding riches is like hugging a venomous snake.

Capitalism leads to alienation and spiritual corruption because of the idolatry of mammon, which is the heart of the capitalist system. Mammon, as the chief end of human life, leads to the alienation of life and the dehumanization of human beings created in God's image. Under capitalism, there is no sacrifice too great for the sake of mammon, not even the human being. Take, for example, the existence of child labor. While the Western world has outlawed child labor—thanks mostly to the courageous efforts of socialists and trade unionists who struggled against it—the global south still practices it. Many consumer products made for the pleasure of the first world are produced by impoverished children in the south. That is because capitalism holds nothing sacred, not even the life of a child, except for profit.

Capitalism cannot exist without the misery of the poor. It is a system that exploits the vulnerable for profit. Moreover, the chief aim of capitalism is to accumulate more and more capital at all costs. It is a system rooted in usury and the Church's critique of usury today should be directed against capitalism.

Usury is murder

 Not new nor negligible is this evil, which is restrained by the Precept of the Old and Divine Law. The people who had despoiled Egypt, who had crossed the sea on foot, is warned to beware shipwrecks from the money of usury. And although it has prescribed once or with many times repeated admonition concerning other sins, most frequently has it referred to usury. You have in Exodus: "But if thou lend money to a ward, to an orphan, to a poor man among you, thou shalt not strangle him nor oppress him with usury" [Ex. 22:25]. It shows what strangling is, that is, oppressing with usury, for, what is even worse, the noose of the creditor strangles the soul. With this word it has expressed the violence of the robber and the suffering of a horrible death. "If thou take of thy neighbor a garment in pledge, thou shalt give it him again before sunset. For that same is the only thing wherewith he is covered, this is the clothing of his dishonor, in what shall he sleep? But if likewise he cry to me I will hear him" [Ex. 22:26]. Have you heard usurers, what the Law says, concerning which our Lord said: "I am come not to destroy the law but to fulfill it?" [Mt. 5:17]. What the Lord did not destroy, do you destroy? "To seek usury," he said, "is to strangle."

This has also been said later by certain of their wise men outside the fold. "What is it to take interest? It is to kill a man," he says. But surely Cato was not before Moses who received the law. He was much later.[12]

— AMBROSE OF MILAN (340-397)

Cato the Elder (234-149 BC) was a Roman soldier, senator, and historian. Ambrose comments on a famous saying by Cato against usury but shows that Moses was earlier in proclaiming God's disdain for usury. Cato's famous saying is this: "What do you think of Usury?—What do you think of murder?" He answers the question with a question to suggest that usury is the same as murder. Thus, Ambrose quotes Cato as saying that taking interest is to kill a man.

Ambrose refers to Exodus 22:25-26 to show that this claim is originally from Moses, not Cato. Cato simply repeats later what Moses already saw, that usury is strangulation. He also stresses that this command against usury in the Hebraic law is with us still today because of Christ's words in Matthew 5, that he did not come to destroy the law.

It is easy today to overlook the brutality of usury (of charging interest) because it is so common, but debt causes suffering for the poor and oppressed. Indeed, debt is a *means* of oppression by keeping the poor bound to their misery. Ambrose also says that the noose is not only material but spiritual; usury threatens the soul. That is because usury forces the borrower to be enslaved by their loan. And because those who must take out such loans often do so because they are struggling to survive, the result is that usury can shipwreck a person's life. It can lead to death, directly or indirectly, because of the added strain on an individual's ability to feed themselves or their family. So it is not far-fetched to compare usury to strangulation and murder, as the psychological effect of living under immense debt is similar to these physiological tortures. It kills both the soul and possibly the body.

Elsewhere, Ambrose recognizes the trap of usury and compares it to a doctor who gives poison instead of medicine to their patient:

> Such, O rich men, are your kindnesses! You give less and you exact more. Such is your humanity that you despoil even while you are helping. even the poor man is fruitful to you unto gain. The usurer is needy: he has what he may render if you compel him, he does not have what he may spend. You are merciful men, certainly, who enslave to yourselves him whom you free from another! He pays usury who lacks food. Is there anything more terrible? He asks for medicine, you offer him poison; he begs for bread, you offer him a sword; he begs for liberty, you impose slavery; he prays for freedom, you tighten the knot of the hideous snare.[13]

The poor face an impossible debt trap; they often have no other choice but to take out a loan, even though they know that the loan will cause them more harm in the future. But they need the loan to survive. That is why poverty is like quicksand. The more one struggles, the more one is taken down to the depths of suffering.

The usurer manufactures this situation to oppress the poor and vulnerable, callously extracting interest from the needy. The vulnerable search for relief but find only poison; they beg for bread and peace and receive only disaster and violence. A central problem with usury is that it turns the poor into a means of profit when they are at their most vulnerable state; it preys on the weak and needy and worsens their situation. It is a trap that keeps the poor bound to their situation. It presents the facade of help while being, in truth, an inescapable trap.

It is important to remember here that usury is simply charging interest for a loan. It seems impractical for us today, but this shows how radically distant we are from the teachings of the Early Church on mammon. The capitalist world cannot exist without interest. The financial system itself runs on usury. It would collapse without the logic of usury. And while that is not something to be hoped for, it is still important to pay attention to what Ambrose is saying in these quotes. Usury leads to death because the rich exploit the poor. They exploit the poor because they have excess riches to profit from their misery. In these simple terms, it is clear that usury today is synonymous with the capitalist system, a system that exploits the poor for the benefit of the rich. The biblical case against usury is the foundation of Christian anti-capitalism.

Profit from distress

> For nothing is baser, nothing is more cruel than the interest that comes from lending. For such a lender trades on other person's calamities, draws profit from the distress of others, and demands wages for kindness, as though he were afraid to seem merciful. Under the mask of kindness he digs deeper their pit of poverty; where he stretches out his hand to help, he then pushes them down, and where he receives them, as it were, in safe harbor, and he then involves them in shipwreck as on a rock, or shoal, or reef.[14]
>
> — JOHN CHRYSOSTOM (349-407)

Usury abuses the vulnerable while wearing a mask of kindness. Today, that mask is sometimes called investor or job-creator. It is said that the capitalist class kindly creates jobs for the poor. But they feign kindness on the surface while acting as the cause of their misery. Underneath this kindness is a brutal exploitation of the poor by the rich. A hand is stretched out to help, but it is the hand of an exploiter.

Another form of this "kindness" is the loan given out to college students, which for most, becomes a decade-long burden. Or we might point to the inhumanity of the American healthcare system and the burden of medical debt. Both loans are given at interest and under duress, first by the student who only hopes for better opportunities in their future or by the patient who has no other choice but to seek medical care or be harmed and possibly die from their ailments. Thus, the heart of capitalism is the inhumane act of usury, profiting off the misery of the vulnerable.

I will follow this quote from Chrysostom and use it to conclude this chapter. Here I want to consider two modern examples of how the logic of usury is at work in capitalism: first, capitalism's obsession with limitless growth and climate change, and second, the extension of capitalist exploitation globally against the poorer nations, which is called imperialism, the highest stage of capitalism.

Climate change

Capitalism is a system bound to the expectation of limitless growth. Thus, usury and capitalism are not only irreconcilable with Christian ethics, but they are also incompatible with the earth itself. Investors expect the stock market to go up every year, but that hope is at odds with the finitude of the planet. Expecting a perpetual return on investment while living on a finite planet is irrational, and the catastrophic threat of climate change directly results from this system. There is no such thing as "no growth" capitalism; profit comes first in every decision.

Just one hundred companies are responsible for 71% of global emissions.[15] Furthermore, the largest single polluter on the planet is the U.S. Military.[16] The solution to climate change will not be found in the same system that caused it. And in practice, capitalism was never designed to solve this problem. Any analysis of climate change that does not confront capitalism as the primary cause of the problem is naive.

Instead of investing in renewable energy, developing public transportation infrastructure to wean us off car dependency, or producing sustainable products for long-term use, capitalism defaults to the most profitable sector. Thus, since there is too much money to be made in oil and too little in renewable energy, we keep polluting our air and ruining our oceans. Because oil is profitable, lobbyists push back against any move to develop public transportation across America because that would mean fewer profits for the car and oil companies. Sustainable products sell only once; cheap, plastic, single-use products require repeat purchases and thus have a built-in guarantee of future profits. Accordingly, our oceans are full of plastic, and our landfills overflow with consumer goods. These three examples out of hundreds demonstrate how capitalism prioritizes profits over anything else.

But limitless growth is unsustainable, and the house of cards cannot last forever. Only by urgently organizing and resisting mammon in all its forms can we hope to stop the effects of climate change before it is too late. People and the planet over profits—that must be our message today.

John Chrysostom recognized that usurers profit from the distress of the vulnerable. That is also an apt description of how capitalism functions by exploiting the poor and weak for profit. Capital accumulation is a zero-sum game. For the rich to grow their wealth, the misery of the poor must increase. We will return to this point in chapter nine, but it is worth stating here that the riches of the wealthy are soaked in the blood of the poor and weak. The poor do not benefit from the rich getting richer, no matter how often this lie has been repeated by "trickle-down" economics.[17] The scenario is not that "A rising tide lifts all boats" because the poor have no boats; rather, the rich get a better view, and the poor drown.

Imperialism

Another example to illustrate the link between capitalism and usury is the mechanism of global imperialism. Usury abuses the misery of the vulnerable for profit. That is true for personal loans between individuals but also true globally, as rich countries lend to poorer nations. Imperialism—the highest stage of global capitalism—causes the third world, via the IMF and World Bank, to become deeply indebted to the richer nations. As a result, the former colonizers of the poorer countries have returned, no longer pursuing conquest and exploitation by military strength but establishing dominance through debt.

These loans often include clauses requiring poorer nations to give richer countries enormous control over their economies, which leads to the exploitation of their people's cheap labor and their farmer's cash crops. So rather than using farmlands to feed their people, these countries must export most of their crops for foreign companies to profit. And these loans often actively hinder any attempt to improve the working conditions of the poor.[18]

That is imperialism: the global monopoly of capital, wherein rich nations use their capital to oppress and exploit poorer nations—often by force.

The United States, particularly the CIA, has not shied away from using military force to suppress the vulnerable and to keep poorer countries in line. They went so far as installing brutal dictatorships (Batista in Cuba, Pinochet in Chile, etc.), supporting the execution of protesting laborers (United Fruit in Guatemala), and funding death squads (Operation Condor) to assert the iron will of global capitalism and protect the interests of the capitalist class.[19]

So we can see in this dynamic how usury profits off the misery of the vulnerable, both individually and globally. Imperialism is the highest stage of capitalism, wherein the rich oppress the poor internationally through military and debt-related economic pressure.

Usury is thus the heart of modern capitalism. It is a tool by which the rich repress the poor individually and globally. The debt imposed upon the poorer nations by rich nations is one side of this, with direct intervention through military operations is the other side. The history of the Cold War offers plentiful examples of these two forms of imperialism.

A total ban on usury would mean the end of capitalism. Thus, we cannot afford to be naive about the political implications of the Bible's ban on usury. The Church's critique of usury is thus not only relevant today but direly necessary. It is not a stretch to direct the rebuke of usury towards a critique of capitalism because it is impossible to imagine capitalism without usury. Usury loans are like a baited hook; the goal is not to help the needy but to further enslave them with their neediness. Capitalism relies on this bait and switch. It presents itself as good for humanity, but under the mask is a brutal system of exploitation that has led to the existential threat of climate change and the present situation of endless war.

Martin Luther King, Jr., said it best, "Capitalism has outlived its usefulness. It has brought about a system that takes necessities from the masses to give luxuries to the classes."[20] The brutal realities of climate change and global imperialism make clear that we must begin working toward a world beyond capitalism because the alternative may be extinction.

7

THE TYRANNY OF MAMMON

We become like what we worship. That is why idolatry—worshipping false gods—destroys the human soul. Yet devotion to God elevates persons created in God's image and reaffirms them as beloved children. The love of God makes us more fully what we were created to be, but the love of mammon makes us more and more like mammon, an inhuman object marked by death. If we worship mammon, we become inhumane, lifeless, greedy, and tight-fisted. Yet when we worship God, we become loving, generous, and more fully human. Thus, idolatry is not merely a matter of God's jealousy over creation but a struggle for our nature as beloved children of God.

Idols demand complete devotion. When a system is designed around mammon, it is total; it permeates every aspect of our lives. Mammon is like a viral disease that violently infects the host until it finally kills it. Accordingly, John Chrysostom often talked about the "tyranny of mammon." He understood that mammon is a rival god—the love of which cannot coexist within the heart of a Christian who calls Jesus Lord. It is like a weed that chokes out the harvest. The quotes in this chapter reflect on this dimension of mammon as a tyrannical master.

What is noteworthy about this concept is how it reflects upon the *systemic* nature of mammon. Mammon is not simply a personal issue. And capitalism is the economic form of the idolatry of mammon. The accumulation of mammon becomes the chief end of human life. In many regards, capitalism *is* the tyranny of mammon in its most perfect form.

Everything in the capitalist system comes second to accumulation; every economist's knee must bow, and stockbroker's tongue confess that mammon is lord. This pathological greed for more and more is at the core of the capitalist system. Accordingly, it is a system deeply rooted in idolatry. Just as there can be no compromise with mammon and God, there must be no Christian compromise with the system of capitalism: it is idolatry in economic form.

A Christian critique of capitalism requires a revitalized understanding of idolatry and its effects on the human soul. What good is it to gain the whole world but lose one's soul? What is it worth if to be exceedingly wealthy, the richest on earth, when the planet becomes unlivable, and millions of poor and needy people die from hunger and disease? What good is sinful luxury if it infects the soul with the illness of discontentment? Is it better to live with a healthy soul that loves God and is made more human by that love or to pursue mammon endlessly while becoming more inhumane by greed? The love of mammon scars the soul and disfigures humanity. Only the declaration that "Jesus is Lord!" and mammon is not can save us.

Insatiable gluttony

> For mammon is, according to the Jewish language, which the Samaritans do also use, a *covetous* man, and one who wishes to have more than he ought to have. But according to the Hebrew, it is by the addition of a syllable (*adjunctive*) called Mamuel,[1] and signifies *gulosum* [gluttony], that is, one whose gullet is insatiable. Therefore, according to both these things which are indicated, we cannot serve God and mammon.[2]
>
> — IRENAEUS OF LYONS (130-202)

This quote is from Irenaeus' great work, *Against Heresies*. It is enlightening to reflect on why Irenaeus considered it important to define and discuss mammon in his famous treatise against heresy. Today, our definitions of orthodoxy and heterodoxy focus on abstract doctrinal issues. But what if serving mammon is also heresy?

The first century Father Ignatius of Antioch (35-108) seemingly agreed with Irenaeus about connecting heresy to mammon. According to González, "Ignatius of Antioch characterizes heretics as those who 'have no regard for love; no care for the widow, or the orphan, or the oppressed; of the bond, or of the free; of the hungry, or of the thirsty.'"[3]

If we remember that mammon is a rival god and capitalism is the religion of modernity, then this makes a lot of sense. Any and every lord we claim to be above or beside Jesus Christ is heretical. All those who prove they serve mammon rather than Christ by their actions are practicing heretics. It is helpful to expand our definition of heresy in this way. Orthodoxy (right belief) has often been disconnected from orthopraxy (right action), but that does not seem to be an original division, nor is it helpful today. Irenaeus' definition of mammon explains why this distinction is problematic. If we focus solely on correct thinking but ignore action, it becomes possible to *believe* Jesus is Lord while being consumed with greed for mammon.

In Matthew 7:21, Jesus makes a similar point: "Not everyone who says to me, 'Lord, Lord,' will enter the kingdom of heaven, but only the one who does the will of my Father in heaven." Our definition of orthodoxy risks this very mistake, but an expanded definition that *includes* orthopraxis (right action) more faithfully corresponds with how the Early Church understood the term.

We cannot serve God and mammon because mammon is like a black hole that consumes and corrupts everything in its orbit. Mammon is an insatiable, gluttonous master. Both God and mammon demand total devotion. We cannot serve mammon innocently, just as we cannot pass by a black hole without being trapped in its gravity. We will be consumed. There is no innocent devotion to mammon; it is a rival god, and capitalism is a rival religion.

Let us not be enslaved

> And I would ask you, if it does not appear to you monstrous, that you men who are God's handiwork, who have received your souls from Him, and belong wholly to God, should be subject to another master, and, what is more, serve the tyrant instead of the rightful King—the evil one instead of the good [...] Who, that may become a son of God, prefers to be in bondage? [...]
>
> Let us not then be enslaved or become swinish; but, as true children of the light, let us raise our eyes and look on the light, lest the Lord discover us to be spurious, as the sun does the eagles. Let us therefore repent, and pass from ignorance to knowledge, from foolishness to wisdom, from licentiousness to self-restraint, from unrighteousness to righteousness, from godlessness to God. [...]
>
> What the bastard, who is a son of perdition, foredoomed to be the slave of mammon, has to buy for money, He assigns

to thee as thine own, even to His own son who loves the Father; for whose sake He still works, and to whom alone He promises, saying, "The land shall not be sold in perpetuity," for it is not destined to corruption. "For the whole land is mine;" and it is thine too, if thou receive God. Wherefore the Scripture, as might have been expected, proclaims good news to those who have believed.[4]

— CLEMENT OF ALEXANDRIA (150-215)

This quote is from Clement's *Exhortation to the Heathens* (or *Protrepticus*). It written to correct the mythological thinking of the Greek and pagan religions. To be more specific, the quote is from chapter ten, in which Clement stresses the necessity of abandoning former traditions when becoming a Christian.

Clement's argument echoes Galatians: "For freedom Christ has set us free. Stand firm, therefore, and do not submit again to a yoke of slavery" (Gal. 5:1). Freedom is ours in Christ, but it must be defended vigilantly. Those former things, which lead to bondage, must be left behind for the sake of this freedom. Clement writes that the former Greek and pagan traditions must be resisted for freedom's sake.

The final paragraph requires some context to understand. Clement contrasts the inheritance of Christ with that of worldly wealth, citing Isaiah 54:17 about the inheritance promised to the children of God. Clement writes, "It is that treasure of salvation to which we must hasten, by becoming lovers of the Word. Thence praise-worthy works descend to us, and fly with us on the wing of truth."[5] The inheritance of Christ is for those who serve the Lord. Clement then quotes Isaiah 55:1, "Ho, everyone who thirsts, come to the waters; and you that have no money, come, buy and eat!" This leads to his open rebuke of those who try to buy the natural grace of land, calling them slaves to mammon.

Clement's approach is interesting. The land is often considered a gift of grace in the Bible, especially in the Hebrew Scriptures. The land was the source of sustenance and thus reflected God's will that all would have the necessities on this earth. Therefore, it is an image that often refers to natural grace. Those who take this natural, freely-given grace and turn it into a commodity, who privatize the land and sell it back to God's creatures for profit, rob from the Lord. They are unfree. But the grace of God is not for sale. What God has given in common belongs to all; only by theft and violence does it become the exclusive property of the few.

Just as the apostles harshly rebuked the man who tried to buy the gift of the Holy Spirit—Acts 8:20: "May your silver perish with you, because you thought you could obtain God's gift with money!"—we should condemn those who today try to monopolize the natural grace of the earth by greedily hoarding the common resources that belong to all. Clement calls them bastard children who try to steal what has been freely given to the children of God. What the rich have turned into a commodity, God has ordained as a gift of grace. It is absurd for the liberated children of God to follow the rich by becoming slaves to mammon. This clearly distinguishes the children of God (who are free) from the bastard children who serve mammon (who are enslaved). The former live by grace and hold the earth in common, while the latter greedily commodify the earth for private gain.

Those who are slaves to mammon buy and sell what belongs to God, particularly the land. Those liberated—*from mammon*—are not like the world. They receive an inheritance freely from the Lord and do not strive to buy grace with money. At the very least, it is instructive here to see the contrast between the liberty of Christ and the slavery of mammon. Those made free in Christ have an eternal inheritance, while those enslaved by mammon demonstrate their slavery by thinking they can purchase what God has given freely for the good of all: the land. Privation of the land is thus a sign of mammon's lordship, meaning it is incompatible with the Lordship of Christ. Mammon as lord brings tyranny; Christ as Lord brings freedom.

Possessed by possessions

> A possession ought to belong to the possessor, not the possessor to the possession. Whosoever, therefore, does not use his patrimony [inherited property] as a possession, who does not know how to give and distribute to the poor, he is the servant of his wealth, not its master; because like a servant he watches over the wealth of another and not like a master does he use it of his own. Hence, in a disposition of this kind we say that the man belongs to his riches, not the riches to the man.[6]
>
> — AMBROSE OF MILAN (340-397)

It has been said that money is a good servant but a terrible master. That is effectively the same point Ambrose is making here. Greed dehumanizes us when money is put in charge of our lives. What we should possess then possesses us. Like Saturn, mammon devours its children. To serve mammon is to be enslaved by it. In the third century, Cyprian of Carthage writes, "You are the captive and slave of your money; you are bound with the chains and bonds of covetousness; and you whom Christ had once loosed, are once more in chains."[7]

We could push this point further and apply it to economic systems. When money is seen as a tool to benefit all, to ensure the needs of all are met, then it is good; but under capitalism, money is an end unto itself, not a tool. It is an idol we serve rather than a tool we use for the sake of helping our neighbor. That is what makes this economic system not only inhumane but pathological. Capitalism serves an irrational master who is never satisfied. The love of money is like a snake consuming its tail. It only leads to devastation and loss.

Capital is the god of capitalism, a tyrannical master that devours its servants. No one is free from the tyranny of this system, which has only one command: accumulate!

Ambrose contrasts "possession" with being possessed. Those who know how to possess money and property use it for the good of the needy. It has a utility, a goal. But those who are possessed by money treat possessions as an end for themselves. Any economic system that forces everything into the role of accumulating is itself a system more possessed by money than in control of it.

Anti-capitalism is not about getting rid of all possessions. The goal is not shared poverty. Rather, the goal is to *properly use* the resources of this earth and the wealth of society in a way that serves human beings instead of a lifeless god called money. An economic system that prioritizes real human need over private gain is the goal. But under capitalism, human beings are but a means of accumulation. Houses sit empty while men and women created in the image of God are discarded as unwanted side-effects of the cult of mammon; food is wasted when it cannot be sold, yet millions of humans go hungry every day. That is the pathological effect of slavery to mammon. That is the fruit of capitalism.

O bitter slavery, and devlish tyranny!

 If then we serve God, we shall not submit to the tyranny of mammon. And truly a bitterer thing than any tyranny is the desire of riches; for it brings no pleasure, but cares, and envyings, and plottings, and hatred, and false accusations, and ten thousand impediments to virtue, indolence, wantonness, greediness, drunkenness, which make even freemen slaves, nay, worse than slaves bought with money, slaves not to men, but even to the most grievous of the passions, and maladies of the soul. [...] O bitter slavery, and devlish tyranny! For this is the most grievous thing of all, that when entangled in such evils we are pleased and hug our chain, and dwelling in a prison house full of darkness, refuse to come forth to the light, but rivet evil upon ourselves, and rejoice in our malady.[8]

— JOHN CHRYSOSTOM (349-407)

The chief end of human life is to participate in God's triune love and joy, to be the beloved children we were created to be, and to extend that love to the world by loving our neighbor as ourselves. Instead, mammon turns human beings into slaves subject to an inhumane idol rather than children liberated into the joy of God. The fullness of life is exchanged for a dead, cold lump of gold. That is, indeed, bitter slavery and devilish tyranny. But thanks be to God, who has liberated us from bondage and into the life that is real. If only we would serve Christ as our Lord and reject mammon.

Chrysostom poetically describes a brutal situation. We are enslaved by mammon, yet we are "pleased and hug our chain." We are addicted to our captivity and prefer slavery to freedom. In the Western world, it is difficult to imagine the end of capitalism because we love our chains. They are comfortable chains padded with an abundance of cheap commodities. But they are chains nonetheless.

That is what makes mammon the most brutal of tyrants. It is subtle and devious. It does not announce itself with fanfare as an idol and a ruler, but it slowly grips our lives and consumes us until we are enslaved by it. That is the bitter tyranny of mammon. But as Marx and Engels famously declared, we "have nothing to lose but [our] chains."[9]

Job did not serve mammon

Tell me not of them that are rich, but of them that serve riches. Since Job also was rich, but he served not mammon, but possessed it and ruled over it, and was a master, not a slave. Therefore he so possessed all those things, as if he had been the steward of another man's goods; not only not extorting from others, but even giving up his own to them that were in need. [...] But they that are rich are not now such as he was, but are rather in a worse condition than any slave, paying as it were tribute to some grievous tyrant. Because their mind is as a kind of citadel occupied by the love of money, which from thence daily sends out unto them its commands full of all iniquity, and there is none to disobey. Be not therefore thus over subtle. Nay, for God hath once for all declared and pronounced it a thing impossible for the one service and the other to agree. Say not thou, then, "it is possible."[10]

— JOHN CHRYSOSTOM (349-407)

In chapter one, we analyzed how Origen contrasted Job with the rich man who mistreated Lazarus. The rich man is named by what he loves, so Job is called righteous because of his love of God, which is proven by his generosity toward the needy.

In this quote, Chrysostom asks how Job could be rich and not serve mammon. The assumption is that the rich became rich through their service to mammon. How is Job the exception? He answers that it is because Job used his wealth to help all those in need—he held it in common. Job knew it was not his wealth but the Lord's and stewarded it accordingly. Job's doors were always open to the poor. He was not enslaved by mammon but used it in a righteous way.

With this, Chrysostom vividly portrays the situation of those under the tyranny of mammon: their mind is consumed by the love of money. So he says do not be subtle in condemning the rich because it is impossible to serve both God and mammon.

Chrysostom highlights how the love of money consumes our minds and crowds out the love of God. But those set free from sin are now the "slaves of God" (Rom. 6:22). Paul describes himself as being "constrained" and "urged on" by the love of God (2 Cor. 5:14). How can we say we love God, who we do not see when we do not love the neighbor we see? Job demonstrated his love and thus proved the way out of the tyranny of mammon.

The word "repent" in Greek is *metanoia,* which means to "change one's mind." One of the worst effects of service to mammon is what it does to our minds, occupying our thoughts with greed, dissatisfaction, and the desire to mindlessly consume more and more stuff. Freedom in Christ from the tyranny of mammon means putting on "the mind of Christ" (Phil. 2:5).

If only I could speak about it every night

And perhaps one of you will say, "Every day thy discourse is about covetousness." [If only] I could speak about it every night too; would that I could do so, following you about in the market-place, and at your table; would that both wives, and friends, and children, and domestics, and tillers of the soil, and neighbors, and the very pavement and walls, could ever shout forth this word, that so we might perchance have relaxed a little. For this malady hath seized upon all the world, and occupies the souls of all, and great is the tyranny of mammon. We have been ransomed by Christ, and are the slaves of gold. We proclaim the sovereignty of the one, and obey the other.[11]

— JOHN CHRYSOSTOM (349-407)

Whenever I criticize capitalism in the name of Christ, inevitably, someone objects, "Stop making the gospel political. It is not about politics. The gospel is about saving souls." But this is an unbiblical understanding of the gospel. The Old and New Testaments speak of God's profound concern for the poor and oppressed. That concern is inevitably political. It is impossible to proclaim "liberty to the captives" or "good news to the poor" without saying something politically subversive about an oppressive, exploitative society.

The objection that nothing is political about the gospel is rooted in a false division between the spiritual and the material. But the Christian critique of mammon is a perfect example of where a theological rebuke of idolatry coincides with a political defense of the poor. God is not only concerned about souls. God cares about human beings, which includes the well-being of their bodies. Where there is hunger, malnutrition, disease, and corruption, God calls us to proclaim a word of hope and liberty. That requires a political word of subversion against the rich and oppressive. I would go so far as to argue that an apolitical gospel is a betrayal of Christ's message.

I love Chrysostom's response to his critics. His sermons were full of rebukes against the rich and greedy. If only the Church had to courage to stand up again and say, "I wish I could speak about it even more!" Indeed, the danger is not speaking *too much* against mammon but *too little*.

The lazy rich

'Anyone who would not work should not eat' (2 Thessalonians 3:10). But the laws of Saint Paul are not merely for the poor. They are for the rich as well [...] We accuse the poor of laziness. This laziness is often excusable. We ourselves are often guilty of worse idleness. But you say, 'I have my paternal inheritance!' Tell me, just because he is poor and was born of

> a poor family possessing no great wealth, is he thereby worthy to die?[12]
>
> — JOHN CHRYSOSTOM (349-407)

The poor are an easy punching bag for those looking for someone to blame. We often read Paul's words and assume that he criticizes the poor (which says a lot about our faulty presumptions). But Chrysostom turns that critique on its head. He even suggests that the idleness of the poor is often excusable. But the rich are also idle. They do not work but often live idly off their inheritance. Paul most likely had the rich in mind with this commandment.

Still today, it is not the poor who are lazy but the rich. They live in luxury off a return on investments and the labor of others. The rich in society are not those who work the hardest but those who have the most capital to invest, while the working class does the work, and the rich earn a hefty return.

It is interesting to note that modern socialists frequently evoked Paul's phrase as a guiding principle for socialism. One socialist government even codified the phrase as law in their constitution: "He who does not work, neither shall he eat."[13] This phrase was elsewhere described as "the prime, basic and root principle of socialism."[14] The criticism that socialism is for the lazy has never been true. On the contrary, it could be argued that capitalism promotes laziness among the capitalist class, who do not work for their luxury but leverage their capital to profit off the labor of others. No capitalist country has taken this version of Paul's phrase as law, but socialist governments frequently have. Those who do not work shall not eat—that is a socialist principle.

Chrysostom is blunt in stating that the rich did nothing to earn their wealth but be born rich or steal from the needy; the rich condemn the poor to death by hoarding their wealth. Mammon corrupts the minds of the rich, causing them to imagine that they *deserve* their luxuries while the poor deserve death. But the rich seldom work for their riches without exploitation. So, Chrysostom takes Paul's word of rebuke against the idle and directs it toward the rich. Socialists in modern times have done the same. It is always interesting to note an agreement between the Church Fathers and socialists.

Systemic fraud

> I do not ask you mercifully to render from what you have plundered, but to abstain from fraud [...] For, unless you desist from your robbery, you are not actually giving alms. Even though you should give ever so much money to the

needy, if you do not desist from fraud and robbery you shall be numbered by God among the murderers.[15]

— JOHN CHRYSOSTOM (349-407)

Notice what Chrysostom identifies as the cause of poverty. It is not the result of individual laziness by the poor, nor is it a result of financial mismanagement. Instead, poverty is a systemic issue. It is the result of *robbery* and *fraud*. Chrysostom goes so far as to call the rich *murderers* for their abuse of the poor. The poor are not poor by accident but are *made* poor by the exploitation and oppression of the rich and powerful.

Modern research agrees with this point. Poverty is the result of systemic structures, not personal choices.[16] These systemic structures include culture, history, law, media, and economic factors such as debt and ownership. All of these causes of poverty can be traced, at least in part, to the capitalist system, which is defined by private property and the exploitation of labor by capital. Thus, those who own property and capital control society and use their power to extort greater wealth from those who do not own property or capital. This leads to systemic injustice, which explains why the rich get richer while the poor get poorer. It is naive to see the increase of wealth among the rich and the immiseration of the poor as accidental facts; these are interrelated.

Chrysostom also brings up an important point about charity. He criticizes the rich for giving back to the needy a portion of what they have stolen. In a capitalist system, charity is a band-aid solution. The same class that hands out charity is responsible for poverty in the first place because they exploit the poor. For example, the same billionaire who funds a charity to help feed hungry children in an impoverished country also builds a factory in that same town to exploit their poverty for profit. Or, the billionaire who funds medical care worldwide lobbies against public ownership of life-saving medicine, thus causing a scarcity of medicine leading to unnecessary deaths. These are just two examples that demonstrate the facade of capitalist charity.

This illustrates the dire need for a systemic change in economics rather than just a temporary alleviation of the effects of capitalism. Cheap philanthropy—often a ploy for good P.R.—is not enough. Only justice, which entails systemic restructuring of society around common need rather than private greed, will do. That is Chrysostom's solution: not that the rich give charity, but that they end their fraud and robbery of the poor.

Today that points to the necessity of anti-capitalism. Band-aid solutions to systemic issues will never be enough. Only a total restructuring of society will lead to lasting change. Historically, this has been demonstrated by the remarkable efforts of socialists to lift millions out of poverty. Without the efforts of socialist policies and governments, the world would be poorer today. The most remarkable example of this is the People's Republic of China, which lifted over 800 million people out of absolute poverty in the twentieth century, making up 75% of global poverty reduction. Furthermore, in 2019, absolute poverty was eradicated in China. These are staggering accomplishments that should impress every Christian who takes the command to feed the hungry and clothe the naked seriously (Mt. 25).[17]

All privation is a diminution

'The love of money is the root of all evil' (1 Timothy 6:10)—if [by 'love of money'] we mean general avarice, by which each desires something beyond what is appropriate, for its own sake, and a certain love of one's own property—which the Latin language has wisely called 'private,' for it connotes more a loss than an increase. For all privation is a diminution.[18]

— AUGUSTINE OF HIPPO (354-430)

A core driver of capitalism is privatization. The origin of capitalism is in the privatization of common lands, and still today, it is the driving mechanism behind monopolization and global imperialism. Augustine's critique of privation can serve as a warning against capitalism itself. If privation is diminution, then a system that tends towards privatization (as opposed to communalization) is headed in the wrong direction. And since this tendency has been essential to capitalism from its inception, we might suggest an anti-capitalist application of these words from Augustine.

Furthermore, it is notable that Augustine criticizes the desire for anything beyond "what is appropriate," such as the love of money and property for private enjoyment. He then stresses that the love of money, which drives privatization, indicates a *loss*, not a gain. The bounty of God's earth is not liberated by privatization but rather oppressed and diminished. Capitalism—the economics of privatization—does not mean freedom. Instead, privation leads to oppression. Only the slavery of Christ, sharing in common of God's earth, and solidarity with one's neighbor will lead to liberation from the tyranny of mammon.

This will bear witness

 How then can gold and silver rust? By being hoarded in excessive abundance; and this very fact will bear witness against them before the divine judgement seat, and proves their lack of mercy. For, having hoarded their abundance of treasure, they ignored utterly those who suffered in want, though with great ease they might have done good to them.[19]

— CYRIL OF ALEXANDRIA (376-444)

Cyril was a fifth-century theologian and Patriarch of Alexandria known for his role in the Christology controversies. This quote is from a homily given on the gospel of Luke. Here, Cyril reflects on the vanity of hoarding what can rust and wither while ignoring the suffering of those who lack.

The desire to be rich often expresses the desire to be free from the burdens of money and to live as we please without worrying about having enough to get by. But that desire for security can only be satisfied by trusting in God. Because, in reality, service to mammon means slavery, not freedom. The rich are not free. If anything, they are *less* free. Their hearts are bound to their riches. The person with much has much to lose and is bound to their gold like a chain. Mammon presents itself as a lustrous beauty, but, like the Siren's Song, it is a trap leading to shipwreck. Hoarded wealth causes us to overlook what is truly valuable—our fellow human beings. Thus, they miss out on the true treasure of good works of justice for the least of these.

The wealthy's rusted riches proclaim a word of rebuke against them. Abundance is a blessing from God, but it becomes a curse when hoarded for private consumption rather than shared freely with those in need. The voice of the poor cries out for justice. The tyranny of mammon has so corrupted their soul that they failed to do right by the poor and needy; thus, they have not served Christ. They are not free but remain under the slavery of sin.

Concluding thoughts on the necessity of Anti-Capitalism

The tyranny of mammon is an apt metaphor for capitalism. For Chrysostom and others, mammon is not simply an issue of the heart. It is a *system*. Mammon is a rival deity and lord demanding complete allegiance or resistance. There is no grey area. Thus, Jesus' either/or is a declaration of war with mammon in the name of God. That places the Church irrevocably at odds with mammon and all its systems. Today, a perfect expression of mammon's unjust lordship over humanity is the system of capitalism, which prioritizes, above all else, capital accumulation. Every institution is aimed toward that end, and thus, the love of mammon has become not only systemic to a capitalist society but indistinguishable from it.

Capitalism is an economic system defined by private ownership over the means of production. The result is that all economic decisions and most of the social and political decisions are predicated upon the drive for more and more capital. The mantra of capitalism is, "Accumulate, accumulate!"[20] That is the chief end of all things in the capitalist system. The result is that the love of mammon is institutionalized into the social framework of capitalism. It is impossible to be against the tyranny of mammon and support capitalism; the two are one.

But it is worth reflecting on how the Church has avoided this conclusion so far. Four objections to this might explain the discrepancy.

The first objection is the assumption that mammon is *neutral*. This approach fails to take Jesus' personification of wealth seriously as a rival deity that must be hated for the love of God. Mammon is explicitly *not* neutral, according to the Bible; it is an active threat to the Lordship of Christ. There can be no compromise with a tyrannical enemy. There is only resistance or compliance.

The second objection is the assumption that mammon is a matter of the heart, which goes together with the first assumption. If mammon is simply an object—not the personification of a rival deity—then the issue of mammon is a question of where we place our trust. But this ignores Christ's either/or approach to mammon. Mammon is not a heart problem *alone*; it is also a systemic one involving the social, political, and economic dimensions.

The third objection is the assumption that mammon is a practical necessity and that another world—a world without the tyranny of mammon—is impossible. The idea is because we live in a fallen world, we should accept it without resistance. But that goes against the resurrection of Christ and the hope for a new creation. In truth, Christianity is even *more radical* than the most revolutionary of the revolutionaries. It anticipates and hastens the new creation of all things in the resurrection. The end of mammon's rule, where capitalism is no longer the dominant economic system, is not only possible but necessary for a Christian to remain faithful to the coming of God in the *eschaton*. We should never accept the defeatism of apathy.

The fourth objection is the assumption that capitalism is not identical to the systems of mammon idolatry. The idea here is that capitalism may be problematic, but it is not *identical* to mammon. Many people live under capitalism without serving mammon, or so it is claimed. But that misunderstands the heart of the anti-capitalist position, which is not about personal ethics but a systemic critique. Liberalism tends to individualize every issue to the lowest common denominator, the self. So the claim is that some people live in capitalism without serving mammon, implying that this exception disproves the rule. But that is not the case.

Capitalism is a system we live in, no matter how we act individually. At its core, the capitalist system cannot be other than what it is. Even if some individuals act contrary to what the system intends, that does not change the system itself but merely demonstrates its adaptability. Or, more precisely, it demonstrates the limit to personal ethics in a system of injustice. We have made this point throughout, echoing the Church Fathers, that personal charity is not enough. We are concerned with establishing justice, a world where Christ is Lord, not mammon. That necessitates anti-capitalism.

8

SOCIOECONOMIC ANALYSIS

My hope in examining the anti-mammon witness of the Early Church has been to demonstrate the dire need for a radical recalibration regarding how we address the questions of wealth, poverty, and economic justice, and to push the Church towards adopting an anti-capitalist political ethic. The themes examined in this book deserve to be at the forefront of how we talk about faith and wealth today. But, unfortunately, we have fallen far from the anti-mammon message of Christ—taking what was *essential* to the first Christians and making it secondary. Yet the anti-mammon impulse remains critical to the gospel, and it must become central to our witness again in the twenty-first century.

But the vital task remains of applying these insights to our situation today. That full burden will not be satisfied here, but perhaps a way forward can be offered, and a few paths indicated. The Church needs a new approach to social and economic problems, one that follows the *spirit* and *intent* of the anti-mammon witness while contextualizing that witness to our life and times. We need a robust socioeconomic analysis of capitalism.

In this chapter, I will examine the necessity of socioeconomic analysis by contextualizing Jesus' critique of wealth. Then I will suggest that we water down Christ's radical critique because we misunderstand the true object of his critique, which is not directed primarily to the middle class but to the ultra-rich and, most of all, to inequality. Finally, I will discuss Marx and his contributions in the next chapter.

Economic justice is vital to the gospel, as we have seen in the teachings of Scripture and the Early Church. Accordingly, we must adopt a radically anti-capitalist approach to politics today if we wish to proclaim Christ's gospel faithfully. My concern is not to promote a "woke" liberal gospel of social justice but a radical ("rooted") gospel of revolutionary change that makes central Christ's rebuke of all idols, chiefly mammon. Thus, what is truly at stake is the very heart of the gospel proclamation itself: Jesus is Lord and not mammon.

Contextualizing Jesus' words

In Jesus' time, most people lived at or below substance levels. By "subsistence," I mean the minimum material resources required to keep one's self and family alive. Thus, it was a daily struggle for most to survive. That is the most striking distinction between our world today, and the ancient world where Christ and the first Christians lived and taught the good news, and it is the first insight that will help us contextualize the anti-mammon witness of the gospel.

90% of the Roman Empire around the time of Christ lived near (22%), at (40%), or below (28%) subsistence. 7% lived with moderate resources, such as merchants and some artisans. 1.4% lived as municipal elites, 1% as regional elites, and only .04% as imperial elites.[1] Thus, 3% of the population hoarded most of society's wealth, while the majority lived with barely enough to survive—and more than *one in four* did not even have that.

Accordingly, the notion of hoarding wealth (or even just saving money for a rainy day) was an impossible hope for the majority of families living in the first century. What does this mean for Christ's rejection of mammon and critique of hoarded wealth? This point demonstrates how the wealth of the rich often meant death for the poorest of the poor—28% of the population—and indicates how we might apply Christ's words today.

Under capitalism, the inequality that existed in the Roman Empire has only sharpened to unimaginable degrees. Today, it is not merely the 3% that are the true "elites" but the 1% of the 1%. *Eight men* own more wealth than 50% of the entire planet combined.[2] That is inequality at a level never seen before. Thus, we might suggest that the object of Christ's critique of "the rich" translates, in our day, to a radical critique of the "capitalist class," who are the driving cause of global inequality at such an absurd scale.

With this historical context in mind, the story of the rich young ruler takes on new significance (Lk. 18). We should not think about his wealth as that of a middle-class worker who saved up his income to buy a nice home or retire comfortably. Instead, the young ruler's wealth was above and beyond what anyone in the crowd could have hoped to achieve in a lifetime. The majority of Jesus' listeners did not have enough to eat—and the young ruler's hoarded riches were possibly a direct cause of their destitution. The Fathers stressed that the rich are rich *because* the poor are poor.

Thus, Jesus' command for the rich young ruler to give away his wealth would have meant salvation from starvation for the needy, many of whom would have been in the crowd. Likewise, his tight-fisted decision to continue hoarding his ill-gotten wealth led to death for the disadvantaged. Jesus was asking him to save the hungry, many of whom were in the crowd. This realization adds a much-needed dose of brute realism to the story. The rich young ruler was not just holding on to what belonged to him but was actively participating in the misery of the poor. The same is true today for every rich person who lives in absurd luxury rather than housing the homeless or feeding the hungry.

The 1% hoard enough resources to feed nearly everyone on earth, while around 9 million people starve to death every year. The sin of the capitalist class is far greater than that of the rich young ruler. "Go, sell what you own, and give the money to the poor" (Mk. 10:21) was more than just a command to test the rich young ruler's devotion to God; *it was a call to save the poor from starvation.* Today, that command remains a perpetual witness against the rich's injustice, and every refusal to help the needy stores up wrath.

We might call the capitalist class the 1% of the 1%. Ownership of the "means of production," or private property, defines the capitalist class.[3] Examples include the owners of large multinational corporations, joint-stock companies, and giant tech conglomerates. It is through the ownership of these large enterprises that the capitalist class hoards such vast riches. And because they monopolize the earth's resources for profit, this class is directly responsible for the misery of the poor and oppressed—many of whom work in their factories and fields to earn the rich their ill-begotten profits.

Subsistence vs. luxury

With this context in mind, I want to clarify what is and is not the object of Christ's critique of mammon. We have seen that Jesus' anti-mammon teachings directly criticized the upper class and privileged elites (i.e., today's capitalist class), not necessarily today's middle or lower working class. If a working-class individual owns an iPhone, a car, or even their own home, that is not necessarily the concern of Christ's anti-mammon critique.[4] In today's terms, these are still within *subsistence*, not hoarding. Thus, the metric of working for subsistence vs. hoarding luxuries points us in the right direction for applying Christ's anti-mammon message most accurately to our times.

This also tells us that the attempt to "soften" Christ's hard words regarding mammon is sometimes motivated by the mistaken assumption that a middle-class person is automatically the object of his critique. The aim of

Christ's anti-mammon message had a specific target: the exceedingly rich who hoarded great wealth while many others suffered from a lack of resources. While no individual is off the hook from Christ's teachings, it is vital to recognize that, according to the historical context, Jesus would not have been concerned so much with *subsistence living* as with *hoarded luxuries*. Drawing a parallel to today means recognizing that most of the "middle class" belongs in the former category rather than the latter. The subconscious urge to soften Christ's critique of wealth to protect middle-class people misunderstands that his concern was not about those living comfortably but the exceedingly rich who hoard more wealth than the average person could dream of accumulating in a thousand lifetimes.

Thus, Jesus was not rejecting wealth as a means of subsistence living, which today includes having a bank account and a 401k (modern necessities to survive under capitalism). Likewise, saving for retirement is not the same as hoarding. Saving for retirement is necessary; it is still within the realm of subsistence.

We should redefine "the rich" for our own time based on Jesus' concept of the rich in his time and direct his critique accordingly. Earlier, I hinted toward a solution by referring to Jose Miranda's concept of "differentiating wealth," which makes the issue of inequality rather than abundance explicit. The Bible frequently praises material abundance as a gift from God—the promised land flowing with milk and honey is a prime example of God's blessing of abundance for God's people. Yet it was a blessing for Israel as a people to be *shared* by all, not hoarded by the few. Thus, the Bible's critique of wealth is against *differentiating* wealth, i.e., inequality, not abundance.

Of course, the working class is not exempt from the danger of serving mammon idolatrously. Still, if we seek to translate this critique into today's terms, it seems the most crucial element here is *inequality*. And the blame for inequality lies with the rich, who exploit the poor. The unequal distribution of God's gifts is sin, and the rich are responsible for this unjust economic order. So we should focus on the root cause behind the injustice of differentiating wealth: the capitalist class.

All of this means that the anti-mammon message of Jesus translates today into a critique of inequality and the systems that create it, namely, capitalism and its driving engine: capital accumulation at all costs. The rich he condemned were the elite 3% of society who lived in luxury as more than a fourth of the population was living in poverty, with the remaining population living "hand to mouth" or "paycheck to paycheck," as we might say today. How much more must we today condemn the 1% of the 1%, over and above the words directed against the ancient 3%? The love of mammon has only led to more deprivation and misery in these two thousand years.

But I want to return to the point that middle-class subsistence radically differs from capitalist-class luxuries. We should not lose sight of the radical disparity between the rich and the middle and lower classes. The chief difference is *ownership*. The ownership of capital (including the means of production) defines the capitalist class. In contrast, the working class owns nothing (in capital and private property) except for their time and labor power, which they must sell to the capitalist class for subsistence living.

Thus, one class works for a living (working class) while the other lives off the labor of others (capitalist class). Paul's rebuke in 1 Thessalonians 3:10 that anyone unwilling to work shall not eat was most likely directed towards the rich, not the poor. The working class cannot afford the luxury of not working and will probably work most of their lives, often even into old age, to survive. Accordingly, the primary difference is each group's relation to the "means of production," i.e., private property.

John Steinbeck once said, "Socialism never took root in America because the poor see themselves not as an exploited proletariat but as temporarily embarrassed millionaires."[5] We often "soften" the critique of wealth because we have a stronger sense of solidarity with the wealthy than with the poor. But it is misplaced solidarity.

If you go to work on Monday morning to pay the bills, you are working-class. And the truth is you are closer to being homeless than being rich. It would not take much to put you or me out on the street—a financial crisis, a family tragedy, etc.—but it would take a great miracle to make us a billionaire. We mistakenly think we have more in common with "the rich" than the poor, but we must rethink this assumption. You and I have more in common with the man on the street than the man in the penthouse.

The point is to redirect Christ's anti-mammon critique toward its actual target. It is not directed towards the majority just barely trying to survive in the conditions given to them, who nonetheless think of themselves as "temporarily embarrassed millionaires." Historically, Christ's critique of mammon is toward the elite class of persons who hoard society's resources for themselves, as the majority toil and suffer with barely enough to survive. That translates today to the capitalist class.

Redirecting our energy towards the true hoarders of wealth frees us to be *united* in radical solidarity for a common cause: liberation from the tyranny of mammon. Our struggle is not against one another but against the capitalist class that hoards enough wealth to live in luxury for a thousand lifetimes while millions cannot even afford to eat. But unfortunately, we are so quickly distracted by the fact that our neighbor has a nicer car, bigger house, or larger retirement fund than we do that we ignore the full picture. We should not fight each other. The working class has a common struggle and goal: a world where everyone has enough to eat and society's resources are used for the good of all, not the luxuries of the few.

We have missed Christ's radical critique of riches because we think it is directed primarily against the working class. Christ's message has relevance for us, of course. No one is free from the temptation of idolatry. But the radicalism of the gospel is downplayed whenever we turn this message into a personal excuse to feel bad about ourselves because we have a few nice things. Or when we judge people simply trying to carve out a subsistence living under an inhumane economic system rather than joining together to rebuke and call to repentance the rich of our time who hoard for themselves far more than they deserve. The goal of society is not to guarantee absurd luxuries for the few but to provide essentials for all. Until that happens, the rich must be perpetually called to repentance, to give what they have to help the needy and poor.

I want to reiterate, however, that I am not trying to let anyone off the hook. Instead, the *primary* aim here is to show how Christ's words against mammon were directed against the richest of the rich—the elites. Obviously, within the global context, the West *is* the privileged elite. But that is not the fault of the working class merely trying to survive in this hostile system. We did not create the conditions for the exploitation of the third world (which led to the West's privileged status in the global community). The truth is, the working class of the West has more in common with the working class of the global south than with the capitalist class in its own country. International proletarian solidarity against exploiting the poor is necessary for a more humane and just future. Thus, I suggest that the proper object of Christ's anti-mammon critique—*when contextually applied to today's world*—is against the capitalist class.

The necessity of socioeconomic analysis

It might be apparent that this conclusion relies upon Karl Marx's socioeconomic analysis of capitalism. Marx scientifically analyzed the nature of class relations under capitalism with more precision than anyone else before or since.

But the necessity of such an analysis is a conclusion we might draw from the Church Fathers examined in this book. As we have seen, most Fathers were not content with accepting poverty as accidental or inevitable. Instead, many Fathers sought to examine *why* the poor remained bound to their misery. And they did not hold back in calling the rich unjust and condemning their greed as the cause of the misery of the poor.

We should follow their lead and again ask today *why* the poor are poor. *Why* do the rich countries exploit poorer ones for profit; *why* does the wealthiest nation on earth fail to feed its children or guarantee subsistence living or housing for its people? And all this in the so-called greatest economic system ever created. These are the questions we must ask ourselves today if we want to not simply repeat what the Scriptures and the Fathers' say but to apply their wisdom to our time.

The lack of a socioeconomic model for analysis has made it difficult for the Church to recognize that the anti-mammon witness of Christ applies today to capitalism. Thus, one of the reasons why the Church has failed to proclaim Christ's rebuke consistently is that it does not know how to translate it to today's economic conditions. We still think in individualistic terms, not political or economic terms. But consider this: If we do not even know who the rich and poor are of our time, then we definitely cannot proclaim good news to the poor. Likewise, if we do not understand why the poor are poor, we cannot feasibly proclaim the Kingdom of God. Thus, we desperately need a method for analyzing our world today to apply Christ's anti-mammon message to our context. One such tool for socioeconomic analysis is Marxism.

It may be a shock to hear this recommendation, but I hope you will give me the benefit of the doubt as I explain why. There are few critics besides Marx who more carefully analyzed the systems of modern capitalism—including how hoarded wealth creates injustice and poverty for the majority of the population as the privileged few live in luxury and extravagance. A significant concern of Marx's work is how capitalism functions and why it creates such misery on the one hand and luxury on the other. An analysis of this sort is valuable for our anti-mammon proclamation. Whatever we may think of Marx as a political theorist, there is no doubt that from a scientific standpoint, his critique of modern capitalism remains one of the most sophisticated and vital tools for understanding our world. Thus, I recommend the scientific Marx, not the "ideological Marx" (if such a Marx even exists). If we seek to contextualize the teachings of Christ into our lives under capitalism—and we cannot afford not to—then we should at least pay attention to the insights of Karl Marx and take them seriously.

Marx devoted his life to *understanding* the world to *change* it.[6] This approach is much needed again today, especially in the Church. We might rightly remind ourselves that the point of biblical study and theological inquiry is not merely to *understand* the Bible or God but to *change* the world, to usher in the reign of the Kingdom "on earth as it is in heaven." The gospel is not understood intellectually; it is lived out as a transformative power. We proclaim a Kingdom of righteousness, not a pie-in-the-sky religious escape; thus, we cannot afford to ignore the conditions of this world as we seek to change them.

Our fear of Marx is often rooted in a failure to understand that he is, first and foremost, a scientific thinker. His magnum opus is the incredible three-volume *Capital*. Many just read (or claim to have read) the *Manifesto* as if that is all Marx had to say—but a pamphlet Marx and Engels wrote in two weeks should not be the only work we read to judge Marxism as a whole. Perhaps that is why so many people think of Marx as a purely ideological figure since their only exposure to his work is found in a forty-page summary while ignoring his actual scientific work. In *Capital*, Marx sought to decipher the nature of modern capitalism and its systems to show precisely why the poor are poor and why the hungry do not have enough to eat even though there is enough abundance to go around for all.[7] These questions are still relevant today, and few have found better answers than what Marx offered.

It is one thing to help the poor, but it is another thing entirely to ask why the poor are poor in the first place—and to refuse to accept the victim-blaming tactics of the powerful. Dom Hélder Câmara once astutely observed, "When I give food to the poor, they call me a saint. When I ask why they are poor, they call me a communist."[8] Today, we are in dire need not merely to give food to the poor but ask why they are poor in the first place.

When the richest country on earth cannot guarantee basic subsistence to its most vulnerable citizens, then there is something seriously wrong with this capitalist system. Marx astutely observed, "There must be something rotten in the very core of a social system which increases its wealth without diminishing its misery."[9] As we saw, the Scriptures and most of the fathers *assumed* that to be rich is to be unjust; Marx *demonstrates* scientifically why that is the case and what we can do about fixing it.

Thus, I would hazard a controversial conclusion: the Church needs Marx's analysis. That is not to say we need to adopt everything he said uncritically. But why not use all the tools available for understanding this world? Of course, I am not suggesting we accept Marx wholesale or that everything done in Marx's name can be justified. But to overlook his conclusions would be like a scientist ignoring Isaac Newton or a physicist neglecting Steven Hawking. These men did not get everything right, but their insights are vital for understanding today's world. The same is true for Marx and his contributions in economics and sociology.

Liberation theologians, such as James Cone, considered Marxism valuable as a *tool* for social analysis, not an ideology. Of course, we can and should keep a critical distinction from Marxism as an ideology because no ideology can take precedence over the gospel. But as a tool for social scientific analysis of the systems of capitalist oppression, we cannot afford to ignore any insight which might help us faithfully proclaim the message of Christ to today's world.

Science helps us navigate the natural world. Likewise, we need a social scientific tool for navigating the tyranny of mammon as it exists today under capitalism. The Early Church readily used "secular" sciences to help it proclaim the gospel. Patristic theologians such as Augustine and Origen studied and engaged with philosophy for that reason. Today, there is a supposed "war" between faith and science, but that was rarely true for the Church Fathers, nor is it appropriate today. Friedrich Schleiermacher understood this well when he called for an "eternal covenant between the living Christian faith and a completely free, independent science, so that faith does not hinder science and science does not exclude faith."[10]

Schleiermacher's insight applies not only to the natural sciences but to social and economic sciences, too. Thus, Christian faith need not fear a scientific analysis of capitalism. The opposite is the case. We can and should recognize ourselves as allies with all those who seek to understand the injustices of this world and strive to overcome them. That includes the insights presented by Marx and Engels.

It is essential to see that this conclusion is not at odds with the teachings of the Early Church but a result of their concern for the poor and their critique of the rich. We repeatedly saw that Fathers such as John Chrysostom, Basil, Ambrose, and even Augustine were not content with accepting poverty as an accident of nature. Instead, they went further and analyzed the conditions that led to inequality and overwhelmingly found fault with the rich and powerful.

That means we cannot afford to neglect the social and economic sciences as a tool for critically analyzing our world and proclaiming the gospel anew. The Bible alone is not enough for us to faithfully *apply* the Bible again today. For example, the Bible does not contain a manual on how to irrigate farmlands effectively to feed the poor. But it commands us to feed the poor. Nor does it contain a medical manual of best practices or a guide for brain surgery. But it tells us to heal the sick. So we must be willing to learn from other scientific tools to fulfill the Bible's commandments.

Thus, as a tool for social analysis, Marxism is just as necessary for us to help achieve Christ's message as tools of medicine and farming. If we do not even understand capitalism—the dominant economic system of our world—then we cannot proclaim Christ's message anew to our time. We will be irrelevant if we continue proclaiming the gospel to a world that no longer exists.

9

ON MARX

Why is Marx worth reading? Even if you are convinced of the need for social analysis, it remains to be seen why Marx is the best resource for such a task. I want to introduce a few notable insights from his work to answer that question. These are not exhaustive but may help establish Marx's value today. Later in the chapter, I will address the main objection to Marx—his critique of religion. But Marx's name has been disparaged so often that I think it is helpful to begin with the benefits of his work before turning to possible objections.

These contributions are especially notable because they correspond to insights we have learned from the writings of the Early Church. These include the insight that the rich and poor exist in a symbiotic relationship, that the poor are not poor by accident but are made poor by the exploitation of the rich. Then there is the point that the origins of wealth are unjust. Additionally, the nature of mammon is to alienate and dehumanize human beings. These insights from the Early Church echo similar points in Marx. Finally, Marx also goes beyond one of the frequently unacknowledged limitations of the Church's historical approach to wealth and poverty.

1. The poor are not poor by accident

We often assume that poverty and wealth are personal choices resulting from hard work or a lack thereof. But the more we analyze the existing systems of capitalism today, the less true that becomes. Indeed, hard work plays a part in wealth and poverty, but the systemic features of capitalism are far more determinative. As a result, the rich often remain rich, and the poor remain poor. The rare exception or two does not disprove the rule: almost everyone will die in the same economic class as their parents.

But this is not accidental. The capitalist class wants the poor to remain poor so they can remain rich and increase their wealth. And they have the power to ensure exactly that. Marx's analysis of capitalism concludes that at its core, capitalism is a class struggle between the capitalist class and the working class. The interests of the capitalist class are at odds with the interests of the working class. That is because the rich become wealthy (and consolidate their wealth) by *exploiting* the poor—by leveraging capital to purchase the labor of the working class, which is the source of profit. Thus, the rich (the capitalist class) have a vested interest in keeping the poor (the working class) bound to subsistence levels or below. They conspire to keep wages low and costs high to extract as much wealth from the working class as possible.[1]

The Early Church Fathers recognized a similar dynamic in their time and called it unjust. That is why they considered giving to the poor an act of restored justice, not charity. As Charles Avila explains, concerning Basil, "He did *not* see the wealth few and the destitute majority existing side by side fortuitously, without a relationship of causality between their two states. He saw that one state caused the other. The enormous wealth and sumptuous living of the few caused the impoverishment and misery of the many."[2] The poor are *made* poor by the hoarded wealth of the rich. On this issue, as we have seen, many of the Fathers agreed.

Marx's central economic theory validates that conclusion, his labor theory of value. Without going into too much detail, Marx's theory demonstrates how capitalist profits are unpaid value generated by the labor of the working class. In other words, the working class generates the wealth of the capitalist class; the capitalist's riches come from exploitation. The rich are made rich by the efforts of the poor, who receive a small portion of the profits they create for the capitalists. Thus, the core of the capitalist system is the theft of value from the working class. Profits are unpaid wages; the rich take what they did not earn from those who did.[3]

The working class sells their labor to the capitalist class (or else they starve, thus, it is through coercion). And in return, they receive a fixed wage. But through their labor, the working class creates far more value for the capitalist than they receive back in wages. Part of that goes into fixed capital, i.e., maintenance of the production process, but a surplus remains and becomes profit, which the capitalists claim as theirs even though they did not work for it. Accordingly, profits are not earned by the capitalists but by the working class. Yet, the capitalists steal their surplus value, which is justified by the capitalist's ownership of private property. That is how the capitalist class exploits the working class.

In this sense, the poverty of the working class is a *direct result* of the riches of the capitalist class. They exist in an essential, causal relationship with each other. The greatest economic myth of our time is that society's wealth might "trickle down" from top to bottom. That has never been the case.[4] The rich leverage their power and influence to ensure their hoarded wealth remains theirs. In other words, they build bigger barns for themselves to hoard their riches.

Under capitalism, the worker who produces a product does not benefit from its sale. Instead, the capitalist, *who did not labor over the product*, pockets the profits created *by the worker*. That is, in brief, Marx's labor theory of value. Through this mechanism, the capitalist is motivated to suppress the worker's wages. Thus, the riches of the capitalist class exist *because* of the poverty of the working class. The luxuries of the rich create misery for the poor. Marx writes:

> Accumulation of wealth at one pole is, therefore, at the same time accumulation of misery, the torment of labour, slavery, ignorance, brutalization and moral degradation at the opposite pole, i.e. on the side of the class that produces its own product as capital [the working class].[5]

Thus, if we are to ask today why the poor are poor, why millions starve to death each year—even though we produce enough food to feed ten billion people—the answer, for Marx, is clear. It is because the capitalist class has monopolized production and distribution solely for their benefit and because capital accumulation is the central priority of capitalism. Therefore, the profits of the rich correspond directly to the misery of the poor because they are generated by the exploitation of the working class. The rich are the *cause* of inequality. Marx saw this clearly and demonstrated it scientifically in his analysis of capitalism.

But, in a more simplistic way, so did John Chrysostom when he wrote:

> Whence, then, does such great inequality arise? It arises from the greed and the arrogance of the rich.[6]

If we wish to help the poor, then we cannot afford to ignore this insight. The poor are not poor by accident but are made poor by the systems of capitalism, by the exploitation of the rich.

2. The origin of capital accumulation is violence and theft

Jerome said that the root of hoarded wealth is injustice. The Early Church did not accept the myth of righteously acquired wealth. Charles Avila explains:

> The fathers of the Church already held what political economists twelve to thirteen centuries later would learn from their researches and analyses. Historically, they said, whenever private ownership of land prevailed, it was always the result of usurpation, arising by violence and force, war and conquest, or outright robbery.[7]

Marx examined the history of capital accumulation and demonstrated what Jerome and other Fathers' intuitively recognized. The rich are wealthy not because of their hard work but because of violence and theft. That is true both historically (in the transition from feudalism to capitalism) and daily as the capitalist class exploits the working class and continually consolidates control over the economy.

José Miranda explains, "In reality the accumulation of capital in a few hands could not and cannot be achieved without an institutional violence exercise over wages and prices."[8] Marx calls this primitive accumulation. As feudalism transitioned to capitalism, the capitalist class stole and privatized the common lands. The economic violence of stealing lands from peasants is one thing, but this transition was also marked by physical violence and brutality in the form of colonialism. Capitalism ravaged the earth for lands and resources to monopolize for profit. We do not reflect enough on how private property is rooted in an original act of theft and violence. And thus, how capitalism, which is defined by this relation to property, is a system founded upon injustice and robbery, not merit and morals. There is no bloodless capitalism.[9]

The American Empire is an apt example. Genocide and slavery are the foundation of America's wealth. It is not an accident that the wealthiest country in the world has such a fraught history of violence and theft because that is how capital is accumulated. Colonizers did not earn the land through hard work or a fair exchange; they did not persuade the natives through logic and morals. Instead, they stole America by force through the violent extermination of the native peoples. Likewise, the profits of southern plantations were not earned by their owners but by the blood and sweat of black bodies enslaved in the pursuit of capital. Even today, the traces of capitalism's origin can be seen in the subjugation of the poorer nations by richer ones, exploiting their lands and cheap labor for profit and exporting cash crops while the people starve.

Jerome approvingly quoted the aphorism that a rich man is either unjust himself or the son of an unjust man. That aptly describes how capitalism began and how the rich remain rich today. The root of wealth is the monopolistic theft of God's earth, which was given for all in common, into the private hands of the greedy. The earth belongs to all of us, yet the rich have hoarded the means of subsistence for themselves.

Thus, Marx's insight corresponds well with the biblical rebuke of the rich, which we explored in chapter one and saw repeated throughout the teachings of the Early Church. Yet he discloses a more scientific explanation of why the root of wealth is injustice, theft, and violence with his analysis of "primitive accumulation" and the daily exploitation of the working class under capitalism. We often think the rich earned their wealth justly, but Marx explains, "In actual history, it is a notorious fact that conquest, enslavement, robbery, murder, in short, force, play the greatest part."[10]

Likewise, Avila places the burden of proof on the rich, not the poor: "Thus, in a situation in which so much wealth lies in the hands of a few, while so many are impoverished, the burden of proof of just acquisition lies with the wealthy."[11] It is more likely that the rich acquired their wealth unjustly than the poor became poor due to moral failure. We often blame the poor for their poverty and fail to condemn the rich for their unjust wealth.

Thus, Marx's insight corresponds with and heightens the witness of Scripture in a modern way. He proved how the riches of the wealthy come from injustice and thus added a scientific basis to Jesus' rebuke, "Woe to you who are rich!" We do not repeat these words because they are holy but because they are true. The rich condemn themselves by their unrighteousness. Truly, woe to the rich who store up wrath for themselves (God and humanity's alike). Their ill-begotten riches are a sign of their sin.

3. Alienation

The effects of capitalism are more than just economic. A system that prioritizes the accumulation of money above all else is idolatrous. And every idolatry involves the dehumanization of the human being. The twentieth-century theologian Karl Barth once described how "the pulling down of God becomes its own punishment" because we become prisoners of our idolatrous constructions.[12] Under capitalism, mammon usurps the throne of God and enslaves humanity to its alien power. While Marx understood this problem in more philosophical terms, calling it "alienation," it is a powerful description of the spiritual degradation of human beings under the tyranny of mammon.

There are four aspects of alienation. First, the worker is alienated from what they produce. Second, the worker is alienated by the process of production itself, by their work. Third, the worker is alienated from what Marx calls their "species-being" (*Gattungswesen*), meaning their labor is out of harmony with their social essence. Fourth, the worker is alienated from their fellow-human.

Marx makes a strong case for understanding capitalism as being at odds with human nature. That is because the capitalist mode of production entails the denial and degradation of human beings, not the fulfillment of their nature. Thus, capitalism, not socialism, is incompatible with human nature, as Marx understands it.

Eric Fromm writes, "For Marx the aim of socialism was the emancipation of man, and the emancipation of man was the same as his self-realization in the process of productive relatedness and oneness with man and nature."[13] And elsewhere, Fromm argues that "Marx's aim was that of the *spiritual* emancipation of man, of his liberation from the chains of economic determination."[14] Capitalism is incompatible with human nature, but socialism is the liberation of human beings from the alienating processes of capitalist production.

Because capitalism has subjected all human life and society to the demands of capital, it is an alienating system. We saw how the tyranny of mammon led to the destruction of one's soul in chapter seven, but here Marx makes a parallel point about labor under capitalism. Capitalist production demands self-denial (denying one's nature), not self-expression (expressing one's nature). Only that which can be exploited by capital is permitted within the production process.

When a worker clocks-in for the day, they deny themselves (second aspect) by submitting to a mechanical and inhumane system. What they produce is not their own product but belongs to another (first aspect). That means their essence as creative and free human beings is denied (third aspect), their species-being. And finally, it means that the worker is alienated from their fellow human (fourth aspect).

To understand this, we will examine these points in more detail.

The first aspect describes how workers produce products and value that does not belong to them. Because the capitalist owns the "means of production," they claim all the value that the worker produces. The worker's efforts are alienated because they do not directly benefit from their own labor; what they produce is another's property. The worker's wage only reflects a small portion of the value they produce with their efforts; the capitalist class takes the remaining value without compensation.

The second aspect describes how the dignity of work is removed by the mechanical process of production that robs the laborer of any self-fulfillment and makes work itself an act of self-alienation.[15] Work entails the denial of the self, not the expression of the self. While previous systems may have included forms of alienation as a feature of work, it is only under capitalism that the human being is a commodity to be bought and sold. Because the working class has nothing to offer—no capital—except their labor power, they must sell *themselves* to the capitalist class in exchange for subsistence.[16]

Capitalism transforms the labor power of the human being into a commodity. Labor is an action, but Marx realized that capitalism has made it a commodity. Our labor, and thus our life itself, is a *product* we sell to survive. Marx recognized that labor is the commodity of commodities; it is the source of all value in the capitalist system because it is the only commodity that does not use up its value in production but creates new value for the capitalist. In short, under capitalism, human beings are now for sale like objects. Workers go to school and put great effort into their resumes to effectively market themselves as a commodity worth buying.

Marxism thus suggests that wage labor under capitalism is barely distinguishable from slavery.[17] A slave is sold once to a master, but a wage laborer must sell themselves daily and hourly to their boss. The laborer has no choice but to sell themselves to the capitalist class as a class, no matter what job or specific employer they choose. That shatters the illusion of "freedom" under capitalism.

The freedom to select a job is only to choose between capitalists, but never to choose *not* to be exploited by the capitalist class, i.e., not to sell themselves like a product to survive. It does not matter that we are free to choose who we wish to be exploited by if we cannot choose not to be exploited at all. So it may seem extreme for Marx to call this a form of slavery, but in reality, the function of wage labor is different only in *quality*, not in *kind* with slavery. Most of a worker's life is still under the control of the capitalist class because they are forced to sell their labor under the threat of starvation.[18]

Furthermore, subjecting an entire economic system to the will of capital is the real problem of capitalism, and no one, not even the rich, are free from its tyranny. Marx compares capital to a vampire—a dead thing that lives off the living labor of the working class.[19] Capitalists continually struggle against each other for dominance in a tyrannical system wherein one must either kill or be killed. Thus, the entire system of capitalism is trapped by the inhuman and demonic will of a dead idol called capital.[20] Therefore, John Chrysostom's concept of the "tyranny" of mammon parallels Marx's concept of alienation at this point.

Finally, alienation under capitalism is also social, as it forces laborers who actually a common cause to compete, leading to animosity. That is because capitalism is fundamentally a "dog eats dog" system, where everyone is concerned with their piece of the pie. Rather than focusing on its true oppressor, the capitalist class, the working class fights amongst itself.

One of the most brutal aspects of this is how capitalism requires a "surplus population" of unemployed or underemployed to keep laborers in a state of competition. The unemployed are a "reserve army" used to coerce the working class into bitter competition with one another.[21] The very existence of a surplus population of unemployed laborers is a perpetual threat to the working class, "Be subservient or end up on the streets."

Furthermore, the relative surplus population asserts pressure on the employed to submit to overwork. The unemployed are a perpetual threat to the employed, which creates the conditions for their being overworked and underpaid by the capitalist class, who knows they have no other options but to obey or starve.[22] In other words, unemployment is not a *bug* in the capitalist system but a *feature*. It retains a surplus population so that the capitalist class might exercise more and more control over the working class.

Thus, under capitalism, we live in perpetual suspicion of our neighbors; we are alienated from our fellow humans because of capitalist competition for resources.[23] But capitalism essentially *manufactures* this competition—we must not forget that we produce enough resources to house, feed, and care for everyone. Socialism envisions a society of cooperation where resources are shared rather than fought over and hoarded. As a result, capitalism alienates the working class, who is too busy fighting among themselves to focus on the real cause of their exploitation.

Another alienating aspect of capitalism is consumerism, which makes the chief end of human life to own things. Yet the pursuit of *having* comes at the detriment of *being*. Marx writes, "The depreciation of the human world takes place in direct proportion to the increase in value of the world of things."[24] Or, more simply, "The less you are, the more you have."[25] In other words, as the value placed on things increases under capitalism, the value of human persons decreases. Thus, the worth of human beings created in the image of God is marred by the value capitalism places on things over people. Capital, a dead thing, is more important than living persons created in God's image. That is the logic of consumerism. Thus, under capitalism, we are alienated from our very humanity as everything is subjected to the tyranny of capital.

In the Christian sense, alienation reflects the spiritual death caused by idolatry. The gospel proclaims new life to precisely this situation. Marx's analysis of alienation is a valuable tool for understanding how the modern world distorts the image of God in every person. A radical critique of capitalism includes concern for persons' physical, mental, economic, *and* spiritual well-being.

4. The poor and oppressed as *subjects*

In addition to aligning with the anti-mammon witness of the Church, Marx can also help elevate the response we have towards the poor. For example, we might critique the Church Fathers for how they often failed to treat the poor as actual *subjects* of history and, more often than not, treated them as *objects* of charity. Susan Holman explains that the perspective of the Fathers tended toward treating the poor as "referents, not subjects." Furthermore, she notes that most academic studies on the Early Church and poverty repeat this error.[26] Accordingly, the poor have become "a passive tool for redemptive almsgiving, a signifier by which the Christian donor may gain honor and divine rewards."[27] Yet this is to ignore, or at least downplay, the agency of the poor in their own lives. Moreover, this approach denies the poor their dignity as historical actors in their liberation.

In contrast, the heart of Marxist praxis is the empowerment of the proletariat—the working class—in their struggle for liberation. Marx and Engels write, "The proletariat alone is a really revolutionary class."[28] Socialism is the liberation of the proletariat from the dictatorship of capital. The *Manifesto* famously concludes: "The proletarians have nothing to lose but their chains. They have a world to win. Workingmen of all countries, unite!"[29]

The Church today still thinks of the poor as objects rather than subjects of their own liberation. That is due to focusing more on hand-outs and band-aid solutions rather than substantial systematic change, which will arise only by empowering the poor and oppressed in their struggle for liberation. Thus, the Church does not properly help the poor by standing above them, offering occasional top-down help. Instead, the Church serves Christ in the poor by joining their plight directly, and by taking up solidarity with the oppressed. Accordingly, the Church is not merely the Church *for* the poor but *of* the poor. This radical solidarity empowers the poor and oppressed, who have been so often subject to the brutalization of powerlessness, to organize and struggle for their rights to life, dignity, and humanity.

Any liberation struggle is twofold: First, the material struggle, which is negatively related to the end of oppression and systemic violence. Second, the struggle for *dignity*, which is positively related to the humanization of the oppressed. Those who have been beaten down and discarded by society for so long can find new dignity and self-worth through their struggle for liberation by becoming subjects of that struggle rather than merely objects in someone else's history. The Church has often overlooked the struggle for dignity—the positive dimension of liberation—but it is central to Marx's understanding of revolution.[30]

This twofold movement of liberation is also found in Israel's history. Their immediate liberation *from* slavery (the exodus) coincided with their lengthy liberation *into* dignity as a people (the wilderness, covenant, and promised land). Today, both sides of liberation are necessary. Marx captures this well in his theory of revolution.

A socialist revolution entails the empowerment of the disenfranchised and the liberation of the powerless. Marx envisions a movement *from below*—by the people and for the people—not a movement *from above*. "All power to the people" is the heart of the revolutionary struggle.[31] This approach to liberation is not identical to the role of the Church, but there are many things that we can learn from revolutionary ethics. Most of all, it is a necessary correction of our tendency to treat the poor as objects rather than subjects. And finally, all this illustrates how fruitful a Christian engagement with Marxism can be.

Liberation theology has grasped this well. The Church historically adopted a top-down approach to liberation. However, liberation theologies were developed in the mid-twentieth century from *within* oppressed communities, not treating them as objects but as true subjects in the liberation struggle. For example, James Cone's Black Liberation theology was born from the black community suffering under white supremacy in America, and Gustavo Gutiérrez's Latin American Liberation theology developed by struggling in solidarity with the poor in the slums of Peru. These theologies offer a necessary corrective to outdated approaches to the poor. While the Church Fathers can be an instructive voice, we have to go beyond them and correct this mistake. It is also notable that both Cone and Gutiérrez cite Marx as an influence on their thinking—although both carefully differentiate Marxism as an ideology or a tool for social analysis.

The oppressed are not external objects for us to help from above; *the poor are what makes the Church Christ's Church.* Therefore, the struggle for liberation is one of empowerment, solidarity, and intersectional dignity. "We" in the Church will not liberate the poor; the poor, as the Church of Jesus Christ, liberate themselves, and "we" must either join them or step aside.

That is why charity alone is not enough. Instead, the emphasis should be on joining the struggle for the liberation of oppressed people. That goes far beyond hand-outs and charity and moves more into the incarnational mission of Christ. Just as Jesus became a human being to take up our cause as his own, we follow Christ by following him into solidarity with the poor and oppressed in their struggle for liberation.

Religion as opium

There remain several objections to Marx to address alongside his contributions. The first and perhaps most frequent objection, at least from the Christian perspective, is his critique of religion. The famous description of religion as an "opium of the people" is one of his best-known sayings. Yet, the meaning takes on far different and perhaps even positive connotations in context. Marx writes:

> *Religious* suffering is, at one and the same time, the *expression* of real suffering and a *protest* against real suffering. Religion is the sigh of the oppressed creature, the heart of a heartless world, and the soul of soulless conditions. It is the *opium* of the people.
>
> The abolition of religion as the *illusory* happiness of the people is the demand for their *real* happiness. To call on them to give up their illusions about their condition is to call on them to *give up a condition that requires illusions*. The criticism of religion is, therefore, *in embryo, the criticism of that vale of tears* of which religion is the *halo*.[32]

We have to reckon with the possibility that there *is* something to Marx's critique. Indeed, there is a significant credibility gap between what the Church professes it believes and what it does in history. Even today, the credibility gap is well known and a significant reason why the Church is dying in the West even while the reputation of Jesus of Nazareth remains high and revered.

It is also important to remember the historical context of what Marx is saying, which had practical significance for the struggle of his time. Marx is not making a universal statement but is suggesting something pragmatic about the misuse of power by religious authorities in the Church. Religion was predominantly reactionary at the time Marx wrote these words. The Church often stood on the side of the empire, the feudal lords, and the capitalist class rather than on the side of the poor and oppressed—as Christ called us.

Marx's insight is also positive because he recognizes how religion can be a genuine expression of suffering and a means for protesting against oppression. Marx's primary concern is how religion tends toward superstition and how it has been used today to justify class privileges. Religion is a *symptom* of the problem, not the main issue. He even has quite positive things to say about religion: it reflects a true expression and protest against suffering as the "heart of a heartless world, and the soul of soulless conditions." The end of religion envisioned here is the end of the illusions that religion often creates, which arise because of the conditions of this world that make such illusions necessary. Thus, the problem with religion, for Marx, is how it has acted to uphold the oppressive status quo, to be merely a band-aid over the wound rather than healing the diseased condition of capitalism.

Despite his late atheism, it is noteworthy that Marx was baptized as a Christian in Trier in 1824, he wrote a school paper on the gospel of John in 1835, and later in life, according to the first-hand account of his daughter Eleanor, Marx also spoke highly about Jesus of Nazareth.[33] She recounts:

> I remember the time I had religious doubts [...] I confided these doubts to the Moor [Karl Marx's family nickname] [...] he narrated to me the story of the carpenter's son who was put to death by the rich, in a way I don't think it has ever been narrated before or since! I often heard him say: despite everything, we can forgive Christianity many things because of the fact that it has taught us to love little ones.[34]

Furthermore, Friedrich Engels, Marx's longtime collaborator, was the son of a Reformed pastor and wrote a lengthy study on Thomas Müntzer and the peasants' war. Both examples show that there was a depth to their engagement with Christianity that goes far beyond the easy caricatures.[35]

Engel's study of Müntzer is especially insightful. Thomas Müntzer was a contemporary of Luther, who helped inspire a peasants' revolt against the feudal lords. Engel's text on Müntzer reveals that the co-founder of a supposed "godless" communism was deeply interested in the *duality* of religion to be at once a reactionary force (Luther, who supported the Feudal Lords) and a revolutionary one (Müntzer).

Religion as opium is a realistic *description* of the Christian faith in history, but it is not exclusive, nor is the dismissal total. The challenge for us today is acknowledging the credibility gap between what we say about the poor and how we act against their interests by siding with the rich. This book has also been critical of how the Church has used religion to suppress the rights of the poor.[36] So, just because Marx and Engels have said something negative about religion does not make their work irreconcilable with the Christian faith.

Another important consideration is that opium was medicine and did not carry an entirely negative connotation during Marx's time. Indeed, Marx took opium for years to help with chronic skin disease.[37] Thus, the connotation of opium as a drug of stupor or a purely negative metaphor is not the immediate idea Marx likely had in mind. Instead, opium was *medicine*, or we might even say it was such *necessary* medicine that Marx himself took it frequently. Therefore, Marx's metaphor is a rather astute meditation of the relation between religion and suffering, which can be a source of healing, yet also lead to paralysis. That again reflects an awareness of the duality of religion.

Marx himself was not religious, but most importantly, Marx did not deny others the right to practice religion,[38] even though he criticized the tendency of religious authorities to hinder progress towards human liberation. And on that account, historically speaking, he was correct.

We should also carefully distinguish between two phrases: opium *of* the people and opium *for* the people. Marx described religion as an opium of the people, i.e., opium that is self-administered, not *for* them as a pacifying drug. Thus, it is clear that Marx considers religion as a means for people to cope with capitalism and the oppression of mammon. That does not immediately mean religion is the problem. On the contrary, the religious are just trying to cope with the inhumanity of capitalism. That is why he describes religion as the heart of a heartless society.

But religious coping can also be a source of resistance; it can mobilize just as much as it can sometimes be demobilizing. The same conditions that lead religion to passivity can also lead it to resistance. The oppressive nature of capitalism also leads the non-religious to soothe themselves with "the society of the spectacle," as Guy Debord observed. Consumerist culture is just as susceptible to being called the opium of the people as religion—perhaps even more so today. But religion also contains the potential for resistance, as Engels demonstrates in his study of Müntzer.

Jan Lochman summarizes Marx's point, "Religion is not the reason for a perverted world, but a perverted world is the root of religion."[39] Marx was more concerned with the *conditions* that lead to religious indifference than religion itself. And while we could argue that he misunderstood religion as purely a symptom, there is a vital insight behind his conclusion. Unfortunately, we miss the main point by becoming offended by his negative tone; but with the same approach, we might miss the prophets.

Further objections

The second primary objection regarding Marx is the issue of communism itself. Critics argue that Marxism has led to the deaths of millions.[40] But there is a double standard. The legacy of Marx receives enormous scrutiny, while we forgive other thinkers in history without a moment's hesitation. For example, why is Adam Smith, the founder of capitalist economics, not condemned for the millions of deaths under capitalism, such as needless deaths from hunger and disease? Or why is John Locke not judged for his role in privatizing the commons, which were the source of vital sustenance for the poor and needy? Indeed, why is Christianity not condemned for its role in slavery or the Crusades?

It is beyond the scope of this book to rehash the debate about communism's legacy. But what can be said in defense here is that an author is not wholly responsible for the actions their words inspire. Nietzsche inspired the Nazis, yet his work is still widely read and studied. Even the words of Christ have been used for devilish ends: from justifying colonialism, genocide, and slavery in the Americas, and even on the belts of the Nazi troops who claimed God was on their side as they committed their atrocities.

Many have rejected Christianity because of the acts of its followers. It is highly ironic for a faith that is perhaps most guilty of this very thing to turn a critical eye towards Marx because of what was done in his name. We Christians are familiar with defending Christ against those who have misused Christ's name. We judge the speck in another's eye while ignoring the log in our own.

Another objection is that Marxism cannot be a tool of analysis without becoming an ideology. The fear is that Marxism will infect the gospel and become a kind of secular messianic hope. The fear is perhaps warranted, but it is still not reason enough to wholly reject Marx.

But to answer the ideology question, think about it like this: You could technically call me a Newtonian because I have good reason to suspect that the laws of gravity are a fact of the created order. But a hypothetical "Newtonianism" is not the ideology that determines my life and faith. Instead, because Newton observed a natural law that God created, I might be called a Newtonian regarding how I understand natural phenomena. Likewise, you could call me a Shakespearean because of my great love for the Bard. But Shakespeare does not determine my life and faith—only my taste in poetry.

So, too, with Marx. His observations of society and economics, like Newton's observations of gravity and Shakespeare's of human nature, are worth taking seriously. That is because he is often right in what he concludes. It is a scientific judgment, not an ideological commitment. Many of his insights have been proven correct empirically, just as others have been proven false.[41] We can and should use whatever tools we have at our disposal to engage with our world. But, whether it is science, art, philosophy, or economics, we cannot rely wholly on the Bible to fulfill the mission of Jesus on this earth. Thus, we need Newton, Shakespeare, and perhaps even Marx to navigate our life and times.

If Marx's observations are false, then let them be false and make no more of it. But to reject them before even testing their validity is irrational. Because his insights have been proven correct and his penetrating analysis of capitalism has the potential to revolutionize the world for the better, he is worth reading and studying vigorously. The Church cannot be afraid of the truth, no matter what corner it comes from—even from the mouth of Marx.

Most other objections against Marx tend to rely on the ignorance of his actual work. However, Marx is not going away if we ignore him or refuse to read him, and the danger in this approach is that we might miss out on crucial insights regarding our world. Dorothee Soelle once compared the neglect of reading Marx to not reading the Hebrew prophets. When asked why she considered herself a Marxist, she replied, "How could you read Amos and Isaiah and not Karl Marx and Friedrich Engels? That would amount to being ungrateful to a God who sends prophets among us with the message that to know Yahweh means to do justice."[42]

In the same way that the prophets offered a critique of the systems of power that dominated their time, so today, Marx may be a prophetic voice against the global tyranny of capitalism that dominates every aspect of our lives. We do ourselves a disservice in the mission to help the poor if we ignore Marx's pioneering work in examining the systems of capitalism. If we care for the poor and strive to liberate the oppressed, we should read Marx.

Conclusion

Followers of Christ cannot ignore the cries of the poor and remain faithful to Christ, who became poor for our sake. To ignore the poor *is* to renounce Christ. Accordingly, we cannot overlook the systemic causes of poverty and should use every available tool to understand capitalism. For that, Marx is a valuable help. As Jan Lochman once observed, "If the Church evades the challenge of Karl Marx, she may easily find herself evading the biblical challenge itself."[43] Indeed, there are numerous biblical themes in the work of Marx that illustrate this point.[44]

The benefit of reading Marx is his scientific critique of capitalism. In studying his work, we realize that mammon's idolatry has today morphed into the idol of free-market capitalism and private property. Thus, the message of Christ today is anti-capitalist.

The similarities between radical anti-capitalism and the Christian faith are many. I have strived to show with this book just how dire it is for the Church to reconsider its approach to economic justice. In my mind, Marxism is a potential ally in that task. I am not suggesting we make Marxism an ideological *master*. Nothing comes before the gospel. But in our effort to proclaim and live out the message of God's Kingdom, Marxism may be a helpful tool for social analysis. To proclaim Christ's rebuke of mammon again today, we need to be anti-capitalist and scientifically analyze the systems of injustice that keep the poor bound to their misery as the rich continue to increase their hoarded wealth.

Marx sought to "overthrow all situations in which men are degraded, enslaved, abandoned, despised."[45] That is a goal the Church shares with Marx, or at least, it should. While we likely will not pursue this goal for the same reasons or in the same manner, we can and should recognize Marx as a fellow traveler down the path toward justice and peace. That is why his insights should be studied more broadly, especially regarding our task to recapture the radical anti-mammon witness of the gospel as found in the Church Fathers.

This proposal may seem out of place in a book on the Early Church, but it is necessary, in my eyes, due to the systemic nature of poverty. And it is also necessary because the questions examined by Marx are strikingly similar to those addressed by the Early Church. Thus, if we want to talk about poverty *superficially*, then, by all means, we can ignore the causes of poverty and, likewise, Marxism as a helpful critic of them. But if we take Christ's command to liberate the captive and proclaim good news to the poor seriously, then we must analyze our world to proclaim this message anew to our situation.

10

CONCLUSION

We began by asking, "Can a Christian be a capitalist?" I think I have more than played my hand in suggesting how I think we should answer. Christ's anti-mammon mandate negates the possibility of accepting uncritically any economic system that prioritizes mammon above all else. Capitalism is a system of mammon worship, where everything serves one aim: capital accumulation at all costs.

The mad pursuit of riches is detrimental to all involved;[1] capitalism is the institutionalized form of that pursuit, where the only thing that matters is accumulating more and more wealth. The real purpose of wealth is to help the needy. But capitalism places accumulation above the needs of the poor. The Christian message is thus inherently anti-capitalist because it is against the idolatry of mammon.

So a capitalist might become a Christian and be saved by Christ (the question was never about salvation, mind you). However, a Christian cannot rightly follow *the way* of Jesus Christ while also following the way of capital/mammon. That is a conclusion about political ethics, though it is not unrelated to salvation. As James realized, faith must bear fruit, or it is not faith. This answer parallels how the Early Church dealt with the salvation of the rich. Can the rich be saved? Yes, all things are possible by grace, but being genuinely repentant will compel them to no longer be rich! So today, we might suggest: Can a Christian be a capitalist? Yes, but after becoming a Christian, a repentant capitalist will follow Christ in solidarity with the poor and needy. Accordingly, they will join the struggle of the working class for total liberation from mammon and the overthrow of capitalism.

My hope in all this has been to provoke thought and challenge the status quo. I made that clear from the beginning of this book—even from the title. Of course, it is unlikely that everyone reading these words will agree with my conclusions, but I hope at least the ideas presented here will be seriously considered and given their due weight. And ultimately, this work is only a preliminary study, which focused mainly on the Early Church by collecting some of their radical sayings. A forthcoming volume will begin where we have left off by transforming the anti-mammon witness of the gospel into a more substantial political ethic. But the goal here has been to provoke more questions than answers, to unsettle the assumed neutrality of the gospel in the face of economic injustice, to refuse to water down the radical message of Christ, and to challenge the Church to reconsider the vitality of standing up against mammon.

Anti-capitalist theses

This book proposes eight theses for a Christian anti-capitalist political ethic. Allow me to summarize these before we conclude.

1. The Bible harshly rebukes riches and forbids the service of mammon as unjust; the gospel is unrecognizable without the prophetic critique of power and wealth; mammon is a rival god and must be condemned for Christ's sake.
2. The Early Church took Christ's anti-mammon teaching so seriously that it debated whether or not the rich can be saved; their general conclusion was this: the rich are sinners who can be saved by faith *but* they must prove their faith by repenting and renouncing mammon through good works of charity/almsgiving.
3. The earth is the Lord's and was created for all in common; riches are unjust because they take what God gave for the sustenance of all God's creatures and turn it into a private means of profit.
4. Accordingly, hoarded wealth is theft from the poor and needy; the rich are murderers of the poor because they have collected for their private enjoyment what God has given for the benefit of all; the poor are not poor by accident but are made poor by the exploitation of the rich.
5. Luxury is incompatible with Christian discipleship; the way of Christ is contentment; economically, this means prioritizing the needs of the many over the luxuries of the few.
6. Usury usurps God's rightful Lordship over time; charging interest is sin and goes against the will of God for creation; capitalism is unthinkable without usury, and therefore, the historical rejection

of usury in the Church must become for us today the basis of a Christian anti-capitalist ethic.
7. Mammon is a rival god that can only be hated or loved; mammon is a system of worship, which today is called "capitalism," and it is a system with one inhumane, ungodly commandment: accumulate.
8. The witness of Scripture and the Early Church points to the necessity of socioeconomic analysis and anti-capitalism; the scientific economics of Karl Marx is a helpful *tool* for the Church's proclamation of the Kingdom of God and the critique of mammon because it analyzes the current idolatry of mammon and corresponds with the historical witness of the Early Church; thus, the Church today must be anti-capitalist to be faithful to the anti-mammon message of Jesus.

Hope

Finally, perhaps most dire today is reigniting our radical hope for the Kingdom to come. *A better world is possible.* Accepting, without struggle, the sinful systems of this world as if immovable, as if this is how things must always be—that attitude goes against the Christian way of hope. The way of hope cannot accept the world as it is because of a radical expectation for what it must become. Thus, in anticipation of Kingdom come, we strive for a world of true justice and liberty without oppression and economic violence. We have no illusions, however. We are not capable of doing any of this by ourselves. But, by God's grace, we can and will work together to end the tyranny of mammon by joining the poor in solidarity in their struggle for liberty. Our radical hope excludes giving up on anyone; thus, while I have and will continue to condemn the rich and powerful, they, too, need liberation from their pathological will to power. But their liberation will come with the liberation of all those they oppress, not a moment before.

Capitalism as a system of sinful injustice and violence may seem permanent, but that is just an illusion; a better world is possible, and it is already in our midst like a mustard seed. Ursula K. Le Guin articulated something of this hope when she said:

> We live in capitalism. Its power seems inescapable. So did the divine right of kings. Any human power can be resisted and challenged by human beings.[2]

Radical hope in the Kingdom of God is essential to Christianity.[3] The forward-looking position of our hope causes us to reject the status quo as unchangeable or unchallengeable. Just because this is how it has been done, because we live in capitalism, does not make the systems of this world immovable realities we must accept without protest. On the contrary, because we hope in the coming reign of God, we contradict this world and its sinful systems of injustice and mammon worship. The Church of Jesus Christ cannot accept systems of oppression and exploitation without giving up its foundational hope.

The greatest threat to our hope is not doubt but indifference and apathy. Our thinking has been infected by what Mark Fisher calls "capitalist realism," which is the belief that capitalism is the *only possible* system. The hegemonic assumption of neoliberalism, sometimes unspoken but often declared with celebration, that no other system is possible. Consequently, there is no hope outside the exploitation of the poor and weak by the rich and powerful in their endless quest for capital accumulation at all costs. Even if this means the end of life on earth as we know it due to climate change, capitalist realism echoes Thatcher's slogan, "There is no alternative." The pervasive atmosphere described by this term is one in which there is no escape from capitalism, that it can only be accepted or reformed but never overcome and replaced.

But to give up hope and cling to apathy is to deny the resurrection. It is to deny the God who raises the dead, having first raised Israel from the hopeless pit of Egyptian captivity. This hopelessness is the total denial of Christian faith. Our task today is not to accept capitalism without protest—to accept the economic idolatry of mammon—but to declare our radical hope with renewed passion. Another world is possible! The Kingdom of God is among us. Change your mind, repent, and anticipate the reign of God.

Jesus is Lord—not mammon!

NOTES

Introduction

1. Oxfam, 2017: https://www.oxfam.org/en/press-releases/just-8-men-own-same-wealth-half-world. Accessed 2/27/23. The gap has only increased since 2017.
2. *Carta* 120 PL 22, Col. 984. Quoted in John C. Cort, *Christian Socialism*, 48. Maryknoll, NY: Orbis Press, 1988
3. I was unable to locate the source of this oft-quoted aphorism, but it is widely attributed to Tutu. For example: https://www.thenationalnews.com/arts-culture/books/2021/12/26/a-look-back-at-desmond-tutus-greatest-quotes-from-kindness-to-forgiveness/. Accessed March 30, 2023.
4. *Communism in the Bible*, 21. Maryknoll, New York: Orbis Books, 1982.
5. Peter Brown, *Through the Eye of a Needle*, 5. Princeton University Press, 2012.
6. See chapter 2 for this illustration.
7. *The Enchantments of Mammon*, 11. Cambridge, Massachusetts: Harvard University Press, 2019.
8. Marx's concept of "commodity fetishism" is relevant here, but a full examination is outside the scope of this book. Many others have commented on capitalism as the religion of modernity. See especially Eugene McCarraher's *The Enchantments of Mammon*, but also Max Webber's *The Protestant Ethic and the Spirit of Capitalism*, and R. H. Tawney's *Religion and the Rise of Capitalism*.
9. Karl Marx and Frederick Engels, *The Communist Manifesto*, 12. New York: International Publishers, 2017.
10. Ibid., 12.
11. Unless otherwise noted, biblical quotes are from the New Revised Standard Version (NRSV), 1989.
12. I expect to complete that book sometime in 2024 or 2025.

1. Biblical Foundations

1. *Atheism in Christianity*, 21. Swann, New York: Herder and Herder, 1972.
2. Cited in *Oscar Romero: Reflections on His life and Writings*, 39. Written by Marie Dennis, Renny Golden, and Scott Wright. Maryknoll, NY: Orbis Books, 2000.
3. See Richard Horsley, *Jesus and Empire*. See page 28 for the use of crucifixion to terrorize the public and pages 129-130 for the case of Yeshua ben Hananiah, a *religious* messiah who was not executed by Rome. Minneapolis, MN: Augsburg Fortress, 2003.
4. *All Things in Common*, 12. Eugene, OR: Wipf & Stock, 2017.
5. *Communism in the Bible*, 68. Maryknoll, New York: Orbis Books, 1982.
6. See Gustavo Gutiérrez: *A Theology of Liberation*.
7. See Hollis Phelps' thorough argument on this point. *Jesus and the Politics of Mammon*. Eugene, OR: Cascade Books, 2019.
8. *Communism in the Bible*, 64. Maryknoll, New York: Orbis Books, 1982.
9. Friedrich Hauck, "Μαμωνᾶς," ed. Gerhard Kittel, Geoffrey W. Bromiley, and Gerhard Friedrich, Theological Dictionary of the New Testament (Grand Rapids, MI: Eerdmans, 1964–), 389–390.
10. Bruce J. Malina and Richard L. Rohrbaugh, *Social-Science Commentary on the Synoptic gospels*, 324. Minneapolis: Fortress Press, 1992.
11. *Carta* 120 PL 22, Col. 984. See chapter two for the full quote.
12. Scholars do not think Israel ever practiced the year of Jubilee. But it is an important concept to Israel's identity, and most of all, it is used by Jesus to define his ministry in Luke 4.

13. See Robert Alter: *The Art of Biblical Poetry*, chapter one.
14. *Theological Dictionary of the New Testament*, IV, 324.
15. I am thinking in particular of the debate between N. T. Wright and John Piper regarding Paul's concept of justification. The merits of that debate notwithstanding, I suspect Paul's words in 1 Corinthians 13 are apt, that knowledge of the mysteries of God without love for the least of these is empty.
16. *All Things in Common*, 122. Eugene, OR: Wipf & Stock, 2017.
17. This global system is called "imperialism." The economic violence of exploitation is enforced by military violence, most recently through the actions of the US military. South American history contains dozens of examples of this tendency. The "free market" is enforced by the barrel of a gun. See *Washington's Bullets* by Vijay Prashad.
18. Quoted in Eugene McCarraher, *The Enchantments of Mammon*, 666. Harvard University Press, 2019.
19. Scholars do not think Paul wrote the two letters to Timothy that we find in the New Testament. But I retain the traditional convention of referring to Paul as the author for simplicity. For our purposes, the authorship of the letter is not the point, but rather what the text says.
20. *The Kingdom New Testament*, 431. Grand Rapids, Michigan: Zondervan, 2011.
21. Quoted in Helen Rhee, *Wealth and Poverty in Early Christianity*, 41. Minneapolis: Fortress Press, 2017.

2. Can the Rich be Saved?

1. *Faith & Wealth*, 116. San Francisco, Ca: Harper & Row Publishers, 1990.
2. See Jürgen Moltmann: *The Way of Jesus Christ*.
3. I discuss this point some in *James Cone in Plain English*. See Cone's *The Cross and the Lynching Tree* and *Black Theology and Black Power*. See also, Willie James Jennings' *After Whiteness*, and Robert P. Jones' *White Too Long*.
4. *The Didache*, §1, §5; *The Apostolic Fathers*, 123, 125. Translated and edited by J. B Lightfoot. Grand Rapid: Baker Books, 1971.
5. https://www.cnn.com/2021/12/11/business/amazon-deaths-warehouse-tornado/index.html. It could be argued that this was not Amazon's fault, but that is to overlook the pattern of abuse. Amazon workers are injured at a far higher rate than other warehouse workers: https://www.bbc.com/news/technology-57332390.
6. *The Shepherd of Hermas*, parable 9, section 20; *The Apostolic Fathers*, 234. Translated and edited by J. B Lightfoot. Grand Rapid: Baker Books, 1971.
7. *First Nations Version*. Downers Grove, IL: InterVarsity Press, 2021.
8. Ziemińska, Agnieszka. "The Origin of the 'Needle's Eye Gate' Myth: Theophylact or Anselm?" *New Testament Studies* 68, no. 3 (2022): 358–61. doi:10.1017/S0028688521000448.
9. *Shepherd of Hermas*, Vision 3, 6; *The Apostolic Fathers*, 174. Translated and edited by J. B Lightfoot. Grand Rapid: Baker Books, 1971.
10. *Homilies on Luke and Fragments on Luke*, ed. Thomas P. Halton, trans. Joseph T. Lienhard, vol. 94, The Fathers of the Church (Washington, DC: The Catholic University of America Press, 2009), 216–217.
11. "Homilies of St. John Chrysostom, Archbishop of Constantinople on the gospel according to St. Matthew," in *Saint Chrysostom: Homilies on the gospel of Saint Matthew*, ed. Philip Schaff, trans. George Prevost and M. B. Riddle, vol. 10, A Select Library of the Nicene and Post-Nicene Fathers of the Christian Church, First Series (New York: Christian Literature Company, 1888), 449–450.
12. González, *The Story of Christianity, Volume 1*, 227. New York: HarperCollins, 2010.
13. *Theology of Hope*, 21. Minneapolis: Fortress Press, 1993.
14. "Homilies of St. John Chrysostom, Archbishop of Constantinople, on the First Epistle of St. Paul the Apostle to the Corinthians," in *Saint Chrysostom: Homilies on the Epistles of Paul to the Corinthians*, ed. Philip Schaff, trans. Hubert Kestell Cornish, John Medley, and Talbot B. Chambers, vol. 12, A Select Library of the Nicene and Post-Nicene Fathers of the Christian Church, First Series (New York: Christian Literature Company, 1889), 76.

15. Quoted in Justo González, *The Story of Christianity, Volume 1*, 228. New York: HarperCollins, 2010.
16. "Homilies of St. John Chrysostom, Archbishop of Constantinople, on the First Epistle of St. Paul the Apostle to the Thessalonians," in *Saint Chrysostom: Homilies on Galatians, Ephesians, Philippians, Colossians, Thessalonians, Timothy, Titus, and Philemon*, ed. Philip Schaff, trans. James Tweed and John Albert Broadus, vol. 13, A Select Library of the Nicene and Post-Nicene Fathers of the Christian Church, First Series (New York: Christian Literature Company, 1889), 374.
17. *Fall of Eutropius*, 2.3. Quoted in John Haughey, *The Faith That Does Justice*, 128. Eugene: Wipf & Stock Publishers, 2006.
18. *The Spirit of Hope*, 10.
19. Peter Brown, *Through the Eye of a Needle*, 142. Princeton University Press, 2012.
20. It is probable that retaining order and a peaceful coexistence with Rome was one of the prime reasons for the pharisees to hand Jesus over to be crucified. The Zealots did revolt eventually, leading to the brutal destruction of Jerusalem in 70 AD. So the fears that Jesus might cause a revolt resulting in a Roman siege were valid.
21. "The Letters of St. Jerome," in *St. Jerome: Letters and Select Works*, ed. Philip Schaff and Henry Wace, trans. W. H. Fremantle, G. Lewis, and W. G. Martley, vol. 6, A Select Library of the Nicene and Post-Nicene Fathers of the Christian Church, Second Series (New York: Christian Literature Company, 1893), 16.
22. This eventually lead to the practice of penance and buying indulgences in the middle ages, a practice the reformers rejected. For a fascinating study on the way Christians understood almsgiving and the afterlife, see Peter Brown *The Ransom of the Soul* (Harvard University Press, 2015).
23. *Vita Pauli* 17, 28C. Quoted in Peter Brown, *Through the Eye of a Needle*, 266-7.
24. Ibid., 267.
25. Quoted Ibid.
26. *Life of Saint Martin*, 24.4-5. Quoted in Peter Brown, *Through the Eye of a Needle*, 217. Princeton University Press, 2012.
27. *Through the Eye of a Needle*, 185. Princeton University Press, 2012.
28. Ibid., 186.
29. Quoted Ibid., 217.
30. The process of giving away his wealth was gradual and likely not as extreme as Augustine says here. Paulinus never become poor in the sense of struggling to survive. But he *humbled himself*, as Christ humbled himself to become human. He spent a good portion of his fortune on a building project dedicated to St. Felix.

3. The Earth is Common

1. https://www.huffpost.com/entry/world-hunger_b_1463429. Accessed August 26, 2022.
2. *Faith & Wealth*, 177. San Francisco, Ca: Harper & Row Publishers, 1990.
3. *Ownership: Early Christian Teaching*, 79. Maryknoll, New York: Orbis Books, 1983.
4. Justo L. González: "Jewish property rights were limited by the rights of God, by the rights of the property itself, which must not be abused, and by the rights of the needy—the poor, the sojourner, the orphan, and the widow. Along these lines the commandment against stealing is to be understood, not as a safeguard for the rights of private property, but rather as a safeguard against abuse that would destroy life." *Faith & Wealth*, 22. San Francisco, Ca: Harper & Row Publishers, 1990.
5. *Paidagogos* Chapter 12, book 2. Quoted in Charles Avila, *Ownership*, 37. Maryknoll, NY: Orbis Books, 1983. Final sentence quoted in Helen Rhee, *Loving the Poor, Saving the Rich*, 171. Grand Rapids: Baker Academic, 2012.
6. Justo L. González. *Faith and Wealth*, 83. New York: Harper & Row, Publishers, 1990.
7. Quoted in Justo L. González, *Faith and Wealth*, 95. New York: Harper & Row, Publishers, 1990.
8. *The Instructor*, 3.6.34 Quoted in Father James Thorton, *Wealth and Poverty in the Teachings of the Church Fathers*, 68. Berkley: St. John Chrysostom Press, 1993.
9. Justo L. González. *Faith and Wealth*, 115. New York: Harper & Row, Publishers, 1990.

10. For more on Sankara's life and the data for these statistics, see Ernest Harsch's *Thomas Sankara: An African Revolutionary*. Athens: Ohio University Press, 2014.
11. *Apol.* 39. Quoted in Justo L. González: *Faith and Wealth*, 120. New York: Harper & Row, 1990. He cites the Latin original of the last two sentences: "*Itaque qui animo animaque miscemur, nihil de rei communicatione dubitamus. Omnia indiscreta sunt apud nos, praeter uxores.*"
12. *The Communist Manifesto*, 27. New York: International Publishers, 2017. Marx argues that the capitalist class makes this objection because they see their own women as mere instruments of production. But the communist goal is to liberate women from that role: "He [the bourgeois] has not even the suspicion that the real point aimed at is to do away with the status of women as mere instruments of production." See Engels, *The Origin of the Family*, for an expanded analysis of capitalism, communism, and the liberation of women. The basic argument is that capitalism has enslaved women (remember this was written long before feminism), and that socialism will be the liberation of women. Thus, from the beginning, socialism was connected with the feminist liberation movement.
13. *The Divine Institutes*, 5.14. Quoted in Helen Rhee, *Wealth and Poverty in Early Christianity*, 49-50. Minneapolis: Fortress Press, 2017.
14. See Helen Rhee, *Wealth and Poverty in Early Christianity*, xxix. Minneapolis: Fortress Press, 2017.
15. *Duties of the Clergy*, 1.132. Quoted in Justo L. González, *Faith and Wealth*, 191. New York: Harper & Row, Publishers, 1990.
16. *Through the Eye of a Needle*, 78. Princeton University Press, 2012.
17. Ibid., 122.
18. Helen Rhee, *Wealth and Poverty in Early Christianity*, xxxix. Minneapolis, Fortress Press, 2017.
19. Smith, J. Warren (2021). "12: *Societas* and *Misericordia* in Ambrose' theology of community." In Gannaway, Ethan; Grant, Robert (eds.). *Ambrose of Milan and Community Formation in Late Antiquity*. Cambridge Scholars Publishing.
20. *Summa Theologica*, II-II, Q 66, Art 7.
21. *On Naboth*, 2. Quoted Helen Rhee, *Wealth and Poverty in Early Christianity*, 105-6. Minneapolis: Fortress Press, 2017.
22. Ibid., 105.
23. *De Officiis Ministrorum*, 1, 28. Quoted in Charles Avila, *Ownership*, 37. Maryknoll, NY: Orbis Books, 1983.
24. *Enarratio in Psalmum CXXXI*, 5, *PL* 37:1718; ibid, 6-7. Quoted in Charles Avila: *Ownership*, 120. Maryknoll, New York: Orbis Books, 1983.
25. Peter Brown, *Through the Eye of a Needle*, 177. Princeton University Press, 2012.
26. Cited ibid., 180.
27. Quoted Ibid., 162.
28. *Letter* 243.2. Quoted in Peter Brown, *Through the Eye of a Needle*, 182. Princeton University Press, 2012.
29. Ibid., 181.
30. Ibid., 179.
31. Letter 243.2, cited ibid., 182.
32. Ibid., 180.
33. Cited ibid., 183.
34. Property rights were central to Roman law, as González notes, "[T]he rights of property owners were the backbone of Roman law[.]" *Faith and Wealth*, 18. New York: Harper & Row, Publishers, 1990.
35. *Homilies on the Psalms*, Ps. 14, 1.6. Quoted in Father James Thornton, *Wealth and Poverty in the Teachings of the Church Fathers*, 84. Berkley: St. John Chrysostom Press, 1993.
36. "Critique of the Gotha Programme" in Marx: *The Political Writings*, 1031. Brooklyn, NY: Verso, 2019. This is one of the few examples of Marx describing an "advanced phase of communist society." He was not prone to speculate about such a society, but this is a rare example of some description of what an ideal communist system might look like after the intermediary stage of socialism, or a less advanced phase.
37. Examples include Gerrard Winstanley (founder of the Diggers), Wilhelm Weitling, Saint-Simon, and Pierre Leroux, among others.
38. *Fidel & Religion*, 15. New York: Ocean Press, 2006.

39. https://www.americamagazine.org/faith/2022/11/28/pope-francis-interview-america-244225. Accessed 2/20/2023.
40. *Fifth Homily on the Beatitudes.* Quoted in Father James Thornton, *Wealth and Poverty in the Teachings of the Church Fathers,* 96. Berkley: St. John Chrysostom Press, 1993.
41. *Race a Theological Account,* 231. Oxford University Press, 2008.
42. *Fourth Homily.* Quoted in Mako A. Nagasawa, *Abortion Policy and Christian Social Ethics in the United States,* 149. Eugene: Wipf & Stock, 2021.
43. For an important analysis of Gregory's argument as it relates to a theology of race, see J. Kameron Carter's *Race: A Theological Account,* 230-251. Oxford University Press, 2008. By no means do I intend to downplay the racial significance of Gregory's argument, but his logic is useful for the modern condition of wage-labor, which is only barely distinguishable from slavery. While this notion of wage-labor can be found in Marx, it is actually instructive to see that it can be traced back further to Gerrard Winstanley and the radical Christian Diggers Movement. See his 1649 pamphlet, *The New Law of Righteousness.* Thus, the argument that wage-labor is a kind of slavery was originally a Christian idea.
44. "Homilies of St. John Chrysostom, Archbishop of Constantinople, on the First Epistle of St. Paul the Apostle to the Corinthians," in *Saint Chrysostom: Homilies on the Epistles of Paul to the Corinthians,* ed. Philip Schaff, trans. Hubert Kestell Cornish, John Medley, and Talbot B. Chambers, vol. 12, A Select Library of the Nicene and Post-Nicene Fathers of the Christian Church, First Series (New York: Christian Literature Company, 1889), 57.
45. "Homilies of St. John Chrysostom, Archbishop of Constantinople, on the Second Epistle of St. Paul the Apostle to the Corinthians," in *Saint Chrysostom: Homilies on the Epistles of Paul to the Corinthians,* ed. Philip Schaff, trans. J. Ashworth and Talbot B. Chambers, vol. 12, A Select Library of the Nicene and Post-Nicene Fathers of the Christian Church, First Series (New York: Christian Literature Company, 1889), 340–341.
46. *In Dictum Pauli,* "Oportet Haereses Esse," 2. Quoted in Charles Avila: *Ownership,* 86. Maryknoll, New York: Orbis Books, 1983.
47. *Pastoral Rule,* book III, admonition 22. Quoted in John C. Cort, *Christian Socialism,* 51. Maryknoll, NY: Orbis Books, 1988.

4. Hoarded Wealth is Theft

1. *All Things in Common,* 60-1. Eugene, OR: Wipf & Stock, 2017.
2. We will return to this point in chapter eight. There are, of course, more complex factors at work in poverty, but most of the time, upon careful analysis, poverty is a necessary fruit of capitalism as the rich exploit the poor. As an economic system, capitalism *needs* poverty.
3. *The Shepherd of Hermas,* vision 3, 9. *The Apostolic Fathers,* 176. Translated and edited by J. B Lightfoot. Grand Rapid: Baker Books, 1971.
4. *Concerning the Rich Man's Salvation,* 15. Quoted in John C. Cort, *Christian Socialism,* 47. Maryknoll, NY: Orbis Books, 1988.
5. Inst. 6.11.18-9. Quoted in Helen Rhee, *Loving the Poor, Saving the Rich,* 136. Grand Rapids: Baker Academic, 2012.
6. Homily 6: "I Will Pull Down My Barns." Quoted in Father James Thornton, *Wealth and Poverty in the Teachings of the Church Fathers,* 80. Berkley: St. John Chrysostom Press, 1993. This is an often quoted saying from Basil. See also Helen Rhee, *Wealth and Poverty in Early Christianity,* 59-60.
7. Homily 7, "To the Rich." Quoted in John C. Cort, *Christian Socialism,* 44. Maryknoll, NY: Orbis Press, 1988.
8. Homily 6, "I Will Pull Down My Barns." Quoted in *Wealth and Poverty in Early Christianity,* Helen Rhee, 57. Minneapolis: Fortress Press, 2017.
9. *Through the Eye of a Needle,* 15. Princeton University Press, 2012.
10. Quoted in Helen Rhee, *Wealth and Poverty in Early Christianity,* 59. Minneapolis: Fortress Press, 2017.
11. Homily 6, *I Will Pull Down My Barns.* Quoted in Father James Thornton, *Wealth and Poverty in the Teachings of the Church Fathers,* 89. Berkley: St. John Chrysostom Press, 1993.
12. *Against Empire,* 208. San Franciso: City Lights Books, 1995.

13. https://forloveofwater.org/water-privatization-the-struggle-to-stop-nestles-groundwater-grab-continues/. Accessed April 3, 2023.
14. Homily 8, *In Time of Famine and Drought*. Quoted in Helen Rhee, *Wealth and Poverty in Early Christianity*, 66-7. Minneapolis: Fortress Press, 2017.
15. *The Condition of the Working Class in England*, 95.
16. Quoted in George D. Herron, *Between Caesar and Jesus* (1899), 111-2.
17. Sources: poverty.com, unwater.org, chop.edu.
18. *On the Love of the Poor*, 19. Quoted in Father James Thornton, *Wealth and Poverty in the Teachings of the Church Fathers*, 93. Berkley: St. John Chrysostom Press, 1993.
19. Ibid, 26.
20. Quoted in Father James Thornton, *Wealth and Poverty in the Teachings of the Church Fathers*, 60. Berkley: St. John Chrysostom Press, 1993.
21. Cited Ibid., 61.
22. *De Nabuthe*, 11. Quoted in Charles Avila: *Ownership*, 66-7. Maryknoll, New York: Orbis Books, 1983.
23. Justo L. González, *Faith & Wealth*, 189. San Francisco, Ca: Harper & Row Publishers, 1990.
24. *Decretum*, I, 47, 8. Quoted in Thomas Aquinas, *Summa Theologiae*, 2a2ae, 77, 7, Vol. 38, 81.
25. *Faith & Wealth*, 227. San Francisco, Ca: Harper & Row Publishers, 1990.
26. *De Nabuthe, Patrologiase Cursus* PL 14. Quoted in José Miranda, *Marx and the Bible*, 16. Maryknoll, NY: Orbis Books, 1974.
27. *De Nabuthe Jez.* 56, PL. Quoted in Justo González, *Faith and Wealth*, 190. New York: Harper & Row, Publishers, 1990.
28. *Catech. Illum*, 1.15. Quoted in Susan Holman, ed., *Wealth and Poverty in Early Church and Society*, 128. Grand Rapids: Baker Academic, 2008.
29. *Homilies on the Rich Man and Lazarus*, 2.4. The second paragraph is quoted in Charles Avila: *Ownership*, 83-4. Maryknoll, New York: Orbis Books, 1983. The rest of the quote is from Helen Rhee, *Wealth and Poverty in Early Christianity*, 87-8. Minneapolis: Fortress Press, 2017.
30. On Lazarus, Homily 11. See also 1 Cor. Homily 10:3. Quoted in John C. Cort, *Christian Socialism*, 45. Maryknoll, NY: Orbis Press, 1988.
31. Quoted Helen Rhee, *Wealth and Poverty in Early Christianity*, 100. Minneapolis: Fortress Press, 2017.
32. Ibid., 99.
33. *Homilies on the First Letter to Timothy*. Quoted Helen Rhee, *Wealth and Poverty in Early Christianity*, 101-2. Minneapolis: Fortress Press, 2017.
34. *On the Trinity*, PL 42, Col. 1046. Latin version: *Iustitia est in subveniendo miseris*. Quoted in John C. Cort, *Christian Socialism*, 48. Maryknoll, NY: Orbis Press, 1988.
35. *Sermon 50*.
36. Exposition on Ps. 147:12. Quoted in Mako A. Nagasawa, *Abortion Policy and Christian Social Ethics in the United States*, 150. Eugene, Oregon: Wipf & Stock, 2021.
37. *In Epistolam ad Timotheum*, 12, 4, *PG* 62:562-63. Quoted in Charles Avila, *Ownership*, 141. Maryknoll, NY: Orbis Books, 1983.

5. Contentment and the Sin of Luxury

1. *Economic and Philosophic Manuscripts of 1844*, Collected Works volume 3, Progress Publishers, 1975. P. 309.
2. For this and the context of clothing in Rome see Peter Brown, *Through the Eye of a Needle*, 27-8. Princeton University Press, 2012.
3. *Address to the Greeks*, IV, 1. Quoted in Father James Thornton, *Wealth and Poverty in the Teachings of the Church Fathers*, 64. Berkley: St. John Chrysostom Press, 1993.
4. *The Shepherd of Hermas*, Mandate 8; *The Apostolic Fathers*, 190. Translated and edited by J. B Lightfoot. Grand Rapid: Baker Books, 1971.
5. *The Shepherd of Hermas*, Mandate 12, 1-2; *The Apostolic Fathers*, 196-7. Translated and edited by J. B Lightfoot. Grand Rapid: Baker Books, 1971.

6. "Irenæus against Heresies," in *The Apostolic Fathers with Justin Martyr and Irenaeus*, ed. Alexander Roberts, James Donaldson, and A. Cleveland Coxe, vol. 1, The Ante-Nicene Fathers (Buffalo, NY: Christian Literature Company, 1885), 464.
7. Paed. 2.13.120. Quoted in Helen Rhee, *Loving the Poor, Saving the Rich,* 170. Grand Rapids: Baker Academic, 2012.
8. See part seven in Marx's *Capital: A Critique of Political Economy, Volume 1.* Translated by Ben Fowkes. London: Penguin Classics, 1990.
9. *Paidagogos,* chapter 8 book 3. Quoted in Charles Avila, *Ownership,* 42. Maryknoll, NY: Orbis Books, 1983.
10. *On Patience, 7.* Quoted in Helen Rhee, *Wealth and Poverty in Early Christianity,* 37-8. Minneapolis, Fortress Press, 2017.
11. Ibid., 36.
12. *To Have or To Be?,* 101. New York: Harper and Row Publishers, 1976. Italics from the original were removed.
13. Ibid., 102.
14. "Fragments from Commentaries on Various Books of Scripture," in *Fathers of the Third Century: Hippolytus, Cyprian, Novatian, Appendix,* ed. Alexander Roberts, James Donaldson, and A. Cleveland Coxe, trans. S. D. F. Salmond, vol. 5, The Ante-Nicene Fathers (Buffalo, NY: Christian Literature Company, 1886), 194.
15. "On the Jewish Meats," in Fathers of the Third Century: Hippolytus, Cyprian, Novatian, Appendix, ed. Alexander Roberts, James Donaldson, and A. Cleveland Coxe, trans. Robert Ernest Wallis, vol. 5, The Ante-Nicene Fathers (Buffalo, NY: Christian Literature Company, 1886), 648.
16. Ibid.
17. *On the Love of the Poor.* Quoted in Helen Rhee, *Wealth and Poverty in Early Christianity,* 71-2. Minneapolis: Fortress Press, 2017.
18. *On the Love of the Poor.* Quoted in Helen Rhee, *Wealth and Poverty in Early Christianity,* 73-74. Minneapolis: Fortress Press, 2017.
19. *The love of the Poor,* 25.3. Quoted in Father James Thornton, *Wealth and Poverty in the Teachings of the Church Fathers,* 113. Berkley: St. John Chrysostom Press, 1993.
20. *The Love of the Poor,* 11.5. Quoted in Father James Thornton, *Wealth and Poverty in the Teachings of the Church Fathers,* 112-3. Berkley: St. John Chrysostom Press, 1993.
21. *De Nabuthe,* col. 748. Quoted in Charles Avila, *Ownership,* 65. Maryknoll, NY: Orbis Books, 1983.
22. "Homilies of St. John Chrysostom, Archbishop of Constantinople, on the Epistle of St. Paul to the Romans," in *Saint Chrysostom: Homilies on the Acts of the Apostles and the Epistle to the Romans,* ed. Philip Schaff, trans. J. B. Morris, W. H. Simcox, and George B. Stevens, vol. 11, A Select Library of the Nicene and Post-Nicene Fathers of the Christian Church, First Series (New York: Christian Literature Company, 1889), 374–375.
23. "Homilies of St. John Chrysostom, Archbishop of Constantinople, on the Epistle of St. Paul the Apostle to the Colossians," in *Saint Chrysostom: Homilies on Galatians, Ephesians, Philippians, Colossians, Thessalonians, Timothy, Titus, and Philemon,* ed. Philip Schaff, trans. J. Ashworth and John Albert Broadus, vol. 13, A Select Library of the Nicene and Post-Nicene Fathers of the Christian Church, First Series (New York: Christian Literature Company, 1889), 308.
24. "Homilies of St. John Chrysostom, Archbishop of Constantinople, on the gospel of St. John," in *Saint Chrysostom: Homilies on the gospel of St. John and Epistle to the Hebrews,* ed. Philip Schaff, trans. G. T. Stupart, vol. 14, A Select Library of the Nicene and Post-Nicene Fathers of the Christian Church, First Series (New York: Christian Literature Company, 1889), 281.
25. Commentary on Psalms. Quoted in John C. Cort, *Christian Socialism,* 48. Maryknoll, NY: Orbis Books, 1988.

6. Usury

1. Quoted in Jacques le Goff, *Your Money or Your Life,* 39. New York, NY: Zone Books, 1998.

2. Cited https://poorwithus.com/2019/06/25/usury-and-the-Church/ footnote 9. Accessed June 21, 2022. The above list of councils that condemn usury is also from this source.
3. {$NOTE_LABEL}. https://www.experian.com/blogs/ask-experian/consumer-credit-review/. Accessed July 16,2022.
4. *Quis Dives Salvetur.* Quoted in Charles Avila, *Ownership,* 44. Maryknoll, NY: Orbis Books, 1983.
5. *Apol.* 39. Quoted in Justo L. González, *Faith & Wealth,* 121. San Francisco, Ca: Harper & Row Publishers, 1990.
6. *Tractatus in Psalm XIV,* PL 9, 307. Quoted in James Simon Watkins, *Religion and the Global Money Markets,* 78-9. Springer International Publishing, 2022.
7. See *Wealth of Nations,* chapter 11. https://www.gutenberg.org/files/38194/38194-h/38194-h.htm#Page_74.
8. *Wealth of Nations,* 21. https://www.gutenberg.org/files/38194/38194-h/38194-h.htm#Page_74. Accessed March 3, 2023.
9. "Prolegomena: Sketch of the Life and Works of Saint Basil," in *St. Basil: Letters and Select Works,* ed. Philip Schaff and Henry Wace, vol. 8, A Select Library of the Nicene and Post-Nicene Fathers of the Christian Church, Second Series (New York: Christian Literature Company, 1895), xlvii–xlix.
10. This is from the *Acts of Thomas,* a third-century apocryphal text. It was rejected by the Church for its docetic connotations. But this story is a fascinating example of the logic behind why almsgiving was considered a saving act. See Helen Rhee, *Loving the Poor, Saving the Rich,* 67-70. Grand Rapids: Baker Academic, 2012.
11. Homily 45. Cited http://forums.orthodoxchristianity.net/threads/Church-fathers-on-usury.66181/. Accessed August 30, 2022.
12. *On Tobias,* 14.46. Quoted at https://lendhopingnothing.wordpress.com/ambrose-on-tobias/, citing primary source: http://www.povertystudies.org/Ambrose_DeTobia_Zucker.pdf.
13. *On Tobias,* 3.11. Cited https://lendhopingnothing.wordpress.com/ambrose-on-tobias/.
14. *Homilies on the gospel of St. Matthew,* 5.9. Quoted in Helen Rhee, *Loving the Poor, Saving the Rich,* 89. Grand Rapids: Baker Academic, 2012.
15. https://www.theguardian.com/sustainable-business/2017/jul/10/100-fossil-fuel-companies-investors-responsible-71-global-emissions-cdp-study-climate-change. Accessed March 8, 2023.
16. https://www.ecowatch.com/military-largest-polluter-2408760609.html. Accessed March 8, 2023.
17. Trickle-down economics has been repeatedly disproven. The reality is that this neoliberal policy creates *more* inequality, not less. http://eprints.lse.ac.uk/107919/1/Hope_economic_consequences_of_major_tax_cuts_published.pdf. Accessed August 30, 2022.
18. This dynamic is sometimes called "economic imperialism." Its other side is military imperialism, but in reality, they are just two forms of the same process by which the global capitalist class asserts dominance over the poor and weak—if on an international scale. John Perkins's *Confessions of an Economic Hit Man* is a direct account of this practice; and while I found his concluding analysis of the situation is lacking, his first-hand account of events is valuable.

    John Perkins was an engineering consultant used by the American government to act as an "economic hitman" in underdeveloped countries. In his semi-autobiographical book, *Confessions of an Economic Hitman,* Perkins outlines how exactly this took place. He argues that economic pressure was the first line of attack. He and other hitmen would go into a country and negotiate for economic restructuring according to the wishes of global capital. Perkins confesses to being the kind face of imperialism, the one who tries the carrot method. But behind him was always the threat of the stick, which was the military intervention method. Thus, both sides of imperialism are seen in this account. Underdeveloped and impoverished nations are given this choice: a debt trap of loans and restructuring via the IMF/World Bank *or* military intervention.
19. All of these occurrences are in the public record and have been admitted by the CIA. But for a detailed account of these and other operations, see *Washington's Bullets* by Vijay Prashad, *The Jakarta Method* by Vincent Bevins, *The Triumph of Evil* by Austin Murphy, and *Killing Hope* by William Blum.
20. "To Coretta Scott," July 18, 1952. https://kinginstitute.stanford.edu/king-papers/docu

7. The Tyranny of Mammon

1. A word of which many explanations have been proposed, but none are quite satisfactory.
2. "Irenæus against Heresies," in *The Apostolic Fathers with Justin Martyr and Irenaeus*, ed. Alexander Roberts, James Donaldson, and A. Cleveland Coxe, vol. 1, The Ante-Nicene Fathers (Buffalo, NY: Christian Literature Company, 1885), 421.
3. *Faith and Wealth*, 101. New York: Harper & Row, Publishers, 1990.
4. "Exhortation to the Heathen," in Fathers of the Second Century: Hermas, Tatian, Athenagoras, Theophilus, and Clement of Alexandria (Entire), ed. Alexander Roberts, James Donaldson, and A. Cleveland Coxe, vol. 2, The Ante-Nicene Fathers (Buffalo, NY: Christian Literature Company, 1885), 198.
5. Ibid.
6. *De Nabuthe*, 15. Quoted in Charles Avila, *Ownership*, 67. Maryknoll, NY: Orbis Books, 1983.
7. *De op. et eleem.* 14. Quoted in González, *Faith and Wealth*, 126. New York: Harper & Row, Publishers, 1990.
8. "Homilies of St. John Chrysostom, Archbishop of Constantinople, on the gospel of St. John," in *Saint Chrysostom: Homilies on the gospel of St. John and Epistle to the Hebrews*, ed. Philip Schaff, trans. G. T. Stupart, vol. 14, A Select Library of the Nicene and Post-Nicene Fathers of the Christian Church, First Series (New York: Christian Literature Company, 1889), 215–216.
9. *The Communist Manifesto*, 44. New York: International Publishers, 2017.
10. "Homilies of St. John Chrysostom, Archbishop of Constantinople on the gospel according to St. Matthew," in *Saint Chrysostom: Homilies on the gospel of Saint Matthew*, ed. Philip Schaff, trans. George Prevost and M. B. Riddle, vol. 10, A Select Library of the Nicene and Post-Nicene Fathers of the Christian Church, First Series (New York: Christian Literature Company, 1888), 147–148.
11. "Homilies of St. John Chrysostom, Archbishop of Constantinople, on the gospel of St. John," in *Saint Chrysostom: Homilies on the gospel of St. John and Epistle to the Hebrews*, ed. Philip Schaff, trans. G. T. Stupart, vol. 14, A Select Library of the Nicene and Post-Nicene Fathers of the Christian Church, First Series (New York: Christian Literature Company, 1889), 280–281. "Would that" has been modernized to "If only," meaning more precisely "I wish."
12. *De Eleemosyna*, 6. Quoted in Charles Avila, *Ownership*, 89. Maryknoll, NY: Orbis Books, 1983.
13. Article twelve of the USSR constitution of 1936. https://www.marxists.org/reference/archive/stalin/works/1936/12/05.htm. Accessed March 14, 2023. This phrase also found its way onto a number of Soviet propaganda posters.
    It is important to note that Paul's phrase is slightly different, "Anyone unwilling to work should not eat" (2 Thess. 3:10). That is because Paul's context is more about those who take advantage of the generosity of the Christian community, not society as a whole.
14. "On the Famine: A Letter to the Workers of Petrograd." May 22, 1918. By V. I. Lenin. Collected Works Volume 27, 391-398. https://www.marxists.org/archive/lenin/works/1918/may/22b.htm?fbclid=IwAR0iXEKWGdfevfKb36t2dULAUfdn-kJ8ZC0KpNElw9lyXs4kOWc9V35SLB4.
15. *De Verbis Apostoli, Habentem Eumdem Spiritum*, 3, 11. Quoted in Charles Avila, *Ownership*, 93. Maryknoll, NY: Orbis Books, 1983.
16. For the theoretical basis of this claim see Michael Parenti, *Democracy for the Few*; Karl Marx, *Capital*; and David Harvey, *A Brief History of Neoliberalism*. For modern research into systemic poverty, see https://www.urban.org/urban-wire/poverty-results-structural-barriers-not-personal-choices-safety-net-programs-should-reflect-fact.
17. For an economic analysis of China's remarkable success and its relation to socialist policy, see John Ross, *China's Great Road*. For a more detailed examination of the socialist program of China, see Roland Boer, *Socialism with Chinese Characteristics*. For those who might claim these statistics are false, see the World Bank—a Western/capitalist institution—which

released a study confirming these figures. https://www.worldbank.org/en/news/press-release/2022/04/01/lifting-800-million-people-out-of-poverty-new-report-looks-at-lessons-from-china-s-experience.
18. *De Genesi,* 11, 15. Quoted in Charles Avila, *Ownership,* 117. Maryknoll, NY: Orbis Books, 1983.
19. *Homilies on the gospel of Luke,* 109. Quoted in Father James Thornton, *Wealth and Poverty in the Teachings of the Church Fathers,* 121. Berkley: St. John Chrysostom Press, 1993.
20. Karl Marx calls accumulation "Moses and the Prophets," meaning accumulation is the basis of everything. See *Capital I,* 742; see also *Capital I* chapters 24-5.

8. Socioeconomic Analysis

1. See the figure 1.1 and table 1.1-2 in *Wealth and Poverty in Early Church and Society,* 20-1. Ed. Susan R. Holman. Grand Rapids, Michigan: Baker Academic, 2008.
2. https://www.oxfam.org/en/press-releases/just-8-men-own-same-wealth-half-world. Accessed July 31, 2022.
3. David McLellan: For Marx, "the criterion for belonging to a class is ownership or nonownership of the means of production." *Karl Marx,* 43. Middlesex, England: Penguin Books, 1975.
4. To clarify, a working class member is anyone who works for a living, no matter how high their salary. Thus, the frequent distinction between a lower and middle-class person—while not unimportant—is relatively meaningless in contrast with the capitalist, owning class.
5. This is likely a misquote, though one with traces in Steinbeck's work. It was popularized by Ronald Wright's *A Short History of Progress.*
6. This echoes Marx's famous eleventh thesis on Feuerbach: "Philosophers have so far been content with interpreting the world; the point, however, is to change it."
7. That is not necessarily Marx's main concern in *Capital*—I doubt he would have phrased it in this way, at least—but for the purposes of this book, it is a helpful result of his work that it answers these questions scientifically.
8. "Quando dou comida aos pobres, chamam-me de santo. Quando pergunto por que eles são pobres, chamam-me de comunista." Quoted in Zildo Rocha, *Helder, O Dom: uma vida que marcou os rumos da Igreja no Brasil* (Helder, the Gift: A Life that Marked the Course of the Church in Brazil), Page 53, Editora Vozes, 2000.
9. https://www.marxists.org/archive/marx/works/1859/09/16.htm. Accessed March 27, 2023.
10. *On the Glaubenslehre,* 64. Chico, California: Scholars Press, 1981.

9. On Marx

1. Recently, an alleged internal memo at Bank of America illustrated this point. The memo effectively stated that worsening economic conditions for the middle class would benefit the bank and its shareholders. This admits that capitalism needs misery, that unemployment is a strategy to suppress wages, and that poverty is a strategic threat to keep the working class under the oppressive thumb of the capitalist class. For the memo, see: https://theintercept.com/2022/07/29/bank-of-america-worker-conditions-worse/. Accessed August 2, 2022.
2. *Ownership,* 58. Maryknoll, New York: Orbis Books, 1983.
3. For Marx's labor theory of value see *Wage-Labour and Capital & Value, Price and Profit, Critique of the Gotha Program,* and *Capital Volume 1.*
4. The trickle down theory has been repeatedly disproven by researchers. Here are two examples of reputable research on the subject: http://eprints.lse.ac.uk/107919/1/Hope_economic_consequences_of_major_tax_cuts_published.pdf and https://wir2022.wid.world/.
5. *Capital: A Critique of Political Economy, Volume 1,* 799. Translated by Ben Fowkes. London: Penguin Classics, 1990.
6. *Hom. in Joh.* 15.3, PG. Quoted in Justo L. González, *Faith and Wealth,* 205. New York: Harper & Row, Publishers, 1990.
7. *Ownership: Early Christian Teaching,* 8. Maryknoll, New York: Orbis Books, 1983.
8. *Marx and the Bible,* 14. Maryknoll, New York: Orbis Books, 1974.

9. With reference to the slave trade, Marx describes how "capital comes dripping from head to toe, from every pore, with blood and dirt." *Capital: A Critique of Political Economy, Volume 1*, 926. Translated by Ben Fowkes. London: Penguin Classics, 1990.
10. *Capital: A Critique of Political Economy, Volume 1*, 874. Translated by Ben Fowkes. London: Penguin Classics, 1990.
11. *Ownership: Early Christian Teaching*, 96. Maryknoll, New York: Orbis Books, 1983.
12. *Der Römerbrief 1919*, 35. Quoted in Amy Marga, "Reading Karl Barth's *Römerbrief 1919* for a Postcolonial Era of Theology" in *Karl Barth's Epistle to the Romans*, 360. Berlin: Walter de Gruyter, 2022.
13. Eric Fromm, *Marx's Concept of Man*, 38. New York: Frederick Ungar Publishing Co., 1970.
14. Ibid., 3. Emphasis mine.
15. The Trappist monk Thomas Merton echoes the challenge of capitalist alienation in spiritual terms: "Work must once again become spiritually meaningful and humanly satisfying." *Life and Holiness*, 96. New York: Image Books Doubleday, 1963.
16. Marx: "The whole system of capitalist production is based on the worker's sale of his labour-power as a commodity." *Capital: A Critique of Political Economy, Volume 1*, 557. Translated by Ben Fowkes. London: Penguin Classics, 1990.
17. *Capital: A Critique of Political Economy, Volume 1*, 719. Translated by Ben Fowkes. London: Penguin Classics, 1990.
18. Even the objection that a worker might have started their own business falls flat. Most businesses will fail, and those few that do not will either be bought out or driven out of business by larger companies with more capital. And in the rare case of a wage-laborer becoming a capitalist, it still does not solve the issue of one class exploiting another. Just because one lucky laborer became the exception and has turned himself into the exploiter rather than the exploited does not mean the system is no longer problematic. The slight possibility of an oppressed member of the working class making their way into the capitalist class and thus becoming the exploiter is not a solution to the issue at hand; it furthers oppression rather than liberating all oppressed persons.
19. "Capital is dead labour which, vampire-like, lives only by sucking living labour, and lives the more, the more labour it sucks." *Capital: A Critique of Political Economy, Volume 1*, 342. Translated by Ben Fowkes. London: Penguin Classics, 1990.
20. That leads us to another important insight for Marx, which also corresponds well with what we've learned from the Church Fathers. For Marx, while the working class is oppressed and the capitalist class their oppressor—according to each class' essential and irrefutable role in capitalism—he nevertheless recognizes that even the capitalist class is not *free* from the alienating effects of capital. Mammon is tyrannical and demonic, a sentiment that Marx very much reflects in his analysis of capitalism. Even the capitalist class, even the rich, are not free from the alienation of capital.
21. Marx "The greater the social wealth, the functioning capital, the extent and energy of its grown, and therefore also the greater absolute mass of the proletariat and the productivity of its labor, the greater is the industrial reserve army [i.e., the unemployed]. The same causes which develop the expansive power of capital, also develop the labour-power at its disposal." *Capital: A Critique of Political Economy, Volume 1*, 798. Translated by Ben Fowkes. London: Penguin Classics, 1990.
22. See *Capital: A Critique of Political Economy, Volume 1*, 789. Translated by Ben Fowkes. London: Penguin Classics, 1990.
23. Thus, capitalism pours gasoline on the fires of racism and sexism because hostility among people benefits the capitalist class by keeping the working class divided. Capitalism leads to sectarianism and the exclusion of the "other." Thus, alienation is social and leads to social unrest among the working class, even among workers at the same job.
24. Marx quoted in Lochman, 54.
25. Marx quoted in Lochman, 62.
26. *The Hungry are Dying*, 12. Oxford University Press, 2001.
27. Ibid., 54.
28. *The Communist Manifesto*, 19. A fuller definition of the proletariat for Marx is "the class of modern wage-laborers who, having no means of production of their own, are reduced to selling their labor power in order to live." Ibid., 9n12.
29. Ibid., 44.
30. It is not primarily Marx, however, who stressed this point. Though his theory of revolution

leads to this, it is a point developed best by others, particularly by anti-colonial and black liberation thinkers. For example, Malcolm X and his concept of black beauty, which inspired the black power movement for dignity in the face of white supremacy. Additionally, Franz Fanon's anti-colonial psychology and Paulo Freire's *Pedagogy of the Oppressed* examine important aspects of the struggle for dignity.

31. This slogan was central to the Black Panther Party. For more on the party's misunderstood history, see the authoritative *Black Against Empire* by Joshua Bloom and Waldo E. Martin Jr.
32. *A Contribution to Hegel's Philosophy of Right*, Introduction. https://www.marxists.org/archive/marx/works/1843/critique-hpr/intro.htm.
33. See José Miranda, *Marx Against the Marxists*, 225-6. London: SCM Press Ltd, 1980.
34. From Eleanor Marx, *Erinnerugen an Marx*. Quoted in Josè Miranda, *Marx Against the Marxists*, 225. London: SCM Press Ltd, 1980.
35. Roland Boer has extensively studied the long relationship between religion and Marxism. See his five volume series "Criticism of Heaven and Earth."
36. Furthermore, Marx's critique does not mean incompatibility with Christian faith. There is a long history of a Christian critique of religion that begins with Luther. Karl Barth, for example, critiques religion in *Church Dogmatics* I/2. The criticism of religion has its place within theology itself.
37. David McLellan: "…like Job he [Marx] was plagued by boils from head to foot. He dosed himself with such extraordinary medicines as creosote, opium, and arsenic, but the boils continued to debilitate him for years on end…" *Karl Marx*, 12. Middlesex, England: Penguin Books, 1975. See also, Andrew M. Mckinnon: "Reading 'Opium of the People'" (2005): https://journals.sagepub.com/doi/10.1163/1569163053084360, and Roland Boer: "What has Religion to do with Marxism?" https://www.youtube.com/watch?v=fOmT5n RSCeE. Accessed August 18, 2022.
38. José Miranda analyzes an interview published in 1871 where Marx states that his atheism is a matter of personal decision, and that he "cannot speak in the name of the society [i.e., the Communist International]." Miranda, *Marx Against the Marxists*, 280. London: SCM Press Ltd, 1980.
39. *Encountering Marx*, 83. Philadelphia: Fortress Press, 1977.
40. The primary source for this claim is *The Black Book of Communism*. But it should be noted that this book has been disowned by several of its authors as an ideological project with dubious research methods. There are many factual inaccuracies in the book, yet it remains the primary source for the claim that communism lead to the deaths of 100 million in the twentieth century. See https://discomfiting.medium.com/debunking-communism-killed-more-people-than-naziism-7a9880696f67 and https://thegrayzone.com/2017/11/22/black-book-of-communism-debunked-antisemitic-nazis/. Accessed March 28, 2023.
41. For example, his theory about periodic crisis in capitalism, the process of monopolization, and the financialization of capital in its higher stages. But a notable insight that has been proven correct is Marx's prediction about the declining rate of profit in *Capital, Volume 3*. It is especially important because this sets a clear limit to the expansion of capitalism. It has been called the "self-destruct" mechanism built into capitalism production. For a good video essay on this, see Hakim: https://youtu.be/SEGGvVinUao.
42. *Against the Wind*, 47-8. Minneapolis: Fortress Press, 1999.
43. *Encountering Marx*, 85. Philadelphia: Fortress Press, 1977.
44. See José Miranda, *Marx and the Bible*. Maryknoll, NY: Orbis Books, 1974.
45. *A Contribution to the Critique of Hegel's* Philosophy of Right, Introduction. https://www.marxists.org/archive/marx/works/1843/critique-hpr/intro.htm.

10. Conclusion

1. Justo L. González explains well the problem with endless accumulation: "To accumulate wealth is to pervert it, not only because real wealth must always be moving and active, but also because the purpose of wealth is to meet human need. Therefore, those who accumulate wealth as if it were an end in itself or who accumulate it in order to live in comfort and

ostentation are misusing wealth." *Faith & Wealth,* 228-9. San Francisco, Ca: Harper & Row Publishers, 1990.
2. From her acceptance speech at the 2014 National Book Awards: https://www.youtube.com/watch?v=5PI1xwT2-74. Accessed July 29, 2022.
3. Jürgen Moltmann perhaps expressed it best, "From first to last, and not merely in the epilogue, Christianity is eschatology, is hope, forward looking and forward moving, and therefore also revolutionizing and transforming the present." *Theology of Hope,* 16. Minneapolis, MN: Fortress Press, 1993.

BIBLIOGRAPHY

Alter, Robert. *The Hebrew Bible*. New York: W. W. Norton Company, 2018.
Avila, Charles. *Ownership, Early Christian Teaching*. Maryknoll, NY: Orbis Books, 2001.
Bentley, James. *Between Marx and Christ*. New York: Verso, 1982.
Bevins, Vincent. *The Jakarta Method*. New York: Public Affairs, 2021.
Bloch, Ernst. *Atheism in Christianity*. New York: Verso, 2009.
Bloom, Joshua, and Waldo E. Martin. *Black Against Empire*. University of California Press, 2016.
Boer, Dick. *Deliverance from Slavery*. Chicago: Haymarket Books, 2017
Boer, Roland. *Christian Communism*. Culture Matters, 2018.
—. *Criticism of Earth*. Chicago: Haymarket Books, 2013.
—. *In the Vale of Tears*. Chicago: Haymarket Books, 2014.
—. *Lenin, Religion, and Theology*. New York: Palgrave Macmillan, 2013.
—. *Marxist Criticism of the Hebrew Bible*. Edinburgh: T&T Clark, 2014.
—. *Red Theology: On the Christian Communist Tradition*. Chicago: Haymarket Books, 2019.
—. *Socialism with Chinese Characteristics*. Springer Nature, 2021.
Boff, Leonardo. *Holy Trinity, Perfect Community*. Maryknoll, NY: Orbis Books.
—. *Introducing Liberation Theology*. Orbis Books, 1987.
—. *Way of the Cross--Way of Justice*. Eugene, OR: Wipf and Stock Publishers, 2021.
Brown, Peter. *The Ransom of the Soul*. Harvard University Press, 2015.
—. *Through the Eye of a Needle*. Princeton University Press, 2012.
Carter, J. Kameron. *Race*. Oxford University Press, 2008.
Castro, Fidel; Frei Betto. *Fidel and Religion*. Melbourne: Ocean Press, 2006.
—. *My Life*. New York: Simon and Schuster, 2009.
Césaire, Aimé. *Discourse on Colonialism*. New York: Monthly Review Press, 2001.
Chomsky, Noam. *The Essential Chomsky*. New York: The New Press, 2008.
Christoyannopoulos, Alexandre. *Christian Anarchism*. Andrews UK Limited, 2011.
Clevenot, Michel. *Materialist Approaches to the Bible*. Maryknoll, NY: Orbis Books, 1985.
Cone, James H. *A Black Theology of Liberation*. Maryknoll, NY: Orbis Books, 2010.
—. *God of the Oppressed*. Maryknoll, NY: Orbis Books, 1997.
Cort, John C. *Christian Socialism*. Maryknoll, NY: Orbis Books, 1988.
D'Amato, Paul. *The Meaning of Marxism*. Chicago: Haymarket Books, 2014.
Dennis, Marie, et al. *Oscar Romero*. Maryknoll, NY: Orbis Books, 2000.
Eagleton, Terry. *Why Marx Was Right*. Yale University Press, 2018.
Engels, Friedrich. *Anti-Dühring*. Peking: Foreign Languages Press, 1976.
—. *Socialism, Utopian and Scientific*. The Leftist Public Domain Project, 2020.
—. *The Origin of the Family, Private Property and the State*. New York: Penguin Classics, 1972.
—. *The Principles of Communism*. A Radical Reprint, 2020.
Engels, Friedrich; Karl Marx. *The Communist Manifesto*. New York: International Publishers, 2017.
—. *Collected Works* (50 vols.). New York: International Publishers, 1975-2004.
—. *The German Ideology*. New York: International Publishers, 1998.
—. *On Religion*. Atlanta: Scholars Press, 1964.
Fanon, Frantz. *The Wretched of the Earth*. New York: Grove Press, 2021.
Freire, Paulo. *Pedagogy of the Oppressed*. Bloomsbury Publishing USA, 2018.
Fromm, Erich. *Marx's Concept of Man*. 1980. New York: Fredrick Ungar Publishing, 1970.
Galeano, Eduardo. *Open Veins of Latin America*. NYU Press, 1997.
Gollwitzer, Helmut. *An Introduction to Protestant Theology*. Philadelphia: The Westminster Press, 1982.

—. *The Christian Faith and the Marxist Criticism of Religion*. New York: Scribner, 1970.
—. *The Rich Christians and Poor Lazarus*. New York: The Macmillon Company, 1970.
González, Justo L. *Faith and Wealth*. New York: Harper & Row, 1990.
—. *The Story of Christianity: Volume 1*. Zondervan, 2010.
Gramsci, Antonio. *Prison Notebooks*. Columbia University Press, 2011.
Gutierrez, Gustavo. *A Theology of Liberation*. Maryknoll, NY: Orbis Books, 1988.
—. *The God of Life*. Maryknoll, NY: Orbis Books, 1991.
—. *The Power of the Poor in History*. Eugene, OR: Wipf and Stock Publishers, 2004.
Harsch, Ernest. *Thomas Sankara*. Ohio University Press, 2014.
Harvey, David. *A Brief History of Neoliberalism*. Oxford University Press, USA, 2007.
—. *A Companion To Marx's Capital*. New York: Verso Books, 2018.
—. *Seventeen Contradictions and the End of Capitalism*. Oxford University Press, 2014.
Hays, Christopher M. *Renouncing Everything*. Mahwah, NJ: Paulist Press, 2016.
Herzog, Frederick. *Liberation Theology*. Eugene, OR: Wipf and Stock Publishers, 2013.
Herzog, William R. *Parables as Subversive Speech*. Louisville: Westminster John Knox Press, 1994.
Heschel, Abraham J. *The Prophets*. New York: Harper Collins, 2001.
Hewitt, Simon. *Church and Revolution*. Durham: Sacristy Press, 2020.
Holman, Susan R. *Wealth and Poverty in Early Church and Society*. Baker Academic, 2008.
Horsley, Richard A. *Covenant Economics*. Louisville: Westminster John Knox Press, 2009.
—. *Jesus and Empire*. Minneapolis: Fortress Press, 2003.
Irvin, Dale T.; Scott W. Sunquist. *History of the World Christian Movement*. Maryknoll, NY: Orbis Press.
Kairos Theologians. *The Kairos Document, Challenge to the Church*. Grand Rapids, MI: William B. Eerdmans Publishing Company, 1986.
King, Martin Luther. *The Radical King*. Boston: Beacon Press, 2015.
Klein, Naomi. *The Shock Doctrine*. New York: Picador, 2008.
Landis, Tina. *Climate Solutions Beyond Capitalism*. San Francisco: Liberation Media, 2020.
Lenin, Vladimir. *Imperialism: The Highest Stage of Capitalism*. Volume 1: *Lenin Selected Works*. Moscow, USSR: Progress Publishers, 1970.
—. *Karl Marx*. Volume 1: *Lenin Selected Works*. Moscow, USSR: Progress Publishers, 1970.
—. *The State and Revolution*. Volume 2: *Lenin Selected Works*, Volume 2: *Lenin Selected Works*. Moscow, USSR: Progress Publishers, 1970.
—. *The Three Sources and Three Component Parts of Marxism*. Volume 1: *Lenin Selected Works*. Moscow, USSR: Progress Publishers, 1970.
Liedman, Sven-Eric. *A World to Win*. New York: Verso Books, 2018.
Lightfoot, Joseph Barber, and John Reginald Harmer. *The Apostolic Fathers*. Grand Rapids, MI: Baker Academic, 2007.
Losurdo, Domenico. *Liberalism*. New York: Verso, 2014.
Lochman, Jan Milič. *Encountering Marx*. Augsburg Fortress Publishing, 1977.
Luxemburg, Rosa. *Reform or Revolution and Other Writings*. Courier Corporation, 2012.
Malina, Bruce J.; Richard L. Rohrbaugh. *Social-Science Commentary on the Gospel of John*. Minneapolis: Fortress Press, 1998.
Mandel, Ernest. *An Introduction to Marxist Economic Theory*. New York: Pathfinder Press, 1973.
Marx, Karl. *Capital Volume 1*. London: Penguin Classics, 1976.
—. *Capital Volume 2*. London: Penguin Classics, 1978.
—. *Capital Volume 3*. London: Penguin Classics, 1981.
—. *Early Writings*. New York: McGraw-Hill, 1963.
—. *The Political Writings*. New York: Verso Books, 2019.
—. *Wage-Labour and Capital & Value, Price and Profit*. New York: International Publishers, 1976.
McCarraher, Eugene. *The Enchantments of Mammon*. Cambridge: Belknap Press, 2019.
McLellan, David. *Karl Marx*. London: Penguin Books, 1995.

McMaken, W. Travis. *Our God Loves Justice*. Minneapolis: Fortress Press, 2017.
Miranda, José Porfirio. *Being and the Messiah*. Maryknoll, NY: Orbis Books, 1977.
—. *Communism in the Bible*. Maryknoll, NY: Orbis Books, 1982.
—. *Marx and the Bible*. Maryknoll, NY: Orbis Books, 1974.
—. *Marx Against the Marxists*. London: SCM Press LTD, 1978.
Moltmann, Jürgen. *A Theology of Hope*. Minneapolis: Fortress Press, 1993.
—. *The Crucified God*. New York: Harper & Row, 1974.
Montero, Roman A. *All Things in Common*. Eugene, OR: Wipf and Stock Publishers, 2017.
—. *Jesus's Manifesto*. Eugene, OR: Wipf and Stock Publishers, 2019.
Morrison, Stephen D. *James Cone in Plain English*. Columbus, OH: Beloved Publishing, 2019.
—. *Karl Barth in Plain English*. Columbus, OH: Beloved Publishing, 2017.
—. *Jürgen Moltmann in Plain English*. Columbus, OH: Beloved Publishing, 2017.
Müntzer, Thomas. *The Collected Works of Thomas Müntzer*. Edinburgh: T&T Clark, 1988.
Murphy, Austin. *The Triumph of Evil*. Fucecchio, Italy: European Press Academic Pub, 2000.
Nagasawa, Mako A. *Abortion Policy and Christian Social Ethics in the United States*. Eugene, OR: Wipf and Stock Publishers, 2021.
Parenti, Michael. *Against Empire*. San Francisco: City Lights Books, 2021.
—. *Blackshirts and Reds*. San Francisco: City Lights Books, 2020.
—. *Democracy for the Few*. Cengage Learning, 2010.
—. *Face of Imperialism*. New York: Routledge, 2011.
—. *Profit Pathology and Other Indecencies*. Boulder: Paradigm Publishers, 2015.
Party for Socialism and Liberation. *Socialist Reconstruction*. San Francisco: Liberation Media, 2022.
Perkins, John. *The New Confessions of an Economic Hit Man*. Alameda, CA: Berrett-Koehler Publishers, 2016.
Phelps, Hollis. *Jesus and the Politics of Mammon*. Eugene, OR: Wipf and Stock Publishers, 2019.
Prashad, Vijay. *Washington Bullets*. New Delhi: LeftWord Books, 2020.
Ragaz, Leonhard. *Signs of the Kingdom*. Grand Rapids, MI: William B. Eerdmans Publishing Company, 1984.
Rauschenbusch, Walter. *A Theology for the Social Gospel*. New York: The Macmillan Company, 1945.
Rhee, Helen. *Loving the Poor, Saving the Rich*. Grand Rapids, MI: Baker Books, 2012.
—. *Wealth and Poverty in Early Christianity*. Minneapolis: Fortress Press, 2017.
Rodney, Walter. *How Europe Underdeveloped Africa*. New York: Verso, 2018.
Roberts, Alexander, et al. *Early Church Fathers*. Peabody: Hendrickson Publishers, 1994.
Romero, Oscar. *The Violence of Love*. San Francisco: Harper & Row, 1988.
Ross, John. *China's Great Road*. New York: International Publishers, 2021.
Rowland, Christopher, and Mark Corner. *Liberating Exegesis*. Louisville: Westminster John Knox Press, 1989.
Schaff, Philip. *Ante-Nicene Fathers*. Peabody: Hendrickson, 1994.
—. *Nicene and Post-Nicene Fathers*. Peabody: Hendrickson, 1994.
Segundo, Juan L. *Liberation of Theology*. Eugene, OR: Wipf and Stock Publishers, 2002.
Shirokov, M. *Textbook of Marxist Philosophy*. Createspace Independent Publishing Platform, 2013.
Sobrino, Jon. *Jesus the Liberator*. Maryknoll, NY: Orbis Books, 1994.
Sölle, Dorothee. *Against the Wind*. Minneapolis: Fortress Press, 1999.
—. *Beyond Mere Dialogue: On Being a Christian and a Socialist*. 1978.
—. *Dorothee Soelle*. Modern Spiritual Masters, 2006.
Stanford, Jim. *Economics for Everyone*. Halifax: Fernwood Publishing, 2008.
Thornton, James. *Wealth and Poverty in the Teachings of the Church Fathers*. Berkley: St John Chrysostom Press, 1993.
Weber, Max. *The Protestant Ethic and the Spirit of Capitalism*. London: Penguin Classics, 2002.

Wolff, Richard D. *Understanding Marxism*. New York: Democracy at Work, 2019.
Yip, Francis Ching-Wah. *Capitalism as Religion? A Study of Paul Tillich's Interpretation of Modernity*. Harvard University Press, 2010.
Zinn, Howard. *A People's History of the United States*. New York: Harper Perennial Modern Classics, 2015.

www.ingramcontent.com/pod-product-compliance
Lightning Source LLC
Chambersburg PA
CBHW070138080526
44586CB00015B/1750